GOOD

CHINESE

WIFE

A LOVE AFFAIR WITH CHINA GONE WRONG

SUSAN BLUMBERG-KASON

 sourcebooks

Published by Sourcebooks, Inc.
P.O. Box 4410, Naperville, Illinois 60567-4410
(630) 961-3900
Fax: (630) 961-2168
www.sourcebooks.com

Library of Congress Cataloging-in-Publication data is on file with the publisher.

Printed and bound in the United States of America.
VP 10 9 8 7 6 5 4 3 2 1

For my family: Tom, Jake, Rachel, and Martin

CONTENTS

AUTHOR'S NOTE

I have changed the names of most people in this book to protect their identities. For the sake of storytelling, I have consolidated a couple of secondary characters and have changed the location of one small scene from Chicago to San Francisco. To keep with the flavor of the story, I have included some Chinese dialogue, most of which uses the pinyin system of romanization that's been prevalent in mainland China since the 1950s. I've also used a little Cantonese romanization and the local Hubei province dialect from my former in-laws' hometown. As I've briefly mentioned in the book, Chinese family names appear first, so Cai Jun's family name is Cai (pronounced Tsai) and his given name is Jun. Thus, his father's and sisters' names also begin with the family name of Cai. Women in China do not change their names when they marry, but it's quite common for non-Chinese women to take their Chinese husbands' names.

PROLOGUE

"Now tell me something," Cai said, holding my hands in his. "What about me do you love?"

"Everything." I could feel my cheeks burning red.

"What's *everything*? I want to know." He rubbed the tips of his long fingers over my nails.

"You're kind, intelligent, funny, modest…and a good communicator," I mumbled, utterly enthralled by him.

He nodded with satisfaction. "Do you want to know why I love you?"

"Yes!" Being a painfully shy Midwestern wallflower, I had never dated anyone for more than three weeks. At times it had seemed unlikely that I would ever have a long-term relationship, let alone marry. I had no idea why an attractive scholar like Cai would be interested in me, but I was thrilled that he was. I felt like a schoolkid waiting for a good report card, but instead of earning grades for classes, I was about to receive them for my personality, for my very being.

"Modern Chinese women are harsh, emotional, and selfish. You're not like them, and you're not like typically loud American women. You remind me of traditional women in China's countryside—kind, warm, and soft."

Just before this, I had been tutoring Cai in English to prepare for a presentation at the university in Hong Kong, which we both attended. Because our engagement happened so quickly, I didn't question why he thought I wasn't a typical American. Or why he deemed loud and emotional Chinese women so unbecoming. I was thrilled that he viewed me as a traditional Chinese woman. I saw it as the utmost compliment.

When walking, look straight, turn not your head;
Talking, restrain your voice within your teeth;
When pleased, laugh not aloud;
If angry, still make no noise.

—Ban Zhao, the first known female
Chinese historian (45–116 AD)
Instruction for Chinese Women and Girls

Chapter 1

A CHANCE MEETING IN HONG KONG

The Chinese University of Hong Kong sits atop a mountain, north of Hong Kong Island and twenty minutes south of the mainland China border. When I arrived on campus in 1990 for a college exchange year, I had imagined Hong Kong would be a city of skyscrapers and neon. But the only lights around the campus came from the occasional barge or leisure boat in otherwise quiet Tolo Harbour. On the weekends, the campus was almost deserted. Local students returned home to their families, and the few overseas students studying abroad left for the bustling expat areas of Kowloon and Hong Kong Island.

Upon my return for graduate school years later, new residential skyscrapers had popped up across the harbor. The campus was beginning to look like what I'd first imagined. But the most significant change on campus was that the mainland Chinese population had blossomed from a handful of people to about two hundred graduate students. I was fascinated by these newcomers and their alluringly mysterious culture, so utterly different from my own.

On one of those still-quiet Saturday nights, a month after I started graduate school, I locked myself out of my dorm room. I was on my way to call a friend, using the hall phone around the corner, and as soon as I closed my door, I knew I had left my key on my desk. My roommate, Na Wei, hailed from Harbin in northeast China, but she slept in her boyfriend's single room most nights and only returned to our room during the day when she needed a change of clothes or a short nap. So no luck there.

Then it hit me. The guard downstairs kept spare keys. I could borrow one from him.

My stomach fell when the elevator opened on the ground floor. The lobby was empty. I inched over to the guard's desk to read a tattered white sign perched upon it. Although I couldn't speak the local Cantonese dialect, I had studied Mandarin, the official language in mainland China. With five years of Mandarin behind me, I could almost make out the meaning of the Chinese characters on the sign: *if*, *need*, *something*, and *return*. But one character came up as a blank. *If you need something, I will return blank.*

If only I could read the one character describing *when* the guard would return. I usually got around Hong Kong without having to resort to my little, red Chinese-English dictionary. Now, the one time I needed it, it was locked away in my room, not far from my coveted key.

I decided to take a seat on a vinyl bench near the front door in case someone came by who could translate that mysterious character. Worst case, I would have to stay up all night until the daytime guard arrived.

And that would indeed be the worst case for me. Other than on long international flights, I had never pulled an all-nighter. I was the type of college student who worked ahead to avoid cramming all night before exams or writing a paper the night before its deadline. Thinking about the daunting prospect of a lobby all-nighter, I looked up, startled, as two men and a woman suddenly entered the building.

Cai immediately caught my attention. Like a movie star, he stood six feet tall with confident eyes and an infectious smile. His hair was cut in the popular Hong Kong men's wedge of the early 1990s—longish on top, tapering down to almost a crew cut a few inches above the neck. He carried himself with the self-assurance of someone used to drawing admiring glances. He looked striking in his stylish brown corduroy pants, short-sleeved shirt, and hunting vest, but I couldn't place his nationality. Based on his more sophisticated appearance, I figured he was from Taiwan, or maybe an overseas Chinese from Japan or another developed country.

His friends, however, weren't so hard to identify. The shorter man wore an olive business suit with the white label still stitched to the cuff, and the woman was dressed in a long, striped polyester skirt and a mismatched floral blouse. Definitely mainland Chinese.

On my first trip to China in 1988 with a group from high school, I had noticed this eclectic fashion trend. Up until the late 1970s, fashion in China consisted of simple "peasant pajamas" or "Mao suits." In the years after the Chairman's death, people started to experiment with colors and patterns, including bright stripes and flowers. So this distinct mainlander fashion was easy to recognize in stylish Hong Kong.

Once Cai's friends turned toward the elevator, I knew I had to act quickly before he left the lobby and I had to face my all-nighter again. "Excuse me, can you read this sign?" I hurried after Cai, speaking in English. No answer. *Oh God, what if he only knows Cantonese?* I thought. But I was determined not to sit on that bench all night, so I repeated my question in Mandarin as I felt a pearl of sweat trickle down my neck.

Cai glanced at the sign and said nonchalantly in Mandarin, "*Tā jiù mǎshàng huílái.*" He will be back soon. His Mandarin was clear and articulate, without the slurring of the northern Chinese accents.

"Oh, thank goodness! I locked myself out and need a key," I explained to this attractive, well-spoken stranger, stumbling in choppy Mandarin. The relief I felt, knowing that I wouldn't have to camp out in the dorm lobby all night, seemed insignificant compared with my sudden desire to know everything about him. I needed to find a way to prolong our conversation.

"*Méi wèntí.*" Don't worry. He nodded slightly, as if locking one-self out happened all the time. "Actually, I need to buy a phone card from the guard." He went to sit on the bench I had just occupied. I couldn't believe my luck.

Without speaking, I joined him, leaving a full arm's length

between us. Although I wanted to sit closer to Cai, I knew from my junior year in Hong Kong and the few times I'd visited mainland China that people in Asia often viewed Western women as loud and loose.

Up until three weeks earlier, I wouldn't have allowed the silly stereotype to cause me any worry. But I had jumped into two consecutive flings with men on campus soon after I moved into the dorm. Now seated next to Cai, I felt sensitive and ashamed that I'd allowed myself to become intimate with people I had no intention of dating seriously.

Doing something like that was so out of character for me. In high school, I didn't date at all. When I moved to Baltimore to attend Goucher College, a few guys asked me out for first dates, but there were never follow-up phone calls. I wasn't too bothered because the feeling was mutual. Conversation with them seemed forced, and our common interests were minimal.

Finally, eighteen months before I returned to Hong Kong for graduate school, I decided I wanted a serious boyfriend. After college, I had found a job in an academic library in Washington, DC. I immediately enrolled in a Mandarin course at the university and became friendly with a Japanese student named Jin. A couple of months into the semester—his last—Jin asked for my number. He wondered if I'd like to join him for dinner one Saturday night during midterms. I wasn't interested in him romantically but didn't think any harm would come of it.

On the evening of our dinner, Jin met me at the library and led me several blocks to his apartment, a low-rise on a side street covered with fallen ginkgo leaves. From afar, the ground appeared to have a light coating of snow. Inside, we spoke about travel, music, and art while he cooked Chinese food and poured me a glass of wine. It was the first time I felt comfortable talking to a man my age. Jin didn't hug or kiss me that night. When I left his place by cab after dinner, I wished he had.

With limited dating experience, I didn't want to tell him that I was starting to have feelings for him for fear of scaring him off. But I had enough chutzpah to phone him most evenings. We would talk for hours about identity, stereotypes, movies, books, travel, and whatever else was on his mind that day. I mainly listened. During those phone conversations, he never mentioned keeping in touch after he left Washington at the end of the semester. So I finally decided to find out what he was feeling.

Our last Chinese class concluded in mid-December. Jin walked me back to the library, like he did after each class. As we started to cross Massachusetts Avenue, I laced my fingers just above his elbow. Keeping my eyes on the ground in front of us, I could feel his arm tense up. Suddenly he tore away from me and raced across the street. Stunned, I froze in utter shame. Had I completely misjudged Jin?

This part of DuPont Circle was full of students I knew from the library, so I continued across the street and didn't dare look around to see who had just witnessed my most humiliating and foolish moment. The walk back to work seemed like miles, although the library was only halfway down the street.

The following afternoon when Jin arrived at the library and settled into a carrel near the circulation desk, I hid among the reserve shelves. But there was only one exit, so I couldn't avoid him when my shift finished an hour later. As I made my way to the elevator, Jin followed me in silence. I prayed that other people would leave the library at the same time, but no one else budged. On the ride to the ground floor, he tried to apologize—complete with the cliché, "It's not you, it's me"—and said he would call. Shaking my head, I didn't want to talk about it. I couldn't stop replaying his mad dash across the street.

I called Jin days later when I did feel like talking. All he said about us was that it would never work out. My shame still raw, I didn't ask him to elaborate. But I mulled it over. Was I too common for his upper-crust family, or was it because I wasn't Japanese? Or did he just not like me that way?

We kept in touch over the phone after he moved, and although the hurt from that December day was still fresh, I hadn't thought there would be any harm in maintaining a connection to him. But eventually, I realized my self-esteem had suffered so much that I severed ties with him and vowed to never put myself in that position again.

Ever since my junior year in Hong Kong, I'd been pining to return there, not as a tourist but as an expat. So after the fiasco with Jin, I decided to leave America for Hong Kong, a place I knew and loved. A place where I felt more accepted and comfortable, and where I better understood the customs than I did Jin's Japanese culture.

I wouldn't admit it at the time, but I also needed proof that I was attractive and desirable. So without ever having experienced a rebound relationship, I jumped into consecutive flings with the first two men I met on campus in Hong Kong. Guo was a PhD student from mainland China who stated up front that he wasn't interested in a relationship, but was rather curious about being with a Western woman.

I convinced myself that if a man could want that, there was nothing wrong with a woman wanting the same. I had never been intimate with anyone before Guo. Unlike most students in the dorm, he had a single room, so we had more privacy than most. At first Guo was charming and spoke about his work back in China. "I'm a poet, a playwright," he crooned as I sat in his lap on his solitary desk chair.

But after our friendship was no longer platonic, I noticed that he bridled the next time I knocked on his door, as if he was impatient for me to leave. I could feel my self-esteem slipping to where it had fallen in Washington, DC. When Guo came to see me the following week, I turned him away, explaining that I needed a committed relationship. Later when we passed each other in the dorm lobby or in the cafeterias, I nodded as I would to any casual acquaintance.

The second fling involved a local Cantonese lifeguard at the university pool where I swam laps most mornings. A week after I'd ended things with Guo, the lifeguard, Yeung, crouched near the edge of the pool as I completed a lap, motioning with his hand for me to stop. I took in his mirrored sunglasses, silky straight hair, and skin darkened from months in the sun. When he asked me out to dinner that night, I agreed without hesitation.

Space is tight in Hong Kong, and like many unmarried adults, Yeung still lived at home. He couldn't bear to tell his mother that he was seeing a foreigner, so for the next couple of weeks, we could meet only when he found time to sneak away. On his day off, he would drive me around the verdant mountains of the New Territories or to the secluded park at the nearby racetrack, where we would stroll, holding hands, our fingers entwined.

Yeung carried keys to the lifeguard hut behind the pool, so we mostly met late at night after his mother had fallen asleep. We would hole up in there until six in the morning, before the campus came to life and we could still return to our respective homes unnoticed.

Those nights with Yeung constituted the bulk of my "Cantonese lessons," meaning I learned almost nothing. Despite having no common mother language, we managed to communicate with bits of Mandarin, Cantonese, and English. After a few weeks, I panicked: I liked him but wasn't in love. And to be honest, I couldn't picture taking him home to my parents. Although they were open-minded about most things, I knew they would worry about the disparity in our education.

Since this was my first semblance of a relationship, I didn't know how to break it off. But I couldn't hurt him the way Jin had disgraced me in Washington. So I started to feign deadlines on papers and exams. By the time I met Cai, I had stopped seeing Yeung late at night.

With these experiences still fresh in my mind, I was determined not to develop a reputation for being an easy American, especially with Cai. When he looked away from me, I stole a quick glance at his face. I couldn't tell his age, but the crow's feet sprouting from the outer corners of his eyes indicated he was older than my twenty-four years. I marveled at his composure in this heat—not a drop of sweat or a hair out of place.

As for me, the humidity wreaked havoc on my frizzy hair, the same hair kids in school teased me about back home in Evanston, Illinois. A tight rubber band couldn't contain my rebellious curls now that I had grown them longer. I wiped the beads of sweat from my forehead and longed for a cool shower, even in my mildew-ridden bathroom upstairs.

As we waited in silence, I wondered whom he would need to call at such an hour. Someone who lived overseas where the sun was still up? Maybe he was like many of the mainland students and had a spouse back home. Resolved to act natural around Cai, I focused on a stream of ants crossing the worn linoleum floor as I tried to think of something to start a conversation. Before I could, the sound of footsteps broke the lobby's heavy stillness. The guard had arrived.

Cai and I sprang from the bench as if on cue and followed the older man to his desk. I thanked the guard in Cantonese (one of the few words I knew in that dialect) as he handed me a replacement key. It felt cool and soothing in my hand. But Cai wasn't so lucky. The guard didn't sell phone cards.

I still knew nothing about Cai but cringed at the thought of seeing him walk away without an introduction or a casual "See you soon." Anything so I could find out more about this attractive, enigmatic man. Then I thought of something. I offered to lend him my calling card.

He smiled gratefully but shook his head. "I can just call tomorrow. It's okay."

"Really, it's no problem." I knew I was taking a risk, trusting a complete stranger with what was essentially a credit card. In America, I never would have lent my calling card to someone I didn't know. But I was lonely and had an inexplicable and irrepressible desire to get to know him—to forge some sort of connection, even if it was just neighborly. Cai clearly lived in the same building, and it would be easy to locate him once I received my phone bill. That way I might be able to find out if he was married or had a girlfriend.

"Are you sure?"

I nodded and noticed Cai reaching for his wallet to pay me.

"Don't worry about that now," I said. "I won't know how much it costs until I get the bill."

As we waited for the elevator, he opened his wallet and handed me his business card. I was thrilled. The purple and gold embossed printing read *Cai Jun, PhD candidate, Department of Music*. (Men in China are often called by their family names, which is what we could call a last name. In China, family names come first.)

"*Nǐ cóng nǎlǐ lái de?*" I still knew very little about him, including where he came from, so I boldly asked him.

"*Zhōngguó, Wǔhàn,*" he answered.

He was from China after all. That surprised me because Cai Jun didn't match what I thought of as someone from Wuhan, an industrial city in the center of the country, somewhat like Chicago, near where I came from. As we continued chatting more and more enthusiastically both on the elevator and after he gave me his card, I wondered if maybe this was what the Chinese like to call *yuánfèn*. Fate had brought two people from the middle of their countries together in a third setting.

Back on my floor, I called my friend Janice from the hall phone. We had become close after Jin left Washington and I realized I hadn't made many friends apart from a few coworkers at the library. Janice and I bonded when we confided in each other one night at happy hour that we both aspired to uproot to Hong Kong. Shortly before I started graduate school, she moved into her relatives' rent-free, sixth-story walk-up in congested Kowloon City and obtained her work visa through a job at her uncle's textile company.

"Susan, you're crazy. You don't even know this guy. He's going to give your access number to everyone in China. You know how my parents lecture me about crossing the border only after I've removed all my gold jewelry. Mainlanders will steal anything."

I could picture her taking a drag on a cigarette and trying to keep cool next to the only fan in her sparsely furnished living room with its original heavy 1960s curtains. Shifting the phone from one ear to the other, I shrugged off Janice's warning. Her parents had emigrated from Taiwan and were wary of everything mainland Chinese. I appreciated where they were coming from, but surely that didn't apply to me.

Without warning, the elevator door opened. Out stepped Cai.

"Can you hang on a second? *It's him*," I hissed. I felt blood rush to my face as I held the receiver away from my ear.

Cai shrugged as he handed back my card. He had removed his vest back in his room and now wore indoor plastic sandals. "I didn't use it. My English is not very good."

"It's hard to understand those phone operators anyway." I tried to sound lighthearted. Remembering the easy, sleazy reputation of Western women, I remained on the phone with Janice so I wouldn't appear overly eager to talk with him. Now that we had made this first connection, I felt confident that I would run into him in the dorm and around campus, and perhaps we could become friends. Cai stepped back into the elevator and waved good-bye.

"He couldn't understand the English instructions, so he didn't even use the card," I told Janice.

"I heard. Still, I don't think you should've given it to him."

"He seems honest."

"You don't know him."

Chapter 2

AN INTRODUCTION TO CHINESE CULTURE

Two weeks after I first met Cai, I noticed a typed flyer in the dorm lobby announcing a mainland student dance on the coming Saturday. *All are welcome*, the bottom of the paper read in English. I hadn't seen Cai since I had locked myself out, but I'd hardly been around at night. Janice and I met almost every night, sometimes for dinner or dancing in Wan Chai, the seedy club district made famous in *The World of Suzie Wong*.

Other times we met for a movie close by in Sha Tin or in the thick of the glitzy Central district on Hong Kong Island. As someone who didn't go out much in high school or even college, I knew I should have been studying. But I couldn't stay away from the temptations of life off campus.

At lunch in the dorm cafeteria, a few expat students mentioned the dance. Some of us had traveled to China over the years and witnessed the ballroom dance craze that had hit the mainland after the Cultural Revolution. I'd stumbled upon such a dance at the Nanjing College of Arts when my high school group stayed there for a few days in 1988. Men danced with men, women with women, and men with women. The vivacious music, none of which I recognized, and the scores of couples waltzing around the dance floor reminded me of a carousel in overdrive.

From the time I entered that Nanjing gymnasium, I couldn't stand still for more than a minute before someone asked me to dance. That trip showed me I could be popular in ways I never experienced at school in the United States. China seemed like a place where I could start over and shed my inhibitions with new people who would never know I had been a wallflower all my life.

Now in Hong Kong, when this group of expats asked for the hands of everyone who would meet at the dance, I raised mine the highest. I was still thinking about Cai and hoped he would go, too.

On Saturday night, I entered the common room of the lower graduate dorm just as the lights were dimmed and a disco ball illuminated. A synthesized version of "Greensleeves" blared from a boom box. I scanned the room and spotted many of the expats I had talked with at lunch, along with some mainland students I'd met on campus.

Thankfully, I didn't see Guo, the student with whom I had the brief fling at the beginning of the year. I wouldn't have left the dance if he had been there, but it would be less awkward if we didn't cross paths. For the most part, mainland students like him didn't mix much with the local Hong Kong Chinese, but I recognized a few of the latter from my dorm.

There was no sign of Cai.

As in Nanjing, these students were dancing elegant waltzes and fox-trots. I was about to join my friends when a mainland student approached, his hand outstretched. Glancing behind me to make sure he didn't mean to ask someone else, I smiled and took his hand. As I tried to keep up with him on the dance floor, I was convinced that no one else would come near me after witnessing my clumsy antics. Thank God Cai wasn't here to see this.

But once "Greensleeves" finished, a short engineering student surprised me by offering his hand to dance, grinning with a row of babylike teeth. He led me to a song that sounded as if it belonged in a military parade. My thoughts flashed to soldiers marching among tanks on a wide boulevard in Beijing, giant red flags flapping in the breeze, and I shuddered as I again tried to keep up.

During "Tie a Yellow Ribbon 'Round the Ole Oak Tree," Cai entered the room with his friends from the night we met. I staggered—trying not to make it too obvious that I was keeping my eyes on him—while my dance partner steered me in an attempted waltz, trying to keep my two left feet from colliding with his graceful ones. After the song ended, I spotted Cai walking toward me and felt my face flush in humiliation. Was he going to make fun of my terrible dancing?

Instead, he smiled and held out his arm as an offer to dance. "Are you still locking yourself out?"

I giggled like a teenager and clasped Cai's hand and shoulder. A full head taller than me, he held me firmly, unlike the others who had only lightly touched me with clammy hands.

"I'm sorry I'm such a bad dancer." I yelled into his ear to make myself heard over "Tian Mi Mi," a song from the Mickey Rourke film *Year of the Dragon*. Cai chuckled, shaking his head as if to say I was crazy for thinking such a thing. We whirled around the common room, the other students a blur to me. When the song petered out, he asked if he could have the next dance. *This can't be happening.*

A Hong Kong love ballad was blaring from one corner and scratchy karaoke from another, so we danced without speaking. Whenever I caught quick glimpses of his face, I noticed that his full lips were turned up in a steady smile. His hair fell gently over his eyes, giving him a sleepy look as if he'd just woken up. And even though the room was dark, those big, beautiful eyes sparkled in the light cast from the disco ball.

He didn't squeeze my hand or give me any other clues to show he was interested in me romantically, yet dancing with him seemed so different than it had with the other men in the room. Suddenly I felt coordinated, even graceful. Maybe it was Cai's height or maybe it was a sense of familiarity from meeting him the night I locked myself out, but I also felt comfortable in his arms, as if he could whisk me away from my past inhibitions and humiliations. I hadn't felt this secure since the night Jin cooked me dinner at his apartment. But if given a chance with Cai, I vowed I would never allow myself to get hurt as I had with Jin and others.

When the music eventually faded, he gazed at the worn carpet. "I really should go back to my friends."

"Yes, of course." I wished we'd dance more, but I couldn't fault his loyalty to his friends. It revealed more about his character: that he cared about others and didn't put himself first. And I was thrilled just to be asked to dance twice in a row.

I got in a few words with my friend Cee Cee before another mainland student led me back to the dance floor. Each time I waltzed with a new partner, I couldn't help glancing in Cai's direction. Later, during a quick breather, I saw him headed toward me, and I knew that he was going to ask me to dance again. Without a word, he tapped my shoulder and led me to the center of the room as a Chinese revolutionary song played overhead, one that denounced America from the Korean War. It turned out to be the last dance. I half expected him to stick around and chat, but Cai said a quick good night as he left with his two friends.

The short good-bye didn't matter. My high from our last dance remained as I returned to my dorm with Cee Cee and some other expats. As we walked back, I replayed in my mind how Cai had asked me to dance three times and how magical it felt to be near him. I couldn't wait to see him again.

Chapter 3
ENTERING A CHINESE
FAIRY TALE

After my first two encounters with Cai—locking myself out and the dance—I wasn't sure when I would run into him again in the dorm or elsewhere on campus. Our departments were on opposite ends of the mountain. And at night, I was usually off campus having dinner or clubbing with Janice. If we stayed out until 3:00 a.m., I would go home with her and sleep on her top bunk. In the morning, we would eat breakfast and watch Bloomberg TV as if we were fancy expats who lived on the Peak and diligently followed the Asian stock exchanges.

But a week after the dance, I found myself face-to-face with Cai in the dorm lobby.

"Susan, *nĭ hǎo*." Hello.

"*Nĭ hǎo*." I hoisted my backpack over my shoulders, suddenly feeling the heat from outside pouring into the dorm. My heart raced. He had remembered my name.

"I was wondering if you could help me with some English pronunciation. I'm going to give a talk at an ethnomusicology meeting on campus in January." As usual, he spoke in Mandarin except for the word *ethnomusicology*, which he pronounced in English, stumbling over the jumble of consonants.

"Of course, I can help you." I had to steady my voice to keep it from going up an octave. Not even in my daydreams had I envisioned this. No, in my mind I had pictured running into Cai in one of the cafeterias or in the main library, gradually getting to know him a little better each time we crossed paths. Now with his request for English tutoring, I pictured so much more: the two of us attending musical performances off campus, followed by long discussions over cups of pu-ehr tea in a *cha chaan teng*, or traditional Hong Kong café.

"*Xièxiè.*" Thank you. "Just so you know, my paper is about Taoist music."

I hadn't a clue about Taoist music, or any Eastern religious music for that matter, but it seemed peaceful and intellectual, something that perfectly suited Cai's gentle personality. I imagined pagodas perched atop narrow buttes surrounded by melancholic gray clouds.

"Can we meet in your room tonight?" he asked, interrupting my reverie. "About seven?"

"My room?" *Was this really happening?*

"Na Wei won't be there, right?" Cai spoke matter-of-factly. "She'll be with her boyfriend."

"How did you know?"

Cai shrugged his shoulders, smiling with a hint of embarrassment. "Everyone knows."

In the midst of the excitement about our new arrangement, I didn't stop to inquire why everyone seemed to know that my roommate was married to someone in China and dating another guy in Hong Kong or, even more significantly, what Cai thought about her situation. I barely knew him and figured it was still early to speak about such intimate matters, even though he was the one who had brought it up. On the other hand, there was no rush to ask him every little question that came to mind. Now that I knew I would meet one-on-one with Cai, there was surely time to learn more about him.

That night I forced down a bowl of rice noodles and pasty, white, congealed fish balls at the dorm cafeteria. Alone in my room, I changed my clothes three times, more nervous than I had ever felt dressing for a first date. Nothing seemed to look right, but as the time crept closer to seven, I finally settled on a pair of wide floral pants, a silk blouse, and a long crocheted vest. Like most people in Hong Kong, I had already slipped into the plastic flip-flops that were only worn indoors.

The digital clock on my mini hi-fi seemed stuck at 6:45. I flipped through one of Na Wei's Hong Kong celebrity gossip magazines, wishing I hadn't eaten so quickly. My Chinese-English dictionary rested on my side of the wall-length desk I shared with Na Wei. Along the opposite wall was our metal bunk bed, where Na Wei's mattress had been untouched for days.

After what seemed like another hour, I heard a knock. When I opened the door, Cai stood before me, smiling widely. He was dressed in the same hunting vest he wore the night we met, but this time he wore a navy blue T-shirt underneath. In one hand he held his paper and a thin Chinese-English dictionary and, in the other, a white floral tea mug.

"Is this a good time?" he asked.

"Yes, of course. I usually stay inside on weeknights." That wasn't exactly true. That night was an exception, as I had canceled dinner with Janice. For my first semester, I had signed up for a full load of graduate-level classes in political theory, public administration, and Hong Kong politics. I would spend this first year in classwork and the second year writing my thesis. If I didn't start hitting the books soon, I knew my grades would suffer. Looking at Cai with his paper and teacup, I sensed that he would be a good academic influence.

As soon as he placed his things on Na Wei's side of the desk, Cai reached into a pocket of his hunting vest and pulled out a small bag filled with dried, green tea leaves.

"Would you like some tea?"

"Sure." I handed him a cup from the ledge above my side of the desk.

Checking myself in the mirror after he left the room, I readjusted my vest and smoothed out my blouse. I saw that my ponytail needed retying to rein in some loose strands. Several minutes later, I heard a knock on a door. "It's me," Cai said. I opened the door to find him grinning again, holding two steaming mugs.

Cai and I sipped our tea, which was surprisingly refreshing in

Hong Kong's hot autumn, while I read a paragraph of his paper for him to repeat. He'd taught himself a little English back in Wuhan, but had never taken a class and could only put a few words together on his own. We had a lot of work ahead of us.

Just as I'd pictured, his paper was filled with descriptions of clouds, trees, ritual music pieces, and Chinese instruments like gongs, two-stringed *erhus*, and bamboo flutes. Translated into English by a local student in Cai's department, his paper centered on a temple in Suzhou, not too far from Shanghai. I had visited both cities on my first trip to China but hadn't seen the temple in his paper. After thirty minutes of Cai repeating each paragraph, he rubbed his eyes. "*Lèile*," he said. I'm tired.

"I'd be tired, too, if I had to read in Chinese for a half hour straight."

"But you speak Mandarin very well."

"*Bùyào kèqì*." Don't be polite.

"No, really, you do. I've never met a foreigner who could say more than *nǐ hǎo*. Where did you learn Mandarin?"

"I studied in America for about four years, but also here in Hong Kong when I was an exchange student a few years back. That's why I'm in Hong Kong now. I loved it so much that I wanted to return. Going to graduate school was the only way I could get a long-term visa."

"Have you been to China? It's much easier to learn Mandarin there."

"Yes, I know. I went in 1988 with a group from my high school. Then I returned a couple times during my study-abroad year."

"Excellent." He sat back in his chair. "Where did you go?"

"The first time to Beijing, Nanjing, Shanghai, Wuxi, and Suzhou, just like in your paper. My dad teaches chemistry at a university in Chicago and has several Chinese students, so I visited their families in Shanghai and Beijing after my year in Hong Kong. Before that, I went back to Nanjing to see my tour guide from the first trip. I stayed with him and his family for Chinese New Year."

Cai's eyes lit up. "Chinese New Year is very loud and exciting. I can't wait to go back home for it this February."

"Your family is all in Wuhan?"

"Actually, I'm not from Wuhan city. I studied and taught there for eight years before I came here last year, but I'm from a small city two hours outside Wuhan called Hidden River. My parents and two sisters are still there. I have another sister who lives two hours in the other direction."

I held my breath, waiting for him to explain that his wife still lives in Wuhan, or that his girlfriend is from there but studying in Germany or Great Britain. Cai had to have a wife or at the very least a girlfriend. He was too good-looking and intelligent to still be single. My jealousy started to boil, and I wondered what I'd do if his wife or girlfriend came to Hong Kong to visit. Would I even be tutoring Cai at that point?

But that was it. Cai had stopped speaking.

This was the perfect opening to inquire about his personal life, but I just couldn't bring myself to ask him. The last thing I wanted was to make a social faux pas and scare Cai away. Since he hadn't asked if I had a boyfriend, I worried it might be premature to bring it up now. Besides, I didn't like feeling jealous, so I stuck to the conversation at hand. "I bet few people from Hidden River have made it to Hong Kong."

Cai chuckled. "That's true. Hidden River is very small for a Chinese city, but it's also a relaxed and peaceful place. Of course, there's no job for an ethnomusicologist there, but it will always stay close to my heart." Again, he spoke the word *ethnomusicologist* in English. I could already hear the improvement in pronunciation. He shifted in Na Wei's chair and took a quick sip of tea. "Aren't your parents worried about you being so far from home?"

"They're fine with it. My mom lived in Japan for a year when she was about my age. My dad has traveled a lot, too. They visited me twice the year I was an exchange student. And now they're planning to come again this December. I think my parents like having me here. It's a good excuse to travel and to see Hong Kong."

What I didn't say, but thought at that moment, was that my parents would like Cai. All of my dad's Chinese graduate students had become close to my parents, joining my family for Thanksgiving every year. Cai reminded me of these students and their spouses: diligent, kind, and curious to learn more, even after they had finished their studies.

"China is becoming more like the United States in that way," Cai said. "Many college students are going to America, and most stay there after they graduate."

"My dad's students have all stayed, and they came to Chicago ten years ago."

He didn't reply and I didn't ask what he thought about Chinese students moving abroad for good. Thinking about my dad's students—all of whom had found good jobs and bought homes—I assumed most young people from China wished to live in the United States.

Cai looked at his watch. "It's late and you must be tired. Is tomorrow night at seven okay with you? I still have so much work to do on this paper. It'll be a miracle if I'm ready by January."

"Tomorrow's great. And of course you'll be ready. It's still early October and we've only met once. There's plenty of time." And plenty of time to get to know him better, I mused.

Cai stood and took his paper, dictionary, and empty teacup. "Good night, Susan. Thank you for working with me."

"No problem. I'm happy to help."

"See you tomorrow," Cai said as he stepped into the hallway.

As soon as I heard the elevator door close, I grabbed my key—I wouldn't forget it this time—and phoned Janice on the hall phone. She would have to go clubbing tomorrow night without me.

The next evening, I saw that Cai's musical background gave him a good ear for languages. Although we continued to use Mandarin in our conversations, his English pronunciation improved faster than I'd first imagined it would.

"I never thought it would be so exhausting to read in English."

"That's just because you're doing really well. If you weren't improving, it wouldn't feel so difficult."

Cai smiled and leaned back in his chair. I wanted to know more about him, so I took this opportunity to ask, "What is Hidden River like?"

He nodded and began to speak of his idyllic childhood full of carefree days roaming the countryside and wading through ponds covered with lily pads the size of Frisbees. He fished and caught frogs with a band of friends, completely free of want. But then he started talking about his adolescence.

"It was a very hard time in China. Just before I finished middle school, all high schools were closed. Teenagers had to work in the countryside so they could learn from the peasants. But I didn't want to do manual labor. I was actually very lucky. One day, a traveling opera group came to Hidden River to hold auditions. This troupe traveled throughout Hubei province to perform revolutionary operas. I'd seen some operas and always enjoyed the colorful costumes and lively music. So I tried out."

"As an actor?"

"No, as a cellist. I played with this opera troupe for seven years and never had to do manual labor."

"Had you played the cello before the troupe came to your town?"

"No. I'd never even seen one before."

What an incredible story. It seemed like something from a Chinese novel or film, especially compared to my predictable childhood in suburban Chicago. My dad's students also grew up during the Cultural Revolution, but they spoke of those days in vague terms, how they stopped going to school and were sent to the countryside to work with peasants. Although I had read similar stories about famous people like actress Joan Chen and author Anchee Min, Cai was the first person I knew who had been saved from this fate through the arts.

He went on to tell me that he was the youngest in his opera troupe and was doted on by the other members, both the men and the women.

They all kept an eye out for him and made sure he was well cared for.

"Everyone was my parent."

"Didn't you miss your family? You were so young when you started with the opera." It must have been difficult to be the youngest. And I couldn't imagine leaving home just as I was supposed to start high school. That age was difficult enough with struggling to fit in. I didn't think I could have successfully navigated those years on my own, far from my family.

"I got used to it. Most teenagers lived apart from their parents back then." He shrugged sheepishly.

A slew of images floated through my mind: his years away from his family, constantly on the road, the thrill of the applause after each performance. Yet something nagged at me. "How could you enter college if you were on the road with the opera for seven years?"

"There's a Chinese saying, 'If a son is uneducated, his father is to blame.' My parents were both teachers, so my dad often sent me homework. He loves to read and study on his own, so he developed lessons for me in reading, writing, and math. When I was twenty-one and finished with the opera, I took the college entrance exams and got into the Wuhan Conservatory of Music."

"That's amazing. Do you still play the cello?"

"No," he chuckled. "I haven't picked one up in years. I don't even own one. After I finished college, I knew I'd never be good enough to play professionally again, so I switched to ethnomusicology for my master's degree. I like the peaceful philosophy behind Taoism and find the music both uplifting and sad. I've even written a few books about Taoist music and will travel to Suzhou this summer to do fieldwork for my dissertation."

His life really was something out of a movie. I felt not just admiration for Cai, but also a newfound respect. I didn't want the night to end, but it was getting late and we both had early morning classes. Before he left my room, we arranged to meet the following evening and every night that week, except Saturday and Sunday evenings.

Cai explained that on Sundays he took the train a few stations north to play the *erhu*, a two-stringed Chinese instrument, in the music rituals at a Taoist temple renowned in Hong Kong's business community. This schedule suited me well. I could meet with Cai during the week and still hang out with Janice on the weekends.

Chapter 4

LEARNING THE CHINESE RULES OF DATING

Several weeks after the magical dance, Cai took a long sip of his tea while he leaned back in Na Wei's blocky, wooden chair. We had been reading through his paper and it was getting late. He looked around the room as if debating whether to say something.

"There's another mainland student dance tomorrow." He made brief eye contact with me. "Do you want to meet there? I have to go off campus before that."

It took me a minute to realize he was asking me to go—with him. All these weeks of wondering how he felt about me, and now this invitation to finally venture out of our dorm together. Ever since we had started meeting nightly, Cai and I had been locked away in my room working on his paper.

"That would be great." I steadied my voice in case he was only asking me as a friend. But would he really ask me if he just wanted to be friends? Could this be a turning point in our friendship? I still didn't know about his personal life and if there was someone back in China or elsewhere. But this invitation to the dance seemed promising.

I didn't wait long after Cai left my room before phoning Janice to tell her about this sudden change. I knew I would sound like a love-struck middle school girl, but I needed to analyze it with someone, and Janice was my best friend. We hadn't seen each other the last couple of weekends because I needed to use that time to write papers or study for exams. Soon most of my contact with her took place over the phone when I could catch her at home.

She continued to go out most nights of the week and sail on junk cruises around Hong Kong's outlaying islands on the weekends. Although I had once aspired to that lifestyle, it no longer held sway. I would rather stay in and talk to Cai every night, and attend mainland dances once a month. By chance, when I phoned Janice that night, she had just returned from a party in the fancy Mid-Levels district on Hong Kong Island.

"Just be careful," she warned me. "You still don't know him very well."

"But we meet every night. And isn't this a chance to get to know him better? I can't wait to dance with him again!" In less than twenty-four hours, Cai would be twirling me around the dance floor, holding me tightly in his arms.

"You're right. It's good you're getting to know him. Just be cautious, okay? I'd hate for you to jump ahead of yourself when it's still so early."

Cai and I had made plans to meet at seven the following evening, so I arrived a couple minutes after that. I didn't want to keep him waiting. The room was filled with mainland students. As I scanned the area, I saw that none of the expats or local students from the last dance had arrived yet. I was so excited to go with Cai that I had neglected to ask my friend Cee Cee if she would be attending this one, too. I found a place to wait for Cai, not too far from the door. Leaning against the peach cinder block wall, I tried to tune out "Rainy Days and Mondays."

Quite a few mainland men who had danced with me last time were now waltzing by with other women. They never once looked in my direction. But it didn't faze me because I wasn't there to be with other guys; I had come to dance with Cai. He should arrive any minute now. More familiar faces swished by—both men and women—yet they continued not to make eye contact. I started to feel invisible, like I did as a young girl in Evanston, when I was the last kid picked for teams in gym class and never got invited to parties. When Cai arrived, I imagined we would dance the rest of the night away.

Maybe the train was delayed or he was still waiting for the campus bus at the bottom of the mountain. Only a small percentage of people had cell phones back then, so we were all used to waiting around an extra half hour or forty-five minutes. It happened all the time when I made plans to meet Janice during rush hour. I decided to wait ten more minutes now before heading back up to my building to check with the guard at the front desk. Maybe Cai had left a message with him.

Air Supply's "All Out of Love" came on, and I wanted to crawl into a corner and hide. The mainland students still hadn't acknowledged me, but surely they saw me and were wondering why I was standing against the wall alone. I hoped they couldn't see my humiliation. Last time I had danced with a lot of men, so I knew they weren't staying away now because they had an aversion to foreigners. What could it be?

And then I saw him.

It was like I was back in the dorm lobby, locked out and desperate to borrow a replacement key. Cai walked into the room and my nerves waned. I almost forgot I'd been standing alone all this time.

He glanced over at me as he adjusted his eyes to the dark room. But instead of joining me, he stopped to chat with a few friends who stood along another wall. Surely he had seen me. Or maybe he wanted to greet these friends before spending the rest of the evening with me. *Please save me!* I wanted to scream into the crowd. Even if I'd been that bold, no one would have heard me over the pulsating synthesized music. A few minutes later, Cai finally made his way toward me. He smiled as if we'd both just arrived at the dance and brought me to the center of the room.

He looked over my shoulder as I tried to follow his box steps. "You look really nice. Sorry I'm late."

"Thank you." His compliment washed away the embarrassment of waiting alone. I certainly couldn't let him know I'd almost suffered a panic attack. "That's all right. I got here a little early."

After we waltzed to a Faye Wong song and "Endless Love," Cai pushed his hands into his pants pockets. "I should probably dance with some people in my department. It looks like they're all alone."

"Sure, go ahead." The irony wasn't lost on me, but what could it hurt to sit out a couple songs now that Cai was here?

I stood back against the wall where I had waited for Cai. Now I watched his graceful dance moves as he tangoed with a couple of older, married women in his department, one after the other. A couple decades younger than these women, I didn't mind that Cai danced with them. They seemed kind and gentle. If I had been in their place, I would have appreciated someone like Cai taking time out to dance with me.

At the end of a Hong Kong ballad, he nodded to his partner. Instead of heading toward me, he turned in the opposite direction, away from the front door. Cai started talking with Yang Xiaoxun, the man he was with the night we met. My eyes bulged in disbelief as he proceeded to teach Yang to cha-cha, swinging his legs along an invisible line on the sidelines.

My first inclination was to storm out, but instead I took a deep breath. I could not let myself come across as needy and immature, although that was exactly how I felt at the moment. As Cai continued to cha-cha with Yang, I tried to stay calm. I couldn't throw away the rapport I'd developed with Cai over the last month just because I felt alone—and abandoned, if I was honest with myself—in a room full of people I barely knew.

The last song, "I Love Beijing Tiananmen," finished and someone flipped on the lights. Now that the dance was over, I remained standing alone, numb. My head throbbed in confusion. How could the first dance, when I couldn't take a breath between songs, differ so drastically with this one, when no one except Cai talked to me? And more importantly, why had Cai only asked me to dance twice this time? Had I unwittingly offended him? Had one of the students told him that I looked miserable before he had arrived?

I loitered around the entrance of the common room while Cai stuck to Yang Xiaoxun's side. When they reached the door, Cai said a quick good-bye to Yang. In silence we ascended two flights to the concrete bridge connecting the lower graduate dorm to the upper one. A fishy aroma wafted up from the Tolo Harbour, the November sky clear and dry. Was Cai going to explain why this dance contrasted so much from the first one? But he remained silent, his eyes directed ahead into dark shrubbery. I couldn't return to my dorm with these matters unanswered.

"Cai," I said, careful to avoid asking a direct question that would be perceived as a personal affront, "it was kind of weird that no one else asked me to dance tonight. Not that I wanted to, but it was so different from last month."

He stopped and looked off to the side, toward the sea below. In the moonlight, his eyes appeared tired and worn. "The mainland students have been talking about us."

"What do you mean, 'talking about us'?"

Cai continued to look away. "They think we're dating." His tone was serious with a sprinkle of embarrassment.

Dating? This was news to me. Of course it was good news if Cai wanted to date me, but humiliating and possibly friendship-ending if he didn't. Was he bothered by this gossip? Was that why he couldn't meet before the dance and why he was so late? Or was he telling me about these students because he really was interested in dating? *Were we dating?*

I wanted to discuss it at length—like I did with Janice—but as with most heavy questions, I was afraid of the answer. After all these weeks of meeting in my room, I was developing an attachment to him that I couldn't think about severing now. I couldn't say anything to turn him away. On the other hand, if he told me about these students, he must have an opinion.

We started again toward our dorm, walking in silence. In the elevator, he hesitated when it reached the fourth floor. "Are we still meeting tomorrow night?" Cai stood waiting for my answer, his eyes wide in anticipation. Something about his look made me think that he doubted I would want to continue our tutoring.

"Yes, of course." I tried to muffle my enthusiasm. Cai smiled and waved good-bye before walking toward his room.

As soon as I reached the eighth floor, I stopped at the hall phone to call Janice. I couldn't wait to tell her about these latest developments. But just as I picked up the receiver, I remembered she was at a party on Lantau Island. There was no one else I could call, so I dozed off on my top bunk, reflecting on how the other students talked among themselves about Cai and me. Together. Dating.

Chapter 5
SHARING SECRETS

In the two weeks since the second dance, Cai and I hadn't spoken any further about our dating status or even about the other students' gossip about us. January loomed on the horizon, and I started to panic that he would end our meetings after his presentation. Or perhaps he had become uncomfortable after revealing that the mainland students were talking about us. But the days passed as usual and he continued coming to my room on a nightly basis, as if the second dance had never occurred. I tried my best to act natural and not show Cai that I worried about the future of our friendship.

Then one evening in early December, as Cai was about to leave my room, he hesitated at my door.

"One of these days, I should tell you a story." He smiled demurely.

A story? Was it the one I'd been waiting to hear all these months, the one that would finally reveal the details of his personal life? Cai couldn't dangle that and leave me hanging. Too anxious to move, I remained in my chair, worried he'd notice my right leg twitching. "Can't you tell me now?" I stammered.

He walked back toward Na Wei's chair and sat down. Smiling, he said, "Guess."

Yes, it could only relate to his personal life in China. Nothing else would be so remarkable that he couldn't just tell me casually. I felt we'd covered every topic except our previous relationships. So I took a quick breath. "Are you married?"

He looked away. "I was."

"You *were?*"

"I was married for five years." He looked down again. "But I've been divorced for two years now."

A wave of relief swept through me. He was available. No one in my immediate family was divorced, but it seemed a far better answer than if Cai had revealed he was married or even separated.

But when I looked into his eyes, he suddenly appeared weary. Maybe the divorce hadn't been his idea and he was still trying to get her back. Was she the one he wanted to call the night we met, the night he meant to buy a calling card at midnight? "Do you still love her?" I asked.

"No!"

Phew. But why would he look unhappy? Most of the married students in our dorm had both a spouse and child back in China. So when I saw dejection on Cai's face, these other students came to mind. Before I could think how best to phrase my question, I blurted out, "Do you have a child?"

"Yes, a daughter." He paused and then smirked. "Too bad, huh?"

I stared at him blankly. It was socially expected for young married couples in China to have a child, so that in itself didn't come as a surprise. My father had been a widowed single father when he met my mother, so the fact that Cai had a daughter wasn't a deal breaker for me. But his comment about his daughter: Did he really think that?

As if guessing my thoughts, Cai chuckled. "I'm only joking about that last part. If you have time now, I can tell you the whole story."

"Of course." I would stay up all night to hear his story.

Before they divorced, Cai and his ex-wife, Wei Ling, had lived in Wuhan with their daughter Ting-Ting and a teenage nanny from the countryside. Out of the blue, Wei Ling announced that she planned to move south to Zhūhâi, a special economic zone— one of several areas designated in the early 1980s as an experiment in free trade—a couple of hours by boat from Hong Kong. She'd found a teaching job there, where salaries were higher and the climate was subtropical.

At the same time Wei Ling announced she was moving south—alone—Cai was waiting for his Hong Kong paperwork to be processed so he could study for his PhD. Wei Ling was aware of Cai's plans to leave Wuhan for several months at a time and only to return for holidays and during the summer.

Because Wei Ling hadn't told him about her decision to move south until after she'd committed to the job, Cai asked Wei Ling if this meant she wanted a divorce. She answered yes. But he told me the divorce didn't come as a surprise, since his marriage had been strained for some time. Even his friends could see it. His family never understood why Wei Ling refused to travel with him to Hidden River even before their daughter was born.

According to Cai, it wasn't until after Ting-Ting came along that Wei Ling started going out at night with her friends, often returning home past midnight. The first time she stayed out late, Cai worried she'd fallen ill or had been robbed. This was well before the time when cell phones—or even private landlines—were common in China, and they didn't have a telephone in their apartment.

He would pace their compact, one-room apartment with no way to reach her and wasn't able to sleep until she returned safely. The teenage nanny provided no reassurance, as she was a child herself and worried about her employer's safety. But when Wei Ling finally walked in the door, Cai saw that she was fine. Wei Ling continued to go out as she pleased, leaving Cai at home with Ting-Ting and the nanny.

Cai and Wei Ling often argued. He didn't think it was right for her to go out so late when she had a baby—and a husband—at home. Wei Ling claimed she simply spent time with a group of men and women at a restaurant. She never confessed to having a boyfriend.

After they split up, two-year-old Ting-Ting moved in with Wei Ling's parents. Cai agreed to this arrangement because he knew he couldn't take care of her once his Hong Kong visa was ready. He didn't mind Ting-Ting living with her grandparents because it was a common arrangement in China when parents worked or studied in other parts of China or even abroad. The official who presided over their divorce required Cai to pay a one-time child support fee of 10,000 Chinese yuan, or about $1,250 U.S.

"So do you visit Ting-Ting when you return to Wuhan?" I expected bittersweet stories of father-daughter outings to large, run-down Chinese parks, the paint from the simple playground equipment faded and peeling away.

Cai looked at his hands. "When I tried to visit Ting-Ting last summer, Wei Ling's parents wouldn't even let me in. Her father said Ting-Ting had a good life and should be left alone."

He hadn't tried to contact Ting-Ting since.

I wanted to hold Cai tightly, to assure him that his luck would change. Maybe he just needed a boost of confidence and a little push to give it another try. If he continued to let me into his life, I would try to gently persuade Cai to visit his daughter. Ting-Ting needed a father, no matter where he lived.

"I hope I haven't shocked you. It's just something I wanted you to know. I haven't told anyone else at the university except a couple of people in my department. So if you didn't say anything—"

"Of course, I won't say a word." I felt so honored he'd confide in me.

In my upper bunk that night, I thought about my father, who had lost his first wife to breast cancer twelve years into their marriage. I understood that people could still hang on to precious memories of a former spouse even years into a new marriage.

But Cai's case was different. He seemed adamant that he wasn't still in love with Wei Ling, so it wasn't likely that he still hoped they'd get back together. In fact, I wondered if he was ever in love with her. From what I was learning about Chinese marriage, I could see how he had felt pressure to marry in his late twenties. So the divorce didn't bother me. The one I couldn't stop thinking about was Ting-Ting.

I'd always pictured myself having a child and could imagine how Cai must suffer from not being able to see his daughter. Did she know he'd tried to visit her last year? I worried for Ting-Ting's happiness if she wasn't allowed to contact her father. Some childhood friends had divorced parents and had become justifiably bitter toward absent fathers. In my own family, I knew what it was like to see a sibling estranged from his family. When my father lost his first wife to breast cancer in the late 1960s, it was difficult for him, but even more so for their adopted son, Danny.

My dad quickly remarried and had two children—myself and my brother, Jonathan. Soon Danny started acting out and threatening my mother, prompting my parents to send him to a special school for children with behavioral issues when he was eleven years old and I was five. Danny never lived with our family again, nor did he have close relationships with either of my parents. Cai needed to fight to see Ting-Ting before it was too late.

I tossed and turned, the gloom of his story weighing down my waking hours. I tried to visualize Cai, Wei Ling, and Ting-Ting as a family back in Wuhan, but the only picture that crept into my mind was a worried Cai pacing the apartment while Ting-Ting slept in a bassinet off in one corner. He must have felt helpless back then.

To clear my head the next morning, I headed to the one place where I knew I could think clearly: the waterfront promenade in Tsim Sha Tsui, the tip of the Kowloon Peninsula. When I was an exchange student and new to Hong Kong four years earlier, I often rode the train forty-five minutes down to the Kowloon harbor front to stand before the dense clusters of modern skyscrapers rising from the base of the island to halfway up the mountain.

Not much of a seafarer, I nonetheless enjoyed watching the boats in the harbor. They came in all sizes: some as small as *wallah wallahs* and some as massive as cruise ships or naval carriers. The harbor had long since become polluted and unsafe for swimming, but one day I noticed a middle-aged Chinese man splashing in the water next to his little sampan. He smiled and waved up to me like an old friend.

With Cai's story on my mind, I gazed out at the green and white Star Ferries chugging across the harbor and wondered how he and

I would interact the next time we saw each other. Had Cai felt like he'd revealed too much, only to retreat inward? My worst fear was still that he'd stop coming to my room for our tutoring sessions. Drawing from my limited experience—and what I thought Chinese culture dictated—I felt like my only choice was to wait to see what Cai would do.

Heading back toward the train station, I almost stopped at a phone booth to call Janice at work so I could tell her about Cai's divorce and Ting-Ting. But then I worried she would form a worse opinion of him if I revealed this new information. It was premature, I reasoned, to discuss these developments with her before I knew if Cai was interested in dating.

On my return to the dorm to pick up my books for my state and civil society class, I entered the lobby and turned toward the elevator. Just then, Cai walked out of the cafeteria.

"Good morning." He spoke in English, a change from our usual Mandarin, and stepped closer, brushing his hair away from his eyes. "Do you still want to meet tonight?"

"Of course." I switched to Mandarin out of habit. "Thanks for talking to me last night. I'm so glad you told me."

"No problem. I'll see you after dinner. Same time, same place." He winked and walked toward the front door.

As I rode the elevator alone to my room, I felt giddy with the anticipation of meeting Cai that evening, of keeping his secret, and of seeing our friendship grow.

Chapter 6

"CHINA IS MY HOME"

Days after he told me about Wei Ling and Ting-Ting, Cai spoke of his postgraduation plans during our nightly tutoring session. It was the first time we'd discussed the future.

"I don't want to move to America. China is my home and I want to return there and teach." He sounded more serious than usual, sitting up straight in Na Wei's chair.

"What about Hong Kong? Would you want to stay here?" It didn't bother me that he wasn't interested in moving to the United States. I had no plans to return there anytime soon and hoped to find a job in Hong Kong after graduation. If he wanted to do the same, we might have a future together.

"I can't. Mainland students aren't able to stay here after our student visas expire. In any case, Hong Kong has no culture. I want to go back to China."

My stomach fell. I could hear what was coming next. Cai would say he liked me but it would never work because he wanted to move back to China and couldn't ask me to give up the comfort of Hong Kong or the United States for a life of harsh conditions. It wasn't difficult for me to picture Cai returning to the motherland, teaching for low wages and serving the people.

However, from my trips to China, I knew I'd feel too isolated to live there long-term, cut off from everything familiar. That's why I had chosen to move to Hong Kong, which to me was a perfect mélange of East and West. But why was I thinking about our future together when we weren't even dating? Janice was right; I couldn't let myself jump ahead like this. He probably wasn't going to discuss a future together with me.

But he did continue speaking. "I just wanted you to know that— and that I have a child—in case we start dating and get married."

Wait. Dating? Married? *With me?* Had he really just asked me about either, especially to possibly *marry* him? Everything in my room suddenly seemed to blur. Cai continued to speak, but I couldn't hear him. Time had suspended with those words "dating and get married." My mind raced back to the night I met Cai in the dorm lobby, the day he asked me to tutor him, the short discussion about dating after the second dance.

I slowly tuned back into the conversation to hear Cai say, "In China, couples traditionally date only if they plan to marry. It's not like in the United States where people date casually until they meet someone they want to marry."

So this was normal, talking about dating and marriage in the same sentence. It was the first time I had heard of this custom, but I trusted Cai. The Chinese way was so different, so straightforward and risk-free. I couldn't imagine finding someone more kind or attentive than him. And by agreeing to marry him, I'd no longer worry about whether he'd still want to meet every night or if he'd run away after he told me about his daughter and failed marriage.

All I could think about was spending the rest of my life with Cai—and that he wanted to share his with me. I didn't dwell on the fact that I didn't really want to live in China. Even after I had a moment to gather my thoughts, I still couldn't speak up. What if he took back his proposal if I didn't accept his terms? That seemed more unbearable than giving up a life in Hong Kong or America. So I blurted out, "Oh, that's fine! I could live in China, too."

Cai bent in closer, peering at me with his gentle eyes. "So would you like to start dating?"

I can't believe this is happening. I was psyched! "Yes, of course," I said, trying to keep my voice calm and collected.

He fidgeted as he looked away from me. "Can I kiss you?"

"Yes." I spoke quietly, yet with newfound self-assurance. When he stood up, I followed his lead, holding on to the desk to steady myself.

Cai drew me to him with his cellist fingers and strong arms. After a drawn-out kiss, he held my hands in his, gazing into my eyes. "Do you have any bad habits?" he asked in the same way someone would whisper sweet nothings into a lover's ear.

I thought it an odd question to ask but felt grateful for his openness. Maybe I'd been wrong to feel so reserved in those first couple months. "Well, I don't like conflict. Sometimes I bottle my emotions inside so I don't have to argue."

He kissed the back of my hands one at a time. "You should always tell me how you feel: what bothers you, what you don't like, what scares you. Remember, I've been married. Communication is vital for a happy relationship."

I gently squeezed Cai's fingers, which still held mine. "What about you? Do you have any bad habits?" I couldn't imagine any. He listens, he understands, he cares.

Cai held my hands still. "Sometimes I get angry and don't like to talk. Don't worry when that happens. I just need time to resolve things myself."

I couldn't picture him getting upset and clamming up. I'd seen him with his classmates that night we met and at the two dances. He was outgoing and upbeat in these social settings, and gentle with me. I looked down at our intertwined hands and felt my cheeks flush. This was all moving so quickly for me. And it seemed so impulsive. Yet I worried I would lose him if I turned him down.

"When were you thinking about getting married?" I asked.

"After we graduate? In a year and a half? Is that okay with you?"

"Yes, of course. It'll be like a graduation party and wedding all rolled into one."

Cai smiled and looked into my eyes. "Can you do me a favor? The other mainland students will be very jealous if they know we're engaged. Just until the end of the summer, can you please not tell anyone on campus? In the fall it will be fine to talk openly about it."

"Do you really think the mainland students even care?"

"Remember how they talked about us before we were even dating? They'll go crazy if they know we're already engaged. They'll probably say I'm marrying you to get an American passport—"

"But you're the only one who wants to return to China. *They* want to go to the U.S." How dare these students label him an opportunist like that? They didn't know him like I did, and I wasn't about to feed their gossip. In truth, I felt a little excited about keeping this secret, just as I had after Cai told me about his former marriage to Wei Ling and his fragile relationship with Ting-Ting.

Cai then asked me why I loved him. It was difficult for me to express complex terms in Mandarin, but I tried my best to say that he was kind, funny, intelligent, and easy to talk to. As he left my room that evening, he kissed me again and whispered, "I love you," before opening the door and returning to his room four floors below.

Chapter 7

CHINESE NEW YEAR IN HIDDEN RIVER

Chinese New Year came two months after Cai proposed. The longest and most important holiday in China, the New Year was a time for people to return to their families no matter where they lived in China. It was also the busiest travel season in Hong Kong, as people either went north to visit their ancestral homes or left the area for the beaches of Thailand, the Philippines, or Malaysia.

As February approached, Cai thought it best to tell his family about me in person—and alone. I was anxious to meet them but trusted Cai's judgment. There would be plenty of chances for me to be introduced, perhaps as early as that summer when he would return to China to conduct his dissertation fieldwork.

When Cai left to study in Hong Kong, it probably occurred to his parents that he could meet and marry a Hong Kong Chinese woman. That was their idea of a foreigner. People in Hubei province didn't speak Cantonese, and in most cases, people in Hong Kong wouldn't understand the local dialects in Hubei. Hong Kong used traditional Chinese characters, along with some characters unique to Cantonese and some English letters, while people in China read and wrote simplified characters that had been introduced in the 1950s to increase literacy after Mao came into power.

And the food in the two regions wasn't the same: Cantonese food didn't use chili peppers, but people in Hubei, just south of fiery Hunan province, were not afraid of spicy foods. Also, women in China didn't change their names after they married, but Hong Kong women did.

Although these differences might seem insignificant to the outsider, they were great enough to cause a cultural divide between many mainland students in Hong Kong and their local classmates. For students like me, who had studied Mandarin in our home countries, it was often easier to fit in with the Mandarin-speaking mainland students than with the local Cantonese students. Thus it was more common for mainland students to date foreigners who knew Mandarin than local Hong Kong Chinese who preferred to speak Cantonese.

But to Cai's parents, I would probably seem like an alien. Upon hearing my nationality, would they think I was a loose American who disregarded the traditional family unit? Would they worry that I would take Cai away from them, whisking him to the United States and changing him into an American? These questions raced through my mind when Cai suggested he return to Hidden River alone this time. I imagined his parents would need some time to digest this news.

A couple of days after Cai left for Hidden River, I returned home one evening from the New Year's market at Victoria Park on Hong Kong Island. Row after row of vendors selling pussy willow branches, kumquat trees, and plum blossom branches lined the spacious park along the harbor. I had met my roommates from my exchange year for dinner and a stroll through the festive market.

In the spirit of the New Year, I purchased a small kumquat tree, the tiny orange fruits bobbing on their lush, green-leaved branches as I lugged it home on the train and halfway up the mountain to my dorm room. Just as I set the tree on my desk, the phone buzzer blasted in my room. I had a phone call.

Picking up my key, I headed for the hall phone around the corner. I was surprised to hear Cai's voice on the other end. He sounded out of breath. Had his family threatened to disown him if he married me?

"I'm calling from the post office and there is a long line, so I can't talk long. I just wanted to tell you that I love you. And that my family is anxious to meet you. I've told them all about you."

"Really? Did you tell them we're engaged?"

Cai still sounded rushed, yet elated. "Yes. They want you to come visit—as soon as possible."

"You mean now? During this break?" They couldn't possibly expect me to buy a plane ticket at the last minute during the busiest travel season of the year. Maybe he meant for spring break.

"Yes, yes! They know everything and want to meet you now. They are so happy for me, for us. When can you fly to Wuhan? I'll meet you at the airport. Please come as soon as you can."

One moment I was returning from a fair with a kumquat tree, and the next I was expected to fly to Wuhan as soon as possible. I had thought that my biggest decision for the rest of the evening would involve whether I would read before bed. Now I had to think about all I'd have to prepare if I were to suddenly leave Hong Kong for a week.

It wasn't that I didn't want to meet Cai's family, but flying up to Wuhan had never crossed my mind. In Hong Kong we only had a three-day vacation, but in China people took off two weeks. My classes would start up in two days and I'd have to miss a week if I suddenly left for Hidden River. And when a billion people travel throughout China during the Lunar New Year, tickets don't exactly come easily. "I'm not sure I can find a flight now."

"Please look," he said gently. "They really want to meet you. There must be some flights still available to Wuhan."

I paused, knowing deep down that I'd do whatever it took to get myself to Wuhan. What was one week of classes compared to meeting Cai's family, my future in-laws? "I'll call my travel agent first thing tomorrow morning. After I find out what's available, I'll phone you at your parents' place."

"*Thank you*. Call me as soon as you buy your ticket."

The next morning I found a one-way ticket to Wuhan that cost as much as a round-trip ticket from New York to Paris. My savings from my research and teaching assistant salary just covered the airfare. I would see Cai and meet his parents the following day. In the meantime, I left a message with the department secretary to inform my professors I'd miss a week of classes. Most of the professors in my department came from Taiwan and, like Janice's parents, were weary of mainland Chinese. So I was grateful I didn't have to tell them in person about my trip and the reasons for it. I knew that some of my professors would not just worry that I had become involved with a mainland student, but that I would marry him.

Several hours later, I stepped out of the Wuhan military airport into a sea of men and women with black hair who wore either dark winter jackets or long, military-green wool coats. The temperature outside hovered just above freezing. Red Chinese character banners draped over the surrounding buildings provided the only color in a monochromatic landscape. Like the other Chinese cities I had visited, Wuhan appeared dilapidated, blanketed by a gray haze.

Cai emerged at the back of the crowd, running toward me. When he reached the front, he embraced me tightly, lifting me off the frozen ground. All around, people stared at us while Cai took my suitcase. With his other hand, Cai held on to mine, leading me away from the masses to a gravel parking lot. He stopped when we reached a black Volkswagen Santana sedan. Two young men leaned against it, smoking cigarettes. The shorter one resembled a Chinese James Dean, with narrow eyes and a cigarette hanging almost limply from the side of his mouth. The taller one was Cai's height and held his cigarette between his thumb and forefinger, like a pencil. Both either sported slight body waves or were growing out old perms.

Cai introduced them as his brothers-in-law, Zhao Yun and Lin Haitao, who had driven with him on the two-hour journey from Hidden River. Something about this scene reminded me of the night I met Cai with his two mainland classmates, Luo Minghui and Yang Xiaoxun. Just like then, Cai's companions seemed at home in China while Cai looked out of place, as if he belonged in a more cosmopolitan setting.

"*Nǐ hǎo, nǐ hǎo*," I said, greeting the men who would soon become my relatives. They nodded as Cai held open the back passenger door for me. An amulet bearing a young, rosy-cheeked Mao Zedong hung from the rearview mirror, protecting the car from calamity. Zhao, the Chinese James Dean, had borrowed the Santana from his *dānwèi*, or work unit. Back then, few people in China owned cars (and today, cars are still somewhat of a luxury in parts of rural China).

The road to Hidden River loomed flat, monotonous, and uncluttered. The empty, rural highway contrasted sharply with Wuhan's cramped city streets, with its masses of bicycles and pedestrians. Besides a few huge trucks, ours was the only vehicle on the highway in either direction. Cai and I sat in the backseat, his arm around my shoulders. With his other hand he pointed out a sputtering tractor and a flock of chickens so scrawny that they appeared not to have eaten since before the Great Leap Forward. Compared to the Hong Kong countryside, the road to Wuhan seemed like a blast back to the 1950s.

We reached Hidden River two hours later, thick clusters of bicycles and pedestrians surrounding us like long-lost relatives. I felt my pulse rush as Cai rubbed my shoulder. The Santana crept through the city of one million people, which looked like a small town with its low buildings, street markets, and wide dusty roads. At his parents' *dānwèi* on the other side of town, Zhao drove under a crumbling, arched gateway. I noticed a few rows of one-story, dilapidated redbrick buildings, as flat and grimy as old condemned motels in America. A handful of adults sat around a card table in front of one door, playing mah-jongg and sipping murky tea from old jars, while a band of children ran in and out of an open doorway.

I almost choked when Cai said his parents had lived in one of those apartments less than two years ago. I couldn't picture myself spending a week in one of the run-down brick shanties, but I would have felt worse for Cai's parents if they still lived that way.

Zhao parked the car in a gravel lot next to a building that looked deserted. Once outside, Cai took my hand while he hauled my suitcase on his other side. As we kicked up clouds of dust with each stride, I felt nervous and excited to meet my future in-laws. Zhao and Lin followed us. Still holding on to my hand, which wasn't a common practice in China then unless it was between friends of the same sex, Cai nodded toward a drab, cement six-story walk-up that looked to be at least forty years old. "My parents live there."

"How old is this building?"

"A year and a half. Just like new."

How was this building, in its Stalinist drabness, less than two years old? Even the run-down buildings in Hong Kong, like Janice's in Kowloon, didn't look this old—and hers really was decades old.

As we walked around to the back of the building, Cai looked up and sang, "*Mama, Baba!*" A plump woman leaned out of an open window, her permed hair dyed as black as night. Cai's mother screeched, "*Yan-er!*" Like many Chinese men, Cai went by his last name. But his parents still called him by his childhood nickname, Yan, the Chinese word for the swallow bird.

Their three-bedroom apartment was no larger than nine hundred square feet, gigantic by Hong Kong standards. I noticed Cai's parents and his three younger sisters still wore their winter coats, and I could see their breath as they spoke. The apartment's mint green and white two-toned paint job reminded me of a hospital. The brown vinyl sofa in the living room offset the naked walls. The smell of coal, cooking oil, and strong, musty cigarette smoke brought me back to a week in Nanjing several years back when I visited the tour guide from my high school trip to China. Cai's parents greeted me by smiling and nodding. They didn't shake hands, kiss, or hug. The sisters talked among themselves and didn't engage me in conversation. But Cai's father spoke to me.

"*Àiwūjíwū,*" Cai's dad said while Cai and I stood holding hands in front of the wooden beads and red silk flowers that hung from the top of the door frame of the middle bedroom. After Cai's dad recited this proverb, he covered his mouth with one hand to hide his teeth.

"That's a traditional Chinese saying," Cai interpreted. "It means, 'Love my house, love the crow on it.'"

As the pungent, metallic smell of chicken blood wafted in from the kitchen, where Cai's mother had returned to chop away at a fresh carcass, I pondered the meaning of this proverb while not breathing through my nose. From Cai's translation, I interpreted it to mean that as long as you have love, you can withstand anything. I took comfort in this idiom; it showed that nothing mattered but the love of Cai and his family, even if it meant living in China and frequently visiting my in-laws in Hidden River, out in the middle of nowhere.

The toughest adjustment that week in Hidden River wasn't trying to convince Cai's family to like me, or getting used to the modest living conditions. It didn't concern the food or the people who stared at me as I strolled down the middle of the main street with Cai and his family. It was the damp, unrelenting cold. We never took our winter coats off inside until it was time for bed. And like the Cai family members, I didn't shower once that week.

"We only take a bath once a week. It's too expensive to turn on the hot water," Cai explained. I didn't care that I would have to wait until I returned to Hong Kong before taking my next shower or taming my tangled hair. I would rather stay warm and covered than unpeel my many layers and expose myself to the freezing temperatures. My saving grace that week was the electric blanket Cai's mother had placed on my bed. Thank goodness it wasn't too expensive to use those. Cai and his parents warmed up at night with electric blankets, too.

But I couldn't avoid cold water all together. When I washed my hands, the icy water sent waves of shock through my system. After a winter of rinsing with frigid water, Cai's family sported chapped purple splotches on their knuckles. To keep my hands warm, I fell back on a trick I'd learned in Nanjing—wrapping my hands around a mug of hot tea—even if I wasn't thirsty. It was my only contact with heat during the day.

The only other way to stay warm when I wasn't tucked under the comfy electric blanket was to eat. I devoured everything Cai's parents cooked—gooey fried bread dripping with pork grease; cooked greens swimming in liquefied fat from huge slabs of pork back; and plates of red and white glistening pork sausage. Normally I wouldn't have eaten any dishes with pork, but I was fine with bending a rule to keep from feeling hopeless against the cold. I also wanted Cai's parents to think I could adapt to Chinese culture, including a central component of that—eating Chinese food.

After our first dinner together, Cai's father asked, "Do you know the term *yuánfèn*?" I nodded. It means fate, something's that meant to be.

"Very few Americans come to Hidden River," his dad continued, "so only *yuánfèn* could bring you to our home."

"*Xièxiè*." I thanked him. Cai's dad seemed to accept me immediately. Over the years, he would turn out to be my strongest ally in Cai's family. He also repeated the crow proverb all week. "Remember, *àiwūjíwū*. I know our conditions aren't very good. It's cold inside and we don't have hot water, but as long as you have love, everything will be all right."

Just like in the dorms in Hong Kong, we slept in separate rooms at Cai's parents' apartment, according to Chinese tradition. But that night, he snuck into my room after his parents fell asleep.

"Your parents are *next door*," I cried. I didn't want them to think I was loose.

"No problem," he whispered, climbing into bed with me. "They're asleep."

"I know, but what if they wake up? And what about protection?"

"We'll be quiet. And everything will be okay. I'll pull out early."

Cai and I hadn't yet had sex. We both had roommates and never knew when they would return. Now in Hidden River, away from the other students, we finally had an opportunity for intimacy. Because of the freezing indoor temperatures, we kept our sweaters on and stayed under the electric blanket, which Cai had turned off as soon as he scrambled into my bed. I'd read about "clouds and rain," a poetic Chinese term for sex, but on this frigid night it felt more like a few sprinkles in a dry desert. I figured Cai kept it quick and quiet because his parents were in their bedroom on the other side of our wall.

He stood up in haste after he'd finished. "I better go back to my room." He sounded as if he were talking to a stranger with whom he just had a one-night stand.

I'd hoped he'd sleep next to me until the early hours of the morning, before his parents woke. "You can't stay here until the morning?"

"Sorry. My parents are next door."

I was disappointed to spend the rest of the night alone, but I understood the cultural norm. And I didn't want Cai's parents to think I didn't respect their customs.

Cai's parents insisted I call them Mama and Baba. Retired and in their fifties, they enjoyed a leisurely life in Hidden River. Most people from their small city had never left China, let alone Hubei province. Baba's travel history corresponded to the first category, having journeyed as far south as Guangzhou, once known as Canton; Mama fit the second.

In the evenings, we sat around the TV watching reruns of the New Year's Eve variety extravaganza that the whole country tuned into and then spent a week discussing, rehashing, and analyzing over their dinner and mah-jongg tables. Toward the end of my stay, during a commercial break in our nightly TV marathon, Baba sucked some air through his teeth and smiled widely. "We think you should get married as soon as possible."

Mama squealed, her eyes bulging. I guess they didn't think I was a slut or a selfish American. Many parents in remote areas of China wouldn't have been so compassionate.

I'd never been opposed to marrying Cai sooner rather than later. There wasn't a day that passed when I didn't doubt my future with Cai. He was the guy I couldn't let get away. I also secretly worried he might change his mind if we didn't marry soon. What if he grew bored with me? Or if he decided our cultural differences were too great and just not worth the trouble?

As if reading my thoughts, Cai gently caressed my knee with his long fingers and turned to me. "It's a good idea. We could travel together in China this summer if we got married first. And we could live together in the dorm come fall. What do you think?"

I looked at Cai, then at Cai's parents' eager eyes. "Yes." I nodded. "I'd like that."

Mama squealed again and Baba placed his hands together, bowing slightly as if giving thanks to a revered deity.

"But what does marriage have to do with traveling together?" I asked, looking from Cai to his parents.

"We can't stay in the same hotel room in China without a marriage license. It's against the law here. So if you come with me to China this summer for fieldwork, it would be easier if we were married."

"Yan!" Mama shrieked. "You and Susan can get married this summer. Since you'll be in China, you can marry here in Hidden River. Susan, maybe your parents can come for the banquet."

"We should first get our license in Hong Kong," Cai interjected, "where it will be written in Chinese and English."

I liked the idea of a civil ceremony in Hong Kong with a banquet in Hidden River. Cai's parents went on to explain that in mainland

China the couple might receive their marriage certificate months or even a year before their banquet, but they still aren't officially married until they drink toasts with their loved ones around tables of Chinese delicacies. So we could obtain our marriage license in Hong Kong at any time, but Cai's family wouldn't recognize our marriage until we held a huge banquet.

These plans seemed perfect for us. My parents had never visited central China, so it would be a unique experience for them. And, I rationalized, what better way to see this part of China than to attend the boisterous wedding party of their own daughter? I became so caught up in envisioning my parents on a once-in-a-lifetime trip to Hidden River that I didn't stop to realize that our plans were rushed or impulsive.

"Is that all right?" Cai asked me in English.

"Of course it's all right." I switched back to Mandarin for the benefit of Cai's parents. "I think my parents can probably come here this summer. They don't teach then."

"Then it's settled," Cai announced. "We'll get our license in Hong Kong this spring, and we'll have our banquet here in the summer."

"We can take care of your baby!" Mama's eyes beamed. I smiled, humbled by her words, but didn't take them seriously. Her offer was probably just a way of saying she couldn't wait to have grandchildren from us.

"Thank you, but we're not sure where we'll live," I said. "It's probably not going to be in Hidden River." If Cai hadn't told his parents that he wasn't coming back to Hidden River after graduation, I didn't want to be the one to break the news.

"I know." Her eyes still radiated from the thought of more grandchildren. "The baby can stay with us. For several years."

What? Never. I felt a wave of nausea collide with a lump in my throat. She wasn't joking, either. There's no way I'd ever let our baby live in Hidden River, with or without me. I had to put an end to this idea now, before she thought I'd agreed. "We don't have that custom in America. Cai and I can take care of our baby." I forced a smile to hide my panic as the TV program resumed.

"But kids don't learn anything until they're five, so we can take care of your baby here." Mama spoke with the authority of the teacher she was before she and Baba retired a couple years earlier.

I would never, ever let her take my baby. With a look of terror, I turned toward Cai, hoping he would stand up to his mother. He nodded as if he could read my mind.

"Mama." Cai put up his hand. "Americans don't do that. We'll raise our own kids."

"Thank you," I murmured to both Cai and his mother. This issue had never crossed my mind back in Hong Kong, but now that Mama brought it up, I was relieved Cai had quickly come to my side.

Chapter 8

A HONG KONG WEDDING

For most twenty-four-year-old American brides, their wedding day is the pinnacle of their lives, the day they've dreamed of for two decades. A white wedding gown, coiffed hair, and meticulous makeup. A maid of honor, mother of the bride, and a cute flower girl and ring bearer to help the bride celebrate her big day. Hours of planning about invitations, flowers, seating charts, rehearsals, and interviews with photographers, musicians, and event space directors. I never paid much thought to those things; I just wanted to find a man who loved me as much as I loved him.

I woke up alone on the day I was to marry Cai in a Hong Kong civil ceremony. Na Wei had slept in her boyfriend's room the night before, and Cai was in his room, since it wasn't culturally acceptable for unmarried couples to spend the night together if they wanted to keep their reputations intact. I was serious about showing Cai that I respected his culture. So I didn't ask him to stay over or object when he insisted on returning to his dorm room alone each night.

A few weeks before our civil service, Cai and I had spent a long afternoon shopping for a dress I could wear to our wedding. It was a little depressing to find that the ones I liked didn't come in a big enough size. And the only dress Cai chose—made of a red and black bandana fabric—seemed more fitting for a picnic. With time running out before our ceremony, I put together a mismatched ensemble of clothes I already owned: a brown sleeveless dress layered with a white linen tunic embellished with frog buttons, topped off with a long black jacket. I looked like a member of a makeshift orchestra.

Not bothering (or knowing how) to style my hair differently from its normal air-dried mass of shoulder-length curls, I left my room and started up the mountain to my morning class. I didn't give a second thought to my clothes and hair, which seemed trivial to the event at hand. Hoping the next few hours would pass quickly, I inhaled the delicate morning scent of campus: lanky ashoka trees, fragrant bauhinia, and mossy greens mixed with the sea smells from Tolo Harbour.

My two-hour political development seminar seemed to last five hours. I had a ready explanation if someone asked about my eccentric outfit—plans after class off-campus—but no one seemed to notice. I was the only non-Chinese in my program, so my local classmates probably chalked up this strange style to my foreignness. We had one eccentrically dressed mainland Chinese classmate who perhaps didn't notice my outfit because it seemed normal to her. But my attendance in class stood out more than any outfit. Because of me, the professor taught in English, not Cantonese.

After class, I flew down the crumbling cement stairs sculpted into the side of the mountain, stepping over giant snails that had come out after the rainstorm the previous night. Cai was waiting with a wide smile at our designated meeting place in front of the student center, halfway down the mountain. He looked stunning in a gray and white herringbone jacket, white dress shirt, gray dress pants, and a red tie.

We grabbed a quick dim sum lunch, but I felt so anxious for our ceremony to begin that I barely touched my usual repertoire of curry squid and shrimp dumplings. Cai paid the bill before we headed down the rest of the mountain to University Station, holding hands the entire way. Approaching the station, we saw our two witnesses seated on a bench near the entrance. I had asked my exchange student friend, Cee Cee, to serve as my witness, and Cai had enlisted his female classmate, Luo Minghui, the woman he was with the night we met.

Two stops away, the Sha Tin train station sat at the edge of a mega mall that faced the sort of town hall, library, and performing arts center found in most satellite towns, or self-contained suburbs far from the bustling business districts of Kowloon and Hong Kong Island. One of the first shops we reached in the mall was a florist's, a space that only fit a couple of customers. Cai ducked in for several minutes. When he reemerged, he was cradling a huge spring bouquet of yellow lilies and peach roses that he handed to me with a romantic smile. I almost melted into the pavement.

At the town hall marriage registry, we checked in minutes before a female official called our names. I half expected to see Janice rush into the lobby, exclaiming that of course she would never miss my wedding. She had recently started a new job with an American consulting firm only one station away, but it felt like she was back in Washington, DC. Just weeks ago, I had called her at work with my big news.

"Are you sitting down?" I asked.

"You're pregnant!" she whispered.

"Are you kidding me? Of course I'm not pregnant."

"That's a relief. So what's the big news?"

"I'm getting married next month."

Silence. Then, *"Shit.* You barely know him."

"We were going to wait until after graduation, but we figured if it was going to happen eventually, why not now?" I explained hurriedly, adding, "Our ceremony is at two thirty on the thirtieth in Sha Tin. It's a Thursday. Could you come for a while? It shouldn't take very long."

I knew Janice would never understand how much I loved Cai or why I knew I needed to seize the opportunity so quickly—before it escaped—to be with this amazing man who loved me back. In truth, deep down I was terrified Cai might change his mind.

Janice paused. "I don't know what I'll be doing that week. I'll come if I can. How about that?"

"Of course." But my gut told me she wouldn't be there.

And sure enough, a week ago she had quickly mentioned that she was swamped at work. I couldn't think too long about her absence without tearing up. It wasn't so much the fact that she disapproved, because I knew I couldn't force her to like him. But she was my best friend, and I couldn't imagine getting married without her by my side. I started to feel her slipping away, going back to when Cai and I started meeting on a nightly basis, and I didn't want to choose between my friendship with Janice and my marriage to Cai.

That's why I still hoped she would come to our ceremony. But Janice didn't show up.

Despite her absence, I was determined not to let anything spoil my big day. I brought up the rear of my group and peered around the room at the other wedding parties. The brides stood out in their white lace gowns and carefully styled hair, pinned up and slightly curled at the ends. They all looked beautiful, but it wouldn't have been convenient for me to do the same. We had a tight schedule that didn't allow for extra time to change in and out of a fancy dress. And I was fine with that; I just wanted to get married.

My party of four followed the marriage official into a small room with plush, red padded walls. A small boardroom table stood in the middle of the room, and a line of chairs flanked one wall. I couldn't imagine how a large wedding party could fit into one of these rooms. Perhaps we were in one designated for those who chose the elopement option, like us.

Mrs. Lee, the marriage official, placed a certificate printed in English and Chinese on a table. I had never attended a wedding in Hong Kong, so I wasn't sure how it would differ from ceremonies in the United States. I grasped my bouquet, which at that moment seemed a little excessive for an audience of two. But I held on to it happily.

Just as with my professors, Mrs. Lee began the ceremony in English because of my presence. She pointed to our marriage certificate and asked me to sign my name above a line that read "spinster." Cai signed his above "groom." She then motioned for Cee Cee and Luo Minghui to add their signatures as witnesses.

Switching to Cantonese, she asked Cai if he took me as his bride. I could only understand a few words, but I breathed a sigh of joy when she asked me in English if I took Cai as my husband. Although the exchange of rings wasn't a tradition in China yet, most married couples in Hong Kong wore them. I was going to have a wedding band; however, Cai was not.

He had explained a month earlier that he would wear a ring if I insisted, but if it were up to him, he would opt not to have one. He didn't like the feel of jewelry on his skin. Since my father didn't wear a wedding ring for the same reason, I thought nothing of it and told Cai to do as he pleased. (I also worried that protesting would make me appear to be a nagging wife even before we were married, something that Cai detested.)

Mrs. Lee turned again to Cai. "Sir, do you have a ring?" She spoke the first word in English.

"Yes." From his inside jacket pocket, he retrieved a tiny, red satin bag fashioned like an envelope. He unsnapped the flap, running his finger along the inside to unzip it. Reaching into the bag, he pulled out a yellow gold ring engraved with the Chinese characters for double happiness or joyful marriage. Mrs. Lee asked him to place it on my finger.

So far, the ceremony mirrored a normal American wedding except for the mix of languages and the bilingual marriage certificate, which were nice touches unique to Hong Kong. From what Cai told me about weddings in mainland China, people simply registered for a license in a government building without an exchange of vows or rings. Yet couples weren't considered truly married until they held a large banquet for family and friends, so we planned to have our banquet in his hometown later that summer. I was grateful to Cai for suggesting this civil ceremony in Hong Kong before going to China, so that we began our married life in this special place where we met and fell in love.

"You may now kiss your bride." Mrs. Lee beamed. Cai brought his lips to mine and kissed me long enough for our friends and Mrs. Lee to clap.

I was his wife.

There was no wedding recessional or thrown rice as we left the room, but I felt just as glorious as a bride being showered with rose petals. Beaming, Cai and I walked back through the marriage registry, hand in hand, as other couples waited for their turns. Outside, we bid good-bye to our friends and thanked them.

"Why don't I take your bouquet back to the dorm? I'll keep it for you until tomorrow," Cee Cee said.

I thanked her and handed over my flowers. Now I wouldn't have to carry them to the hotel where Cai and I would spend the night. Even though we needed to return to campus the following morning so he could make his weekly appointment with his PhD adviser, Dr. Tsang, I wasn't bothered about our abbreviated honeymoon. All I could think of was one thing: the next twenty hours would be ours.

Chapter 9

HONEYMOON IN HONG KONG

As man and wife, Cai and I headed for an abbreviated honeymoon in Tsim Sha Tsui, the district that sits at the tip of the Kowloon Peninsula. We were staying at the Mira Hotel on Nathan Road, only a mile up from the waterfront promenade that overlooks what I consider to be the most breathtaking skyline in the world. My mom and her family had traveled to Hong Kong in the 1960s and usually stayed in the same area. The Mira was a popular hotel back then, but I had never heard any of my family members speak of it. Still, I pictured them walking down this street thirty years earlier, dressed in suits and shift dresses, and poking their heads into the tailors and jewelry shops that lined the road.

Among the traffic congestion and crowds of students, pajama-clad grannies, and tough teenage boys with blond-tipped hair, Cai and I slowly inched our way from the Jordan train station south toward the hotel. I felt graceful and special holding Cai's hand. We had not spent much time in this area together, although it was one of my favorite spots in Hong Kong. When we reached a nondescript mid-rise building with a Wellcome supermarket in the basement, Cai turned to me. "I forgot something. Let's stop in here for a minute."

I followed him down the steep cement stairs. What could he have forgotten? We had planned on bringing nothing but his wallet and my purse. I figured the hotel could lend us a couple of disposable toothbrushes and a small tube of toothpaste. Neither of us drank or smoked, so it couldn't be cigarettes or champagne that he sought.

We came to the produce aisle, followed by the Chinese dry foods section. Cai and I walked single file past shriveled mushrooms, cracked scallops, and stinky abalone.

He led me through the beverage aisle where we glimpsed cans of soda, plus Chinese jelly concoctions, Vitasoy, and drink boxes of chrysanthemum tea and lemon tea. I remembered the thrill of trying these new beverages for the first time when I arrived in Hong Kong as an exchange student. It took a while to get used to the new tastes and textures of these drinks, but now I preferred them to American soda.

I thought that if the person I was back then—a girl excited by the change a different type of soda brought into her life—could only see me now, she would be amazed by the remarkable things that had occurred in my life: graduate school, marriage to the man of my dreams, and in a few minutes a luxurious honeymoon, thanks to the generosity of my parents in Chicago.

"What are you looking for?" I asked.

"It's around here," he answered vaguely. His drooping shoulders revealed frustration.

In the toiletries section, Cai carefully eyed the items, row by row, column by column, as if scanning a newspaper. "I don't know where it is," he mumbled.

"Where *what* is?"

Again, no answer. I was confused as to why he wouldn't tell me what he wanted and started to feel a bit impatient but kept my mouth shut. We reached the end of the toiletries and entered cleaners and paper products. Cai headed toward the checkout lines, but then stopped before a small display of batteries, film, and condoms. Reaching for a black-and-silver box of Trojans, Cai grinned like a mischievous teenager.

"I forgot to bring these."

I almost had to laugh. So that's what he needed. He must have been embarrassed to say so. But it was also odd. Cai never mentioned condoms two months earlier when we were visiting at his parents' apartment—the first and only time we'd had sex. Now that we were married, it seemed strange that Cai suddenly cared about birth control. But I didn't argue; I assumed we were going to wait at least another year until we graduated before starting a family.

Continuing down Nathan Road, we reached the grand Mira Hotel, which almost took up a full city block across the street from the northern entrance of Kowloon Park. In the hotel, the marble floors and murky crystal chandeliers revealed a lobby from its 1960s heyday. Registration was easy, and the front desk staff congratulated us on our marriage. Because mainland couples were required to present a marriage certificate to stay in the same room, Cai opened our pink envelope to show our certificate, but the man at the front desk said there was no need. The hotel only required a passport or Hong Kong identification card, which all residents needed to carry.

Minutes later in our room, Cai inspected the bathroom, as I opened the blinds to peer down on the frenetic road below. Double-decker buses competed with taxis and luxury cars on Nathan Road. As dusk swept over Kowloon, the colorful neon street signs lit up the scene below. Staying in the Tsim Sha Tsui district was an exciting change from the stillness I was accustomed to in the New Territories.

"It's very nice," he called.

Removing my black jacket, I lounged in an oversized chair, a luxury for someone used to living in a dorm. I felt grateful that my parents had insisted we take this one-night honeymoon—extravagant for poor grad students—and that they wanted to pay for it. When Cai came out of the bathroom, he held up the box of condoms.

"We should try these now."

I smiled.

After a late dinner at a Shanghai restaurant around the corner—the green-and-white-checked tablecloths contrasting to the opulence of the Mira—I couldn't wait to get back to our hotel room. Since we brought no change of clothes, I crawled under the fluffy bedding in just my underwear. Cai entered the bathroom to take a shower but soon returned fully dressed, holding a plush white hand towel.

"Susan, is this okay?"

"What do you mean?"

Àizĭbìng."

"*AIDS?*"

He nodded. "Do you think this towel is clean?"

"Of course. You think you can get AIDS from a towel?"

"Foreigners have AIDS, and they stay at this hotel."

What? How could Cai, who was studying for a PhD (albeit not in a scientific field), believe that AIDS could be contracted from a hotel towel and that AIDS cases originated from foreigners? What about me, his foreign wife? He had never inquired about my sexual history or if I'd ever contracted a sexually transmitted disease. And I'd never asked about his history because I feared he would change his mind about me if I told him about the two flings I'd had just before we'd met.

"You can't get AIDS from a towel. Or by drinking from the same glass as someone who has AIDS."

"Really?"

"Yeah. Scientists have proved it." I tried to remain patient, careful not to sound haughty. There were bound to be times when I would be the one who didn't comprehend something about foreign cultures. "It's okay to use the towel."

He looked somewhat convinced, flipping the towel over his shoulder. "I'm going to shower now." Ten minutes later, when he came out of the bathroom stripped down to his underwear, he joined me in bed and reached for the television remote.

"Hmm," he murmured, as he found pay-per-view. "I've never seen this before."

"What's that?"

"Number three movies." Cai switched to speaking in English for the first time all day. In Hong Kong, movies were rated one, two, or three. One was similar to G- and PG-rated movies in the United

States, two was PG-13 and mild R-rated movies, and three was soft porn. I'd never seen porn, but if it was really Cai's first time to view it, I thought it best to go along with it rather than be a nag. Perhaps all men jumped at the opportunity to watch porn. I didn't know because I'd never shared a hotel room with one until now.

Still, I wondered, did he have to watch it on our honeymoon? It was our first time sleeping in the same bed together, because we both had roommates, and also probably our last for the next two months, when we would leave Hong Kong to spend the summer in China for Cai's dissertation research and our wedding banquet. But what choice did I have? I could either prohibit him from watching it and risk starting an argument on our honeymoon, or I could go to sleep and leave him to the porn.

After a long day, I could feel my eyes closing. So I shifted my head on the fluffy pillow in preparation for a night in a bed substantially larger and more comfortable than the camp-cot-esque one in my dorm room.

He clicked on Pay and said gently, "You go to sleep." A nude Japanese couple in a simple room got down to business without so much as a prelude.

My thoughts immediately went to my parents. When I thanked them for the honeymoon, there was no way I could tell them about this. I would have to lie—to pretend I had a once-in-a-lifetime evening of bliss off campus—because the truth was too embarrassing to admit to anyone: Cai was more interested in watching porn than being with me. At least that's what I thought as I fell asleep to the woman's monotonous whimpers, while Cai's eyes remained glued to the television.

Father and mother-in-law
Are your husband's family.
When you arrive at their threshold
You become a new woman;
Reverence and serve them
As your own parents.

—Ban Zhao
Instruction for Chinese Women and Girls

Chapter 10

SUMMER VACATION IN HIDDEN RIVER

We wasted no time departing Hong Kong at the end of our semester. After completing the first year of my master's program in political science, I was free until fall and planned to enjoy my first summer of being married by catching up on pleasure reading while Cai conducted his dissertation research. Our luggage, including one suitcase and a carry-on each, allowed me to bring along six paperbacks, mostly classics bought cheaply at the university bookstore.

Since China was Cai's territory, I was happy to leave our summer planning to him. And as we discussed the cities we would visit, Cai grew especially animated when he spoke about all the places we would go, including some cities I had visited before. Although I would miss Hong Kong, I looked forward to traveling with Cai for three months and seeing these places from a new perspective.

Our first stop—for six weeks—was to visit Mama and Baba in Hidden River. Their *dānwèi*, or work unit, was like a campus unto itself: clusters of living quarters, classrooms, and administrative offices spread out over an area that included a park for tai chi and a rundown playground. Though private housing was becoming popular in the larger coastal and southern cities, most people in China's interior still lived, worked, and studied within the confines of a *dānwèi*.

Summers in Hidden River were scorchers, often reaching above 100 degrees Fahrenheit. Mama and Baba's apartment had ceiling fans in each room, but only one air conditioner. In preparation for our trip that summer, they had bought it for the room where Cai and I would sleep.

Apart from that quick, weeklong meeting during Chinese New Year months earlier, I was still getting to know my in-laws when we arrived that June. At our first dinner in Hidden River that summer, we sat around a wooden card table in the small dining area between the kitchen and living room. I looked forward to Mama's home cooking. The food in China was more rustic than what I ate in Hong Kong, but over the years, I'd grown to enjoy simple Chinese fare.

In the hot dining room, Baba reached over to spoon a ladle full of rice into everyone's dish. Cai served me some green beans and a piece of black chicken, a delicacy. It looked fresh and delicious. Mama followed his lead by plucking a golden-brown rice cake, dripping in pork grease, with her wooden chopsticks. That was something I would pass on, I thought.

In college, especially during my junior year in Hong Kong, I had started to feel sickened by the smell and taste of pork. Some form of pork, including lard, always seemed to make an appearance in many types of Chinese food: bread, pies, vegetables, meat dishes. Although my parents both came from Jewish families, we often ate pork when I was growing up. In Asia, I quickly grew to understand the reasoning behind the Jewish custom of refraining from pork and started to abide by that practice. I also tried to stay away from fried foods, which often inflicted mayhem on my intestines.

When Mama lowered the rice cake toward my bowl, I put my hand up as if to stop traffic. "*Bùyào.*" I don't want it.

Mama's face rotated quickly toward Cai. Her compact face made me think of a crabapple doll I owned as a child. "*Mo shi?*" In her Hidden River dialect, she asked what was going on.

"*Tā bù chī yóu zháde.*" He calmly told her that I didn't eat fried food.

"She ate lots of it over the Chinese New Year. Does she not like my cooking anymore?"

"Of course she loves your cooking. It's just that she normally doesn't eat fried food—or pork. Last time she ate it because she wasn't part of the family and didn't want to be rude. Don't worry so much." Cai returned to the chicken foot in his rice bowl.

"She doesn't eat pork? Who doesn't like pork?" Mama spoke to Cai as if I wasn't in the same room with them, sitting next to her. I stared into my bowl, willing this conversation to end. This wasn't what I thought would happen when I refused the rice cake.

"*Bùyàojǐn.*" Don't worry, Baba interjected, coming to my rescue. "So she doesn't like pork. Now let's eat!"

Mama scrunched her lips together in concentration—as if she were trying to solve a difficult puzzle—and plopped the rice cake into her mouth. When I'd finished eating half a dozen other dishes, my favorites being steamed spinach and sautéed eel, Mama's eyes bulged as I stood up with Cai to clear the plates.

"*Tā bù chīfàn!*" She hasn't finished her rice, Mama shrieked. My rice bowl wasn't empty.

"*Ma, tā chī bǎole,*" Cai said. She's full. He sounded tired.

I figured it was best to just smile, to say I was stuffed, and then drop it. I wanted to respect Cai's culture and show his parents that I enjoyed their cooking and appreciated their hospitality, but at the same time, I feared I'd grow resentful if I didn't start standing up for myself. I knew they were observing everything I did, taking mental notes of my likes and dislikes so they would know what to prepare in the weeks to come.

My parents would have done the same with guests or new family members back in Chicago. But if I didn't make these preferences known early on, it would be almost impossible to change later when they'd already formed their impressions of me. This wasn't easy since food is such a central component of Chinese culture, and people are expected try a bite of every dish.

In the living room after dinner, Baba peeled a tart apple with a rusty pocketknife he kept on a bookshelf that also held a small plaster bust of Chairman Mao. As he skinned the apple, the peel materialized in one long ribbon. Holding the apple with his thumb and pinky finger, Baba handed it to me, his eyes almost disappearing into his face as he smiled. His salt-and-pepper buzz cut stood at attention, counterbalancing his gentle demeanor. I bit into the cool apple, grateful for Baba's acceptance. Besides the tea I had allowed to cool off to room temperature, the apples Baba peeled for me after lunch and dinner provided a reprieve from the heat and stickiness of the day.

At night, once Cai and I retired to our bedroom, I felt some relief from the summer humidity as we switched on the air conditioner. Its gentle breeze cooled the backs of my bare legs while I slept on a bamboo mat, which kept my skin from sticking to the sheets. Like a rough cousin of the tatami, these mats felt smooth to the touch, but at night my hip bones, knees, and ankles collided with the stiff wood as I shifted back and forth from my stomach to my side.

When Cai first suggested this trip to China, I pictured us venturing out on our own to visit the countryside where he had spent his youth or idling outdoors with his friends, perhaps going to a picnic spot for lunch like I did when I went out with my friends in Hong Kong. Instead, when Cai and I left Mama and Baba's, we walked from apartment to apartment to visit his friends. The men played cards in these dark, cement-floored homes while I sat by Cai's side and struggled to follow their quick conversations in the Hidden River dialect.

"Can I try a hand?" I asked Cai late one morning, hungry and hoping we would break to eat soon. I was also growing bored watching the cards fly back and forth from hands to table and back to hands, and thought I would enjoy the days better if I could participate.

"You don't understand the game and it would only slow us down," he replied.

Cai was so accommodating in everything else during my stay in Hidden River that I didn't find his words offensive. If we were in the

United States and I was with old friends, I knew I would appreciate some uninterrupted time with them. So I understood where Cai was coming from. I would just have to find something to occupy my thoughts as they chatted and played cards.

Sometimes during the monotony of those days, I wished I had brought a book to the card-playing sessions. But I also feared running out of reading material. What would I do for the rest of the summer if I had nothing to read? My books became godsends on the days when we didn't leave Mama and Baba's.

Most people took a siesta after lunch for a couple of hours. Called *wǔjiào*, or noontime nap, it was a common practice across China, and they were a relief during the oppressively hot summer months. Unable to sleep the entire *wǔjiào*, I would read while Cai watched television and his parents napped. It was during a quiet afternoon about five weeks into our stay in Hidden River, when Mama and Baba had retired to their room for *wǔjiào*, that I finished the last book I'd brought from Hong Kong.

"Cai," I asked as he channel-surfed the television, "can we go to a bookstore sometime? I don't have anything to read now."

"What about all those books you brought?"

"I finished them. Do you know of any stores that sell English books?"

"Nothing in Hidden River or Wuhan." He squinted his eyes in thought. "There's a foreign-language bookstore near the Shanghai train station. We can go there before we take the train to Suzhou."

It would be another week until we'd arrive in Shanghai for a quick layover on our way to Suzhou, where we'd stay for ten days while Cai, his PhD adviser Dr. Tsang, and a trio of professors from the Wuhan Conservatory would help conduct fieldwork for Cai's dissertation. I could wait another week. In the meantime, I fantasized about entering the foreign language bookstore and finding a sizable English section. I would flip through the brittle pages of seldom-touched books, probably paperback classics like I had bought in Hong Kong. It didn't matter what I bought—anything in English would do.

After Mama and Baba resurfaced from their nap, Cai pulled a thin paperback book titled *Beijingers in New York* from his father's bookshelf.

"Until we get to Shanghai, you can read this book. I think you'll like it." He handed it to me and massaged my shoulders lovingly.

The novel was printed in Chinese on rough gray paper, scattered with simple sketches of scenes from the story. In college I had once tried to read *Jane Eyre* in Chinese but didn't get past page thirty. *Beijingers in New York* would certainly last me until we reached Shanghai.

Chapter 11
SOJOURN IN SHANGHAI

On my first trip to China, my high school group visited Beijing, Nanjing, Suzhou, Wuxi, and Shanghai. It was June 1988, twelve years after Mao died, nine years after the United States and China restored relations, and one year before the tragedy at Tiananmen Square. It was also four years after China and Great Britain signed the Joint Declaration that paved the way for Hong Kong's return to China in 1997. As a recent high school graduate, I only sensed part of this history, but I could feel that China was in the throes of change.

Shanghai was our last stop that June. It was supposed to be Hong Kong, but the cost to include that city was so exorbitant that it would have rendered the trip unaffordable for our group of six students and nine teachers. After two weeks in a Beijing Soviet-built hotel and rudimentary university dormitories in smaller cities, we arrived in Shanghai. It seemed like another country. Although the city was a skeleton of what it is today, back then it had an understated charm that was apparent in the colonial architecture along the Bund, or Huangpu River waterfront.

People got around by riding bicycles or long, accordion buses, but they carried themselves with a sophistication I hadn't seen before, even in Beijing. We stayed at the international students' dormitory at the Shanghai Conservatory of Music, housed in the old French Concession. A few years after that trip, I returned to Shanghai for a week with my father to visit two of his students' families. We stayed with one in their urban apartment, the tall ceilings and frayed French windows a gentle reminder of the opulent years before 1949.

I was anxious to return to Shanghai with Cai the summer we married. When it came time to bid Mama and Baba farewell after a month and a half, I didn't look back. To reach Shanghai from Hubei province, Cai booked us passage on a two-day boat ride, embarking from Wuhan, that would sail down the Yangtze River to the City on the Sea.

"It'll be nice for you to experience China by boat," he said. "You can't see the same areas when you fly or take the train."

It sounded like a good idea when he suggested it. I pictured a romantic journey as the lone Western woman among hundreds of Chinese, bound for Shanghai. When we boarded the boat, the rails were packed with passengers waving good-bye to their families and friends on the ancient dock below. I felt like I was on location for a film set during the Nationalists' flight from China's coastal cities for the safety of Taiwan as the Communists took over in 1949. The romance of this thought fluttered away as I stepped over passengers camped across the steerage floors.

Cai gripped my hand, leading me through the masses to the bare floors of second class—the most luxurious section in China at the time. The concept of first class was still taboo, because back then people were supposed to be equal in China, regardless of profession or family background. Our portion of the boat consisted of two dozen berths, each with two beds, and two Western-style toilets to be shared by all second-class passengers. Cai and I occupied a couple of metal chairs outside our berth, seated along a railing overlooking the mighty Yangtze. To pass the time, I flipped through my Chinese-English dictionary, trying to decipher the many characters I didn't recognize in *Beijingers in New York*. Cai chatted casually with a middle-aged man and his twentysomething daughter from the berth next door.

As the sun began to set across the Yangtze, I took leave to find the bathroom just inside an interior corridor. When I opened the door to the first Western bathroom, I saw pieces of brown paper towel floating in the toilet. I checked the second, but that door was locked. On it hung a handwritten sign that read, "Closed for repair." I returned to the first toilet. At closer glance, I noticed muddy footprints on the toilet seat rim. Though I never sat on public toilets, this time I took extra care to squat as far from the seat as possible.

After nightfall, I returned to the one functioning toilet, but discovered it, too, now had a repair sign on the door. Both toilets were out of order.

I had no problem using the squat toilet at Mama and Baba's apartment, or even the grungy, rust-covered one at the dilapidated apartment Cai still kept in Wuhan. But how would I manage the squat toilets used by five hundred people in steerage? There must be another Western bathroom we didn't know about. I ran-walked back outside to find Cai and our neighbors, the father and daughter, still sitting on lawn chairs on the deck, which was illuminated by dull, bare lightbulbs hanging outside our rooms.

"*Cai.*" I tried to catch my breath. "The two toilets are both out of order now. Is there another Western one somewhere else?"

"No, those are it." He stood up and caressed my shoulders. "You'll have to use the main cabin toilets. They're going to be terrible. I'm sorry."

What choice did I have?

"Do you want me to walk you there?" he asked, taking my hands in his.

I looked out onto the dark river. The smell of burning fuel and rotten fish further punctured my idyllic vision of this voyage. He couldn't go into the ladies' room with me, so there was no point in him leaving our cabin. "It's okay. I can find it."

The steerage corridors had transformed since we'd boarded that afternoon. They were still teeming with standing-room-only passengers, but now some had rolled out thin bamboo mats and were resting on those, while others were curled up on newspapers they had spread out. I followed my nose to the toilets. As the stench grew stronger, I knew I was getting closer.

Inside the windowless ladies' room, I was besieged by a dozen eyes peering at me from the troughlike lavatory. The room was illuminated by a tube of head-splitting fluorescent light. I slunk to the very back of the trough so as not to draw attention to myself. Divided by three-foot-high wooden partitions, the toilet was accessed via narrow, wooden horizontal planks, to be straddled while running water and human waste flowed down the center. I didn't dare breathe deeply; I opened my mouth just enough for the bare minimum of stagnant air to creep in. Practically gagged, I tugged my pants down, trying to balance without holding on to the partition in front of me, all while the boat rocked gently back and forth on the Yangtze.

Quickly rinsing my hands with icy water—there was no soap—I hightailed it out of there. As I made my way back to Cai, I heard passengers rudely commenting on my long nose and ghostlike skin. But those voices quickly faded as I returned to the tranquility of the second-class cabin where Cai greeted me with a wide, understanding smile, enveloping me in his arms and planting a kiss on my head of tousled curls.

"You're really a *hǎo tóngzhì*, a good comrade."

Once in Shanghai, Cai and I strolled hand in hand along the Bund. With its familiar Hong Kong drugstores and colonial architecture, Shanghai still seemed the oasis of civilization I had remembered from my two previous trips. I soaked in views of the tree-lined avenues and tattered mansions of the former French Concession. And I felt at home along the quiet elegance of once-sophisticated Huaihai Road, which in my romantic daydreams I still thought of as the pre-1949 Avenue Joffre, where trams cruised down the center of the street, and Chinese and Europeans shopped together in Jewish Russian-owned clothing boutiques.

For the first time all summer, I found and bought postcards for friends and family in Hong Kong and the United States. Cai reserved us a room at the Shanghai Conservatory of Music's international student dormitory, the same building where I had stayed during my first trip in 1988. Coincidentally, that was also the summer Cai had finished an exchange semester at the Shanghai Conservatory. Much to my dismay, we would only spend one night in Shanghai before heading on to Suzhou so he could start his dissertation fieldwork in Taoist ritual music.

Rain descended upon the city that evening like a much-needed shower. Cai and I hailed a pedicab to the art deco Cathay cinema, where we saw the romantic Hong Kong film *Red Rose, White Rose*. It all seemed so lavish compared to six weeks in Hidden River and that stinky boat ride. I felt like a privileged honeymooner, even though we had already been married for three months and had our one-night honeymoon in Hong Kong the night of our civil ceremony. I drifted off to sleep that night feeling content for the first time since we arrived in China that summer.

I could easily have spent another two weeks at the Conservatory, exploring the remnants of Old Shanghai. We had only covered a small part of the city the day before. But it was out of my hands because Cai's professors were awaiting our arrival in Suzhou. The plus side of leaving Shanghai so soon was that I'd finally be able to visit the foreign language bookstore near the train station. Besides the arrival of my family from the United States and my wedding banquet later that month (different from the small ceremony in Hong Kong three months before), I'd been looking forward to this day the most.

At the Shanghai Railway Station the next morning, Cai worked his way to an outside ticket window, blending easily into the crowds, while I stood in the plaza. Car exhaust and an open sewer assaulted my senses, but I didn't care. I scanned the surrounding buildings, which were dwarfed by a red banner promoting a better tomorrow. It didn't take long for me to locate the foreign language bookstore housed in a blocky, concrete, Soviet-era building. I'd only need ten minutes.

But when Cai returned from the ticket window, his tense eyes focused not on me, but beyond where I stood, toward the red Chinese character banner above the station entrance. Had he run into a problem buying tickets? Foreigners paid a higher price for many things, including train and plane fare. Perhaps the ticket seller had charged him an outrageously inflated price for my ticket. Or maybe she'd scolded him for marrying a foreigner. Something wasn't right.

"*Hǎole, zǒu ba.*" He sounded as though we were running late and nodded toward the station entrance. Let's go.

I stood still. "Aren't we going to the bookstore?" It didn't seem possible, but perhaps he'd forgotten about it.

"No time. Our train leaves in fifteen minutes." He looked toward the entrance and took off the White Sox cap he had bought in Hong Kong, shoving it into his fake-leather shoulder bag.

The weight of Shanghai's humidity descended on me like the abrupt summer monsoons in Hong Kong. Nothing unusual had happened at the ticket window. Cai simply couldn't be bothered to go to the bookstore. Didn't he remember how he had suggested it back in Hidden River? I continued to stand in place, my shoulders bent like a woman in mourning.

"We've been talking about it for weeks," I said more to myself than to Cai.

He turned toward me, his lips nearly vanishing. "Susan, you have to think less about yourself all the time. You can't always get what you want. This is *China*. My professors will be waiting for us, and we need to get to Suzhou. Let's go."

The scalding Shanghai heat couldn't compete with the hot flush that spread over my face. Where was this coming from? He had never raised his voice to me. One of the world's largest cities, Shanghai back then only had two or three foreign bookstores. Considering this, how hard would it be to let me do the one thing I asked for—to spend a few minutes in the bookstore, especially since I'd never asked for anything else these past six weeks?

Surely there was a later train that would still get us to Suzhou in time. There were probably a few such trains. I stared at the ground of the station plaza, afraid I'd cry if I looked him in the eye. Cai exhaled an annoyed sigh and started for the entrance, fading into the throngs that moved en masse like an unstoppable, unthinking herd. Much as I hated to allow this behavior, I had no choice but to follow. He held our passports and our money.

Chapter 12
THE TRAIN TO SUZHOU

The eleven forty to Suzhou crept along the tracks, chugging away from the hazy Shanghai skyline. I sat on a hard seat sandwiched between two young Chinese men, our legs touching. As the train picked up speed, I felt desperately alone among the hundred travelers pouring into the aisles. Holding back tears, I turned to *Beijingers in New York*. The clunky characters seemed more foreign than usual. I flipped through my tattered red Chinese-English dictionary with trembling hands, balancing the novel on my lap.

Seated opposite, Cai stared out the window, his almond eyes full of displeasure. A loud belch from a woman across the aisle distracted me from his icy glare, but only for a moment. He seemed furious with me for a reason I couldn't fathom. In the middle of all these people, I couldn't possibly start a scene with Cai.

Was my tone of voice too harsh back at the train station? Was it wrong of me to ask about the bookstore? And if either or both were true, couldn't he at least tell me that rather than pretend he didn't know me?

A middle-aged woman in a physician's white coat and matching floppy surgical hat entered our car, pushing a metal cart piled high with Styrofoam-boxed lunches. All around, passengers stepped up to the cart, ordering a lunch of pork ribs, boiled cabbage, and steamed rice. Even if I consented to eat pork, I wouldn't be able to order one because I didn't have a single Chinese yuan. Cai kept our cash and passports in his money belt.

Without so much as glancing in my direction, Cai paid for one lunch. "*Yī,*" he said. One. He slurped his rice from a plastic spoon as the lunch lady moved through the car. If we'd been on normal terms, I could picture Cai handing me a lunch with both hands and apologizing that the meal contained pork. He'd ask if I could eat the rice and cabbage for now, and would promise that we'd find something else after arriving at our destination.

But he remained silent. When was Cai going to look at me again? I just hoped he'd snap out of it by the time we reached Suzhou.

After the grueling train ride to Suzhou, Cai's eyes lit up as we approached the administrative offices of the Temple of Mystery, or *Xuánmiào Guān.* The building stood on a dusty Suzhou street with heavy bicycle traffic and appeared to be a colorful remnant of the prerevolutionary era, before chunky, gray Stalinist-style architecture became commonplace. Without speaking to me, Cai entered the temple first. A young receptionist led us to a typical Chinese receiving area with a large boardroom table and oversized chairs draped with faded, white crocheted antimacassars. A narrow air-conditioning unit hummed in a corner. Soon the temple leader and administrative staff filed into the room.

"I heard from your professors, *Xiao Cai.* They should be here in a few hours. Dr. Tsang will arrive this evening." The Taoist leader called Cai "little" in reference to his young age of thirty-three.

We could have gone to the bookstore in Shanghai after all. I bit my lower lip as two office ladies served us hot tea, even though the outside temperatures had reached the low nineties. Carefully lifting the lid off the tall, white porcelain mug, I saw dozens of long, thin, green tea leaves floating in the steaming liquid. The staff greeted me like a familiar friend and complimented my Mandarin. "*Zhōngguó xíguàn ma?*" An older female asked if I'd acclimated to China.

After Cai's silent treatment on the train, I didn't know what to think about living in China. Cai never acted this way in Hong Kong. Was he nervous about working as a peer now with his revered professors? And why had he allowed me to sit mutely by his side as he played cards with his friends all those weeks in Hidden River? Glancing around the room, I understood that I couldn't speak up. The temple staff knew Cai and his academic reputation. I was just a foreigner, an outsider, a stranger.

"She's not accustomed to everything," Cai chortled without looking at me, as if sensing my hesitation. "But she's trying."

As soon as we took leave of our hosts and went to find our room in the guesthouse next door, Cai reverted to his cold, commanding demeanor. Sulking, he entered the room first, stepping onto thin, red carpeting covered with black splotches. It looked like someone had purposely poked lit cigarettes into it. Guesthouses were bare-boned accommodations reserved for Chinese citizens only.

Because I was married to Cai, I was allowed to stay with him as long as we presented our marriage certificate to the manager. But had I been married to a non-Chinese, we wouldn't have had to show proof of marriage to stay at a hotel. The Chinese government didn't allow its citizens to cohabitate with people of the opposite sex other than their spouses, in theory, but didn't care what non-Chinese couples did.

"We're going to find something to eat." Cai broke his silence, his eyes still full of contempt.

How long could he keep this up?

I followed him outside to a symphony of bicycle bells. The cyclists pedaled in rows of six, all keeping a constant rhythm. We dodged bikes in both directions under the singeing midafternoon sun and entered a small restaurant across the street. Except for two waitresses, we were alone.

"You have to eat now." Cai spoke as though granting a prisoner's reprieve.

A dusty clock on an oil-stained wall read three o'clock. I hadn't eaten since before we left Shanghai, but my stomach still felt twisted. I sat in silence, afraid to make eye contact with Cai.

"What do you want to order?" he snapped.

"I'm not hungry." I looked down in disgrace. He can't force me to eat, I thought, as my shame turned to anger and then to defiance.

"*Xiǎojiě.*" He addressed the waitress in the stern and demeaning tone he had started using with me back in Shanghai that morning. "One plate of *kǔ guā*, one bowl of rice, and a pot of *wūlóng* tea."

I usually devoured bitter melon—a crunchy, cucumberlike vegetable sautéed with black bean sauce—but this time I looked away in disinterest when the waitress set the plate of *kǔ guā* on our table.

"*Chī,*" Cai ordered. Eat. He took quick slurps of tea, staring at his empty plate. I was brought up not to waste food, so I forced down a few pieces of the *kǔ guā* and a mouthful of rice. Cai stared off to the side and looked as if he wanted to be anywhere but at this restaurant. After a few bites, I had completely lost my appetite. Without speaking, I rested my chopsticks on the table.

"Why aren't you eating?" he snarled.

"I'm not hungry." I could barely hear myself.

Cai threw some bills on the table with a huff and stood up. We left the restaurant in silence.

At dinner that evening, we ate with Cai's PhD adviser, Dr. Tsang, and Cai's college professors from Wuhan: older gentlemen by the names of Shi, Xiang, and Wu. In their company, Cai had turned back into his old cordial self. Again, I thought that perhaps Cai was nervous about meeting up with his old professors. I could understand how he might feel pressure to show them that his research was sound and feasible. As I dug into a platter of Chinese broccoli at the temple's restaurant, I figured there must be some explanation for Cai's earlier outburst.

A boisterous Xiang turned to me, called out my Chinese name—Su Shan—and raised his glass. With his bushy eyebrows and permanent smile, he seemed the most outgoing of the Wuhan professors.

"No, thanks," I said in Mandarin. "I'm not a big drinker."

"Come on," he roared jovially. "All Americans love beer. This is China's best beer, from Qing Dao. Have a glass with me."

"Really, I don't want to. Thank you anyway." I smiled and continued to pick around the pork that highlighted most of the dishes.

Xiang raised his glass to toast me a few more times that evening, but I politely refused to drink with him. Thinking back to my eating differences with Mama, I feared that if I gave in to Professor Xiang once, I'd be setting a precedent and would be expected to drink beer at every meal. And if later I wanted to stop drinking, it would be more difficult than if I'd just refused up front.

I also worried about the fact that I still hadn't bought a dress for the large wedding banquet Mama and Baba were planning for us at the end of the month. Although considered thin in the United States, I was larger than most Chinese women and knew it would be difficult to find a dress that fit. I couldn't afford to gain extra weight.

Xiang drank his beer and returned to his conversations with Cai and the other professors. He appeared to harbor no bad feelings. After the final course of sliced oranges, he turned to Cai and me. "*Míngtiān jiàn.*" See you tomorrow.

Back in our room, Cai's scowl was gone and he didn't avoid eye contact. We probably just needed more time alone, I reasoned. Staying with his family for six weeks didn't afford much personal space. If other couples were presented with the same scenario, I was sure it would strain their relationships, too. Now we had some coveted time to ourselves. Envisioning a quiet evening watching television snuggled next to Cai, I reclined on one of the two twin beds and waited for him to do the same. But he remained standing, his hands hidden in his pockets.

"Don't wait up for me." He spoke matter-of-factly. "I'm going to my professors' room now."

He was leaving me alone in the room? Had I missed something back in the restaurant? I could have sworn that Xiang had wished us both a good night. Dr. Tsang had booked a room at a Hong Kong–run hotel on the outskirts of town, but the Wuhan professors were staying on the floor above us in the same guesthouse.

"Wait a second," I said as Cai grabbed the room key. "Why are you going there? And why alone?"

"Just to play cards and do chatting," Cai said in English. "They'll only be wearing their underwear. If you come with me, *tāmen bù hǎoyìsi*." They'll be embarrassed.

What? He was going to spend a whole week with these professors. Was it really necessary to play cards with them at night? And why would they be in their underwear? The previous evening in Shanghai—the stroll along the Bund and the romantic film at the Cathay cinema—seemed a lifetime ago. But after Cai's behavior that day, I felt like my hands were tied. I couldn't bear to set him off again and deal with another episode of him not speaking to me.

☕☕☕

When Cai handed me some spending money the next morning and suggested I stay back to explore the city while he and his professors trekked to a Taoist temple thirty minutes away for their fieldwork, I didn't argue. Although I'd felt abandoned the night before, I suddenly was looking forward to time alone. On my first trip to China, I'd scaled the arched bridges over Suzhou's fabled canals and roamed beautiful gardens with round Chinese doorways and walls that curved on top like a dragon's back.

Now I would set off to wander the city as if I were a local. Perusing the outdoor fruit markets, I selected the choicest peaches for an after-dinner snack and bargained down the price, per the Chinese custom. Without Cai at my side, it felt good to speak Mandarin on my own. When I thought about it, this was the first time I had been alone in China and able to speak Mandarin fluently. In the past, I couldn't speak it at all or was still in the beginning stages. Back then, conversing in Chinese seemed like a burden. Now it felt liberating.

In a nearby post office, I proudly handed over my postcards with the scratchy Chinese characters for *měiguó* or beautiful country, which translated into "United States," scribbled at the bottom. Stamps and cards in hand, I headed to a high table where I carefully adhered old-fashioned paste—which resembled the rubber cement my father kept on his basement workbench—to the back of the stamps.

These small tasks brought me great joy, as they allowed me to communicate with the *lǎobiǎxìng*. Ordinary people. I wished I had enjoyed such opportunities all those weeks back in Hidden River. If only I had had a chance to mix with the town folk on my own, I probably wouldn't have felt so isolated there.

At noon, I met up with Cai and his professors at the guesthouse restaurant. Almost as soon as we sat down, Professor Xiang again raised a warm glass of beer and motioned for Professor Wu to pour me one.

"*Bùyào, xièxiè.*" I don't want any, thank you. I truly liked Xiang and didn't want to hurt his feelings, but would he ever get the picture?

"Come on," he said heartily in Mandarin. "Just one drink. When I studied in Moscow many years ago, I always drank vodka with my Russian friends. Now it's time to drink beer with my new American friend."

"No, really, I just want tea. I'm sorry." I smiled bashfully and blew on my scalding green tea. Cai didn't drink alcohol and never received criticism from his friends and colleagues over it, but Xiang seemed persistent. Although I managed to end another meal without taking a drink, it felt like a hard-won battle.

While the professors enjoyed *wǔjiào*—their afternoon nap—Cai took me to the silk museum gift shop to look for a *qípáo*, a Chinese formfitting dress with a high mandarin collar. I had told Cai that I wanted to wear one to our banquet, which was now just weeks away. On my first trip to China, I never once saw a woman in a *qípáo*. Over the last couple of years, I'd noticed that restaurant hostesses in southern China wore them. But it still wasn't common for brides to don this sensual dress that first turned heads in the 1930s.

Without much time to spare before Cai's afternoon meeting at the temple, we rushed through the store to a small rack with silk *qípáo*, and spotted the sole red one. Red was the traditional color for brides in China before 1949. In recent years, fashionable brides had begun wearing poufy pink or white Western wedding dresses. With three-quarter-length sleeves and a hem that fell halfway down my calves, the red *qípáo* was embroidered with yellow and white peonies down the front. The tag read size medium, so I held it up to my shoulders and waist, shrugging as if to ask Cai what he thought.

"It looks perfect," he said.

Outside the museum with our purchase in hand, Cai and I squeezed into the narrow seat of a pedicab. The driver pedaled through the bustling main streets in the direction of the guest-house. We passed vendors squatting along the curbs, selling fresh bananas and melons, candied apples, and skewers of meatballs from makeshift carts. I didn't know when I would get another chance to speak with Cai alone, so I decided to talk to him about Xiang in the privacy of the pedicab.

"I wish Professor Xiang wouldn't pressure me to drink beer all the time. He keeps asking and it makes me uncomfortable."

Peering over Cai's shoulder as we rode by colorful stands of red apples and green pears stacked into neat layers, I waited for him to offer to speak to Xiang. But when I looked back at him, I trembled. His eyes had turned fiery.

"These are my old professors, *Susan*," Cai snapped. "You have to respect them, and respect *me*. Who cares if you drink one glass of beer? It won't kill you." I noticed he failed to mention how he brushed people away when they offered him alcohol, but I kept my mouth shut.

Silent, I felt a cold shiver despite the oppressive July heat.

"I know what it's like to have problems in a marriage," he continued in English so the pedicab driver wouldn't understand. "You must be very careful. If you're not, big trouble can happen to the family. I know."

Feeling even more alone than I had on the train to Suzhou, I finally understood his message: if I didn't comply with his wishes, we were headed toward divorce. And if he divorced me, what would I tell my parents and my friends? It never crossed my mind to threaten Cai with divorce if he didn't start treating me better. But even if I'd been stronger, I wouldn't have given up after just three months of marriage. Surely everyone needed time to get used to living with another person.

As the driver pedaled toward the guesthouse, I thought back to the Chinese University of Hong Kong and how other mainland students there often spoke of the drastic changes taking place in China. They all lamented how it wasn't the same country of their childhoods in the 1960s and 1970s. Cai just needed time to acclimate, I told myself. I would make a bigger effort to understand his culture and his background. With careful choreography, I would also try to dance my way around future eruptions.

To take my mind off these troubles, I started counting down the days until my family flew into Shanghai to be there for our wedding banquet. My parents, Uncle Jeff, and brother Jonathan could get time off from work for the ceremony or the banquet, but not both, so when Cai and his parents stressed the importance of the banquet, my family chose to come for that.

That evening when Cai announced he was going up to his professors' room to chat and play cards again, the burn from the pedicab lecture still hurt. I told myself that Cai had few chances to see his Wuhan professors, so this was just a temporary diversion in our married life. I never felt needy in Hong Kong, where I kept myself busy with friends and classes. But this wasn't the case in China, where I felt lonely and isolated.

So to while away those evenings in the dingy guesthouse room, I found refuge in a soap opera called *Russian Girls in Harbin*. The noticeably foreign women on the TV show lived in northern China and encountered cultural differences every day—at work, with friends, and in love. I fancied myself one of them, learning the complexities of Chinese culture by trial and error. Clinging once again to images of our happier days in Hong Kong, I vowed not to let cultural differences taint our marriage.

When a girl leaves her father's house,
Her husband thereafter
Is her nearest relative.

—Ban Zhao
Instruction for Chinese Women and Girls

Chapter 13
A CHINESE WEDDING BANQUET

A couple weeks after our trip to Suzhou, I squeezed into my red silk *qípáo*. Standing in the bedroom Cai and I shared at his parents' home in Hidden River, I slowly zipped the dress above the high slit on my left side, careful not to burst a seam. I could have used the next size up, but this one would have to do. Cai opened the door, ducking under the fake flowers hanging from the top of the door frame. He looked impeccable, sporting the same gray business pants, white button-down shirt, and herringbone jacket he wore to our Hong Kong ceremony, only now it was accentuated with a synthetic red poppy pinned to his lapel.

Cai picked up my hands and held them in his. "I'm so glad both our parents support our marriage. As long as we have love, our lives will be very happy." When I told my parents about my engagement, they gave me their unconditional support, explaining that their own marriage had been met with resistance from my mom's family. My dad was too Jewish for my mom's Reform family. He was also too old, a widower, and a single father. My parents didn't want me to experience the same opposition. Mama and Baba, on the other hand, not only backed our engagement, but they had encouraged us to marry as soon as possible.

I gazed into Cai's beaming eyes, thankful for our families' support and for his love. I knew I'd remember this day for the rest of my life. After all, how many of my classmates back in Evanston could say they got married in central China? This was a day I'd reminisce about with my children and grandchildren, recalling the stifling heat, the lone red dress in Suzhou that was destined to be mine, and the lavish wedding banquet. Jittery about being the center of attention and eager at the same time, I felt proud to appear in front of all these people with Cai at my side.

Cai guided me down the crumbly stairs of his parents' apartment; I took short strides so to not tear the dress. We ambled across the *dānwèi*'s gravel road to one of four waiting vehicles, all decked out with large red velvet bows above the front bumpers, as clusters of spectators looked on. Compared to our quick civil ceremony in Hong Kong, banquets clearly were a big deal in China. My family would be waiting for us at the restaurant, along with two hundred of Mama and Baba's family and friends. I didn't care that I didn't know most of them. It was my day, one that I couldn't have scripted even six months ago.

I followed Cai into a white Volkswagen Santana, his parents got into a Jeep, and his siblings and their families went in two vans. A fifth car had already left to pick up my family at their hotel. Children of Communist Party members could only include a few cars in their wedding processions, but since I was a foreigner, those rules didn't apply. We rode down to the front gate of the *dānwèi* grounds, along patches of a weed-infested courtyard, and turned onto a dusty, unpaved road leading to a five-street intersection.

Continuing at a funereal pace through the downtown area, we reached the Hidden River Hotel restaurant. When Cai stepped out of the car, he held out his hand to take mine. His brother-in-law Lin took a last drag from his cigarette and touched its tip against the wick of a two-foot-long strand of firecrackers numbering in the hundreds. He repositioned the cigarette in his mouth and stood back while Cai led me up the stairs, escaping the deafening explosions of the firecrackers. The smell of sulfur tickled my nose as we entered the musty building.

We strode into the cigarette-smoke-filled restaurant, twenty tables filled with family, friends, and Baba's Communist Party comrades. Party members' children weren't allowed more than ten tables at their wedding banquets, but again, the rule could be bent for a foreigner. I examined the spacious room and recognized a few of the people staring back at me. On each place setting sat a pack of Red Pagoda Hill cigarettes, the party favor.

Dressed in shorts and T-shirts, my parents, uncle, and brother blended in with the two hundred other guests. When my mom had emailed me back in Hong Kong to ask about the wedding's dress code, Cai stressed that it would be casual. Now I could see that for myself. Many men had donned wifebeater shirts and tattered dress pants belted above their waists. The older women wore housecoats and the younger ones polyester sundresses, some so sheer I could see through to their underwear.

Cai and I shared a table with his sisters and their families. My family followed a Cai family friend—one of the few in their *dānwèi* who could speak English—to an adjacent table. At first I could feel a cool, comfortable breeze from the air-conditioning unit mounted on an adjacent wall. But soon the body heat of two hundred people overpowered the cool air.

Waiters swarmed the tables with the opening dish. We started with a plate of sliced pig ears. I sipped my pink plastic cup of warm orange soda and waited for the next dish. Cai and his family didn't drink, so I was thankful for the plethora of orange soda bottles. Soon the waiters brought out platter after platter, including a whole steamed fish, sautéed eel, fatty pork braised with pickled greens, chicken soup, blackened chicken stew, Chinese water spinach, and steamed rice bringing up the rear. While this amount of food was standard for Hong Kong banquets, I had never seen so many dishes served at one time in China. Before I could serve more than two of these into my bowl, Cai took my elbow and nodded toward my cup. "It's time to *hējiǔ*, to drink toasts." He grabbed his cup.

We first reached Mama and Baba's table. Surrounded by their closest *dānwèi* friends, Cai's parents gleamed. Lifting our cups toward theirs, we toasted them and thanked them for all they'd given us. We then raised our cups above their friends at the table. When we moved over to where my family was seated, I noticed special dishes of dump-lings shaped like birds, flowers, and baskets, some filled with savory minced beef or pork and others with sweet lotus or red bean paste. My parents, Uncle Jeff, and my brother Jonathan stood up to toast us.

"This is wild," Uncle Jeff mouthed through the voices of two hundred people speaking all at once. Although his real name was Jeffrey, we all called him Budgie. Fifteen months older than Jeff, my mom couldn't pronounce his name when she was a toddler. It came out as Budgie and had stuck ever since.

Cai and I moved on, making our way to the seventeen other tables. I took small sips so my flat orange soda would last until we reached the final table, but the heat and the stale, smoky air scratched my throat. About halfway through the toasts, I felt faint and started to see black spots in front of my eyes.

I pulled on Cai's shoulder. "I need more soda."

He took one look at my lackluster appearance and rushed to the next table, reaching over for a half-empty bottle to refill my cup. A baritone started singing karaoke off in a corner, the melody barely audible. Cai held my arm until we finally returned to our table. The wait staff was in the process of clearing the dishes, but I didn't mind. I wasn't hungry in this heat and thick air.

I thought that maybe now Cai would chat with his sisters about the banquet and this big day, while I slipped off for a few minutes to talk to my family. Looking up, I noticed that people were making a mad dash for the exit. It was as if a fire had broken out in the opposite corner and they were running for their lives.

"What's going on?" I asked Cai.

"It's over." He smiled, placing his hand on my shoulder. "Time to go home."

In Hong Kong, people also left banquets as soon as they finished the last dish, but I hadn't realized the same held true for weddings. Although there wasn't much else to do at the banquet but talk with each other, I was sad it was ending so quickly. I hadn't had much time to enjoy my own wedding.

Cai and I returned to his parents' apartment, where we were to stay for the remainder of our trip in Hidden River. After the banquet, my family returned to their hotel to rest up after the heavy dinner in scorching temperatures. Mama turned on the television while we four rehashed the highlights of the banquet. Baba sounded like a government official when he stated with pride that never before had an American woman married a man from Hidden River, and certainly no American had ever held a wedding banquet in the town, at least to anyone's recollection.

"You are *míngxīng* here," Mama said proudly. Famous, like a movie star. I did relish the idea of being known to strangers as the only American in Hidden River. It made me feel like a pioneer, like someone special. Just as I started to daydream of people in Hidden River pointing me out as the American bride while I shopped along the main street, Mama and Baba changed gears and started to scrutinize all that had gone wrong. The food was mediocre, the special dishes on my family's table didn't look fresh, the air-conditioning didn't work, and the final bill was too expensive.

My parents had offered to split the costs, but Mama and Baba knew they had paid thousands of dollars to fly to China and then for hotels and other travel expenses once we left Hidden River. So they gave my parents a figure much lower than half the cost of the banquet. I didn't want to embarrass Mama and Baba by telling my parents the true cost of the banquet, so I kept quiet.

But I vowed to myself to help Cai's parents in any way I could. It wasn't just because they gave us a wedding banquet; I had also been touched by their support and good blessings ever since Cai told them about me. While they decried some friends for paying less than the standard wedding gift amount, I could feel myself starting to doze off on the living room sofa. I stood up and said, "Time for bed."

The three of them nodded good night as they remained sitting and continued their conversation. Even though this afternoon had been extraordinary, now it seemed like any other night in Hidden River.

Chapter 14

VISIT FROM "JAPANESE FATHER"

To differentiate my mother and father from his, Cai named our sets of parents. In fact, we had three. Mine were known as American parents. Mama and Baba were our Hidden River parents. And a Japanese professor named Yoshimoto, whom Cai had met in China and gotten to know mainly through weekly letters, was Japanese Father.

Professor Yoshimoto was a Buddhist scholar from Kyoto in his early sixties. He was estranged from his wife and his adult son, but still spoke to his grown daughter. Yoshimoto could converse in Mandarin and had traveled to the Wuhan Conservatory two summers earlier for a conference on Chinese religious music. It was there that he had met Cai. A couple weeks before my family had arrived in Shanghai for our wedding banquet, Baba walked into the apartment, waving an airmail letter.

"Yan, it's for you."

Cai glanced quickly at the envelope. "It's from Japanese Father!"

"*Ay, lǎotóu hěn cōngmíng*. The old man is brilliant," Mama said, gushing like a schoolgirl. Yoshimoto had visited Cai and his parents in Hidden River the previous summer and clearly left Mama with a strong impression.

Cai carefully tore one of the short ends of the envelope and pried the letter out like recovered treasure. He pinched his brows together as he read in concentration. When he finished reading, he looked up with a wide grin. "Japanese Father wants to come to our banquet, but is busy that day. He'd like us to change the date."

Change the date? Our wedding was planned for July 25. Not only had my family already booked tickets to arrive days before July 25, but my brother Jonathan was only able to get a week off work and had to be back in Washington, DC, by August 1. If we moved the banquet back even two days, Jonathan would miss it.

"I think we can do that," Cai declared.

Mama and Baba smiled and nodded. I could feel my stomach turn into knots. We were not going to shift our wedding date for some guy I didn't know, especially when my family had arranged their whole summer around our banquet. And who was this Yoshimoto person to ask us to change our date?

Baba turned to me. "Susan, your family will still be here in early August, right?"

"My brother won't."

"*Nà bù hǎo.*" Baba agreed this new plan wouldn't work. But Cai and his parents knew Jonathan's schedule very well. After all, they'd arranged outings for every day of my family's visit, which included Shanghai, Wuhan, Hidden River, Chongqing, and a river cruise down the Yangtze to see the Three Gorges. Jonathan would leave right before my parents, Budgie, Cai, and I would fly to Chongqing for the river cruise.

Cai sucked air through his teeth. "I'll just write him back and say we need to keep the date because Susan's family has already booked their tickets. He should understand."

Crisis averted. Since we were going ahead with our wedding banquet as scheduled, I saw no reason to make a fuss about Yoshimoto's request to move it. But it was difficult for me to comprehend Cai's parents' devotion to Yoshimoto. Baba was born at a time when the Japanese occupied northern China. And Mama was born two years after Japan invaded many other parts of China, two years after the Rape of Nanking.

The older generation in Hong Kong still held resentment toward the Japanese, so I figured the same age group in China would feel the same or even stronger. Mama and Baba must be very accepting of others, I reasoned. And though Japanese Father wasn't family, he was an elder and a professor—two Confucian factors that warranted respect. But I still couldn't get around how Cai and his family were willing, for a moment, to put Yoshimoto's wishes above my family's. I couldn't help but feel like the typical lowly daughter-in-law I'd read about in classical Chinese novels.

Japanese Father wrote back a few days before Cai and I left Hidden River for Shanghai. He grasped that we couldn't change our plans, and said he would fly to Wuhan a couple of days after our banquet. We would spend a week in Wuhan and Shanghai with him.

On the day of his arrival, Professor Yoshimoto entered Mama and Baba's apartment like a timid recluse. With dyed black hair, slicked back and as shiny as a beetle, he conversed in Mandarin with Cai's parents in short, quick sentences. He barely glanced at my family and me, even though Cai had boasted of the professor's English proficiency. I figured Yoshimoto wanted to focus his attention on Mama and Baba during his short visit with them. We would get to know one another after leaving Hidden River.

In Wuhan the following day, which we chose to visit so that Yoshimoto could shop for cheap clothes, Cai booked us rooms in a three-star hotel on a busy intersection in the old Hankou district. For entertainment that evening, he led us to a cocktail lounge on the hotel's first floor. Cai's friend and former classmate, Rui, joined us in the lounge. Short and a little plump around the waist, Rui had a kind smile and wavy, permed hair.

When Cai explained that Rui was planning to study in Kyoto with Professor Yoshimoto, he added that he had been Yoshimoto's first choice. Cai chose not to follow Yoshimoto to Japan because he'd already committed to study in Hong Kong with Dr. Tsang. Rui was the professor's second choice and would leave for Kyoto at the end of the summer.

Our party of eight converged on a table facing a large dance floor. A stage sat on the other side. Soon the lights went out and a thin woman dressed in a tight minidress and stiletto heels sashayed onto the stage to wild applause. She shooed off the emcee, first winking at him and then at the nightclub audience. A karaoke song appeared on the screen behind her, and the woman sang a few words as another rush of applause burst out. Yoshimoto slithered around to look at the singer and sat mesmerized for several minutes.

Jonathan leaned toward me. "I think that's a man."

"Huh?"

"Look closer. You can see her Adam's apple."

And there it was. I scrutinized the singer's body and saw no hips. Her tight calf muscles bulged in the fishnet stockings, and her makeup rivaled that of any drag queen.

Japanese Father turned his back to the stage and stuck his pointer fingers in his ears like a two-year-old who no longer wished to listen. He sat with tightened lips, staring down at the table.

Facing the stage, gaping along with the rest of the audience, Cai moved his head to the beat of the Chinese folk song that blared from the speakers while Rui mouthed the lyrics. But Japanese Father continued to sulk with his fingers in his ears. For once, I sympathized with Yoshimoto. He obviously didn't want to sit through this performance. So I tapped Cai's shoulder, prompting him to snap around, eyeing me as if I were interrupting a concert at Carnegie Hall.

"I think Professor Yoshimoto wants to leave," I screamed, barely audible amid the roar of the audience.

"Really?" Cai turned his head to see Japanese Father with his fingers plugged in his ears.

I leaned into Cai's ear. "He thinks it's too loud. We should leave."

"Rui and I will take him back to his room," Cai shouted to me above the cheering.

I rose to join them, but Cai held up his hand. "You stay with your family. I'll meet you back in the room later."

Given his nightly chats with his Wuhan professors, I wasn't surprised when Cai returned just after midnight, stirring me from a light sleep as he turned on a small lamp and headed toward the bathroom to take a shower.

"Japanese Father wanted to do some chatting." Cai spoke in English as he climbed into bed five minutes later. "He likes the quiet environment."

Just as Cai settled into bed, the phone rang. In my head I cursed Yoshimoto. Could he not give us one evening of peace? I imagined he was calling with some urgent message for Cai that couldn't wait until the morning. Or perhaps he suddenly wanted to go out for a midnight snack. It must be Yoshimoto, because after Cai answered the phone, he spoke in a familiar way, as though he knew the person on the other end. I turned my head and tried to fall asleep, but Cai was wide awake, as energetic as if it were noon and not midnight.

"She's right here," he said in Chinese, "right next to me." He giggled and tsk-tsked the way mainland Chinese do to show endearment.

"It's true," Cai playfully chided, as if Yoshimoto didn't believe I was in the room, in the same bed. Where did the professor think I was? And why was Cai acting so flirtatious?

But then something clicked.

Cai wasn't speaking in Mandarin. He was using the Wuhan dialect. Yoshimoto spoke decent Mandarin, but I could bet money he didn't know *Wǔhàn huà*.

So who was on the other end of the conversation?

"Yes, she's American," I heard Cai say when I started paying attention again. "Do you want to talk to her?"

Cai nodded at me, as if I was in on the joke with this mystery person. His relaxed eyes told me not to worry, that everything was under control. He giggled and tsked-tsked for five more minutes. When he finally hung up, Cai exhaled loudly and leaned back into the headboard as if he'd just won an evening of high-stakes poker.

"*Hǎowán*." That was really fun.

"Who was that?" Had Rui called him from home to play some

kind of joke? Or was it an old girlfriend? It certainly couldn't be his ex-wife, Wei Ling, could it? I was utterly confused and couldn't imagine who would know we were staying at this hotel besides my family, Rui, and Yoshimoto.

"*Jìnǚ*," Cai said, as if it was someone we both knew.

"A prostitute?"

Cai nodded as he fluffed his pillow.

"Why would a hooker call our room? Do you know her?" And why had Cai spoken to her in such a familiar manner?

"Of course not." He sounded as if I was the one who had just crossed a boundary. "They all call from the hotel lobby. This is *China*."

This was certainly a custom I'd never heard of before (nor had we experienced it in previous Chinese hotels). "Why did you talk to her for so long? No wait, why did you talk to her at all?"

"It's funny." He sighed joyfully and turned off the light.

I didn't know what was so fun about talking to a prostitute he had no intention of meeting. Had he spoken to hookers before? Had he been with a prostitute? Was that the reason he was afraid of HIV/AIDS? I knew I might be being paranoid, but the thoughts had to cross my mind. Before I could ask anything further, though, I heard gentle snoring.

Porn was one thing, but talking to a prostitute was definitely unacceptable for a married man. Or was I being too prudish in worrying about an innocent phone call? I had to close my eyes to keep my head from spinning. When I met my family the next morning, I knew I could not tell them about this phone call. If I did, I knew they would develop a bad impression of Cai. It was one more thing that I had to keep inside.

✎ ☕ ✎

The next morning, I woke with a start to what seemed like the sound of running water. Groggy, I squinted at the clock. A few minutes past 6:00 a.m. It was then that I realized Cai wasn't beside me. He must be in the bathroom. But why so early? He couldn't have slept for more than six hours. Just then, he reappeared, full of energy and dressed in his button-down shirt and black khakis.

"Where are you going?" I asked.

His eyes showed his surprise. "I didn't know you were awake."

"Well, I am now."

"Japanese Father gets up early. He wants to meet for breakfast."

"*Now?* It's only six."

"That's okay. You sleep and meet parents, Jonathan, and Uncle at nine. I'll take Japanese Father to do shopping after breakfast. We'll meet you later." Once my family arrived in China, Cai started speaking in English. Now that we were alone, he continued to speak in my native tongue and would use English in most of our conversations from that point on. When I stopped to ask him why he rarely spoke in Chinese with me, he said he wanted to practice his English for future trips to the United States and for interactions with people in Hong Kong who didn't speak Mandarin.

I sat up. I didn't know whether to be more upset that Cai was going off alone with Yoshimoto or that he'd meant to sneak out while I was sleeping without telling me his plans. And why couldn't Rui take Yoshimoto out this early? *He* was the one who would soon be the professor's student. But I feared another confrontation so I only asked, "Where should we meet?"

Cai sat on the bed next to me and caressed my legs over the covers. "Sorry, but Japanese Father has his own ways. Can you just take parents, Uncle, and Jonathan to the sights?"

I suddenly felt petty for wanting Cai to stay with my family and me. Yoshimoto was only in China for a week and depended on Cai to get around, even though he could speak Mandarin and read Chinese characters. I figured this would be the first and last time I'd ever see Yoshimoto. They could have their time together.

"Let's meet back at the hotel for dinner at six o'clock," Cai said, slowly standing up.

"Sure." I smiled.

"Oh, by the way, Japanese Father and I were talking last night after Rui went home," he chirped. "He thinks it's not good for the health to have sex relations more than once a week."

"*What?*"

"Japanese Father says—"

"I heard what you said," I snapped. "Why's he telling you this?"

"He just wants to help," Cai replied defensively.

"Help with what? I didn't think there was a problem."

"Of course there's not a problem," he barked. "Since I'm a scholar, he thinks I should concentrate on my research and not use all my energy on other things."

"I've never heard of that. Besides, it's none of his business."

Cai nodded as if in agreement before leaving the room. I tried to fall back asleep but couldn't get this bizarre conversation out of my mind. Cai's relationship with his Wuhan professors was weird enough, but now Yoshimoto was distributing sex advice. In Hong Kong, Cai was adamant about keeping our private life to ourselves. So why did he think it normal and even appropriate to discuss it with someone who was little more than a pen pal? And how had this conversation with Yoshimoto even come up?

What had Cai told him about our sex life? That we didn't use birth control and Cai had a wait-and-see attitude even though we didn't have jobs or know where we'd live after graduation? Was that why Yoshimoto told Cai to hold off? I couldn't wait until Japanese Father went home to his real family, or to those in Japan who were still speaking to him.

◖ ◣ ◗

I led my family around the old city of Hankou, now part of Wuhan, to see the colonial architecture along the water. We found lunch at a small, out-of-the-way restaurant near the Han River and shopped at a Friendship Store, the government-run department store where foreigners were encouraged to spend their money. I enjoyed this time alone with them, not having to worry about Yoshimoto or even Cai.

Since my family had arrived in China, Cai's outbursts in Shanghai and Suzhou seemed like aberrations. But I had to admit it was sometimes more relaxing to speak at a normal pace, telling my family about my life in Hong Kong and listening to them relay news about relatives back in the United States. We shopped leisurely and spontaneously stopped for a cold drink, taking our time. When Cai took us around, he was a perfect tour guide, but we were always in a rush with predetermined time slots for meals and sightseeing.

That evening when my family and I entered the hotel restaurant at six, Cai and Yoshimoto were just standing up from their cluttered table.

"You're leaving?" I asked. Had I mistaken our meeting time?

"Sorry. We just finished. Japanese Father likes to eat early and to go to sleep early. We've been up since six this morning."

I didn't know what to say. Japanese Father obviously didn't get to bed early the night before. And why tell me to meet at six when they were leaving at six? Although I figured it was beyond Cai's control, I was beginning to feel like I was the only one who thought the situation bizarre.

The next day, we left Wuhan for Shanghai to spend a couple days in the city before Jonathan flew back to the United States and Yoshimoto returned to Japan. Our flight to Shanghai was to leave at four in the afternoon, so we arrived at the new Wuhan airport an hour early. Once we took seats at the gate, Cai looked into the distance to listen to a muffled overhead announcement.

"The flight is delayed." Cai strained his voice to stay upbeat. "It should only be an hour late."

With the drooping shoulders of a lost puppy, Yoshimoto leaned over, speaking to Cai so softly I couldn't make out a word. Sitting across from Cai and Yoshimoto, my parents took out their books, while Budgie, Jonathan, and I rehashed the details of the many wedding banquet dishes. Out of the corner of my eye, I saw Yoshimoto lower his head until it rested on Cai's shoulder. Japanese Father gently closed his eyes. Cai didn't flinch.

Budgie opened his eyes wide, catching my attention. *"Huh?"* he mouthed, so as not to disturb the resting pair.

I shrugged my shoulders. Why in the world was Yoshimoto resting his head on Cai's shoulder? Up until now, everything between them had seemed like everyday Confucian teacher-student interactions. But this was different. Again, with my family present, I felt like I had to be strong for everyone. If I spoke up now or in private, I knew Cai would either give me the silent treatment as he had on the train to Suzhou or would chastise me as he had in the pedicab. Although Jonathan would fly back to Washington, DC, in a couple days, my parents and Budgie still had another week in China. I couldn't let them think that I wasn't in control of my life, that inside I was barely hanging on.

Chapter 15

WOMEN ARE DIRTY

Like most Americans, I liked to start the day off fresh with a hot shower. During my first trip to Hidden River at Chinese New Year, I went without a shower all week because that was what Cai and his family did. I wasn't used to waiting for so long between showers, but I also knew nothing awful would happen besides my hair tangling in knots. That was something I could fix when we returned to Hong Kong.

But summers in Hidden River sweltered. A cool shower felt refreshing, a chance to wash away the grime and sweat from days of hundred-degree heat. Just as in Hong Kong, I had enjoyed a daily shower that summer: at Mama and Baba's, at the guesthouse in Suzhou, and at the dorm and hotel in Shanghai and Wuhan. Some days I even bathed twice.

It was early September and we needed to collect official papers in Wuhan for Cai's green card application before returning to Hong Kong for our final year of grad school. Since Cai was still employed by the Conservatory and on leave while he studied in Hong Kong, he was able to keep the apartment where he'd lived with Wei Ling and Ting-Ting on the Conservatory's campus. So we stayed there.

I found it difficult to sleep well in the bedroom with roaches peeping out of the cracks at all hours, but the rustic bathroom scared me even more. It wasn't just the squatter toilet, resembling an old urinal that had fallen flat on the floor, or the outhouse décor: naked cement and spiderwebs dotted with gray egg sacks. Or even the large red plastic basin, turned upside down and kept over the toilet.

"What's that for?" I asked Cai.

"To keep the rats out."

I cringed, imagining diseased rodents poking their pointed snouts out of the squatter toilet. But when I looked up at the showerhead that hung loosely from a crumbling cement wall in the narrow stall, I realized that to take a shower I would need to uproot the red basin and straddle the toilet, trying to balance so as not to step in the hole, one stratum from the rats' underground nest.

The overwhelming sewer stench made me want to gag each time I opened the flimsy wooden bathroom door. I could wait a few days until we returned to Hidden River before taking another shower. Luckily I'd brought enough deodorant for the summer, a product I had yet to find in a Chinese store outside of Shanghai.

One afternoon, Cai and I returned to his apartment after lunch. The excruciating heat had left me worn and sluggish. "*Wǒ lèi sǐle.*" Collapsing onto Cai's platform bed, I wasn't actually tired to death, but I liked this Chinese expression and thought it a good prelude to *wǔjiào*, or afternoon nap. Much to my delight, my brother Jonathan had brought me a few paperbacks. I looked forward to reading for a bit after my nap.

Instead of joining me on the bed, Cai stood firm, peering down at me. "You haven't taken a shower in a while."

Huh? "You haven't taken one either," I replied.

The skin between Cai's nose and upper lip inflated like a balloon. "Women are dirty." He eyed me carefully. "Especially in the summer."

What? For the first time in weeks, we could finally enjoy some time alone away from his family and professors, and this is what he chose to emphasize? His tirade took me by such surprise that I was left speechless and could only look down at the naked cement floor in shame. Did he really think I was dirty?

"You should take a bath now," he ordered.

Cai walked around me, as if I were a filthy street urchin he would avoid in the congested Wuhan streets. He stepped into the bathroom and uncovered the toilet, tossing the red basin right side up on the cement floor. It landed with a thud in the small space between the bathroom and his bedroom. The sound of the plastic colliding with the floor broke the silence in the room.

Cai marched into the kitchen and filled a kettle with water from the sink, which resembled the washbasin in my parents' unfinished basement. While the water boiled, Cai used a cooking pot to transport tap water to the basin. He dumped several pots of water into the basin, mixing it with boiling water so my bath wouldn't be cold to the touch. I looked on in disbelief; none of this made sense. Cai stepped into the bedroom and sat on his bed, watching over me like a prison warden.

"It's ready now."

Although I knew that I should stand up to his misogynist behavior, I felt so embarrassed that he was insisting I bathe that I could barely look at him. Though Cai had never spoken of this before, I suddenly wondered if he was right. Why else would he say it? So I did as I was told.

The apartment had no interior doors except for in the bathroom, and that was a thin piece of wood hung by a couple of rusted hinges. He had placed the basin outside the bathroom, so that one door did me no good. If I wanted to move the basin back a few feet for privacy, it wouldn't be able to rest on a flat surface since the squatter toilet took up most of the tiny floor space.

Numb, I continued to stand there and wonder if our cultural differences were greater than I could handle. Somehow this summer had gone all wrong: the Shanghai Railway Station, the train to Suzhou, Cai's interactions with his Wuhan professors, Yoshimoto's bizarre behavior, and Cai's phone conversation with the prostitute.

Was it China, or was I was the one at fault? Plenty of foreigners had braved the rough conditions in China, but I had opted for the comforts of Hong Kong. Was I just not cut out for the mainland? Maybe I was nothing but a spoiled American. If my own husband could see it, wasn't that proof? It was hard to know what to believe without the support network of my friends in Hong Kong or those back in the United States.

I had no one to talk to in China that summer besides my family, although even they were now out of reach and I hadn't spoken to them about my problems. Still, I wasn't sorry I had kept these worries from them. If they had known the truth, I knew they would have insisted that I return with them to the United States. But I had only been married a few months and couldn't give up so soon.

"*Ay yo*," Cai exhaled as he stood up in haste and walked back over to the basin—and to me. "Don't you know how to take a bath?" His words sounded like a reprimand.

"Actually, no. We don't use this in America." I stared at the dirty basin, imagining the thousands of rats that had made contact with it in their many attempts to break free from the sludgy sewer.

Cai squatted next to the basin and pantomimed splashing water upward onto his crotch. "Like this." He glared at me while he continued his miming. "Chinese peasant women take baths like this." And then he repeated, with a snarl, how women were dirty, especially in the summer. He returned to the kitchen and reached for something. On his way back to the bedroom, he tossed me a worn bar of hand soap, black stains ingrained in its ridges.

Bent over and defeated, I undressed and stepped into the warm water as a flush of shame crept over my skin like a fresh layer of sunburn. I no longer felt like his wife; I was a filthy vagrant, crouching in disgrace as I tried to mimic the way he splashed water in his pantomime. As I squatted in that red basin, I knew I wouldn't be able to keep it together without one central prerequisite: *I cannot live in China with this man*. I could not wait to return to Hong Kong.

Back in Hong Kong, Cai and I moved into a double room reserved for married couples or foreign students. Identical to the one I'd shared with Na Wei the previous academic year, our room stood at the end of the second-floor hall, a floor designated for men only. The university thought it best for married women to reside on a male floor rather than a married man on a female floor.

Cai turned our room into a makeshift marital chamber every night by converting our thin bunk bed mattresses into a queen-size futon, placing them side by side on the floor so we could sleep together. We bought a small refrigerator and on top of that placed a new television with a built-in VCR. It was still a dorm room, but it felt like a cozy home.

One warm autumn day after class, we rode the train a couple stops to the Sha Tin mall and wandered into the KPS Video Express rental store. "Why don't you choose a movie and I'll choose one, and then we can watch both tonight," Cai suggested.

"Sounds good. Let's meet back here in five minutes."

I scoured the foreign film section and pulled the tape jacket for *Blue*, the first in a trilogy by director Krzysztof Kieślowski. Back in Washington, DC, I'd watched *The Double Life of Véronique* two times the night I rented it. I wanted to see another Kieślowski film, and since all movie rentals in Hong Kong included Chinese and English subtitles, both Cai and I could understand them.

But when I returned to our meeting place, Cai was nowhere to be seen. Gazing above the low shelves and scanning the shop, I couldn't see him anywhere. Had he left the store? It didn't seem like something he would do without telling me, so I made for the back of the store, in case he was hidden there. Just as I reached the little room off to the side that housed porn, Cai stepped out, startled to see me.

"Did you find something?" he asked.

I showed him the jacket for *Blue*.

"I don't want to see that."

What? What was the point of us each choosing a movie if he vetoed my pick? I was hesitant to make a scene, especially since the porn room was filled with middle-aged businessmen who could probably speak fluent English.

"Let's get something else," Cai muttered as he headed toward the front, carrying *Sex & Zen*. Before we reached the checkout counter, Cai stopped and picked up *Apollo 13*, as if he had planned to choose it all along. He continued on to the register.

That evening after we'd finished *Apollo 13*, Cai turned to me. "You can sleep," he said, popping *Sex & Zen* into the VCR. "I'll watch this movie alone."

Although surprised he had chosen porn, I focused more on his rejection of my movie pick rather than on the warning signs of a future problem in my marriage. It was just a movie, I told myself, not a life-and-death situation. And it was the first time Cai had lived apart from other mainland students since he arrived in Hong Kong two years earlier. Maybe he was just taking advantage of his newfound independence. I just hoped it wouldn't become a habit, that his preference for porn over me wasn't going to be constant. As on our honeymoon, I fell asleep to Cai staring at the television screen and the phony groans of porn stars.

The next time we traveled to Sha Tin, Cai headed straight to the porn room again. Within a few minutes, I found a movie—Hong Kong director John Woo's masterpiece, *Hard Boiled*—and ended up waiting almost a half hour while Cai perused the porn tapes lining the little room from floor to ceiling. When he finally emerged, he smiled sheepishly.

"I'm going to write an article for a newspaper in China to introduce people there to these movies," he said as we headed toward the checkout register.

"Aren't they illegal in China?" I thought back to my first trip to China in 1988. Arriving in Beijing that summer, my suitcases were searched not only for porn, but also for banned American books. I couldn't imagine things having changed so extremely in just seven years.

"Yes, but people still get them from Hong Kong, Taiwan, and other places."

I thought it a little juvenile for Cai to think he could write a newspaper article about porn—and a bit unrealistic since I was fairly sure it wasn't officially allowed in China—but I didn't question him because I didn't want to be a nag. I figured it was normal for most men to look at porn, so why should Cai be any different?

As the weeks and then months passed, I sometimes thought about Cai's article as he continued to rent porn once or twice a week—sometimes more—when we ventured out to the mall. But since he didn't veto my choices after the Kieślowski film, it seemed like a fair deal. We'd watch one movie together, and after I went to sleep, he'd pop in the porn. He never did write that article.

Chapter 16
THE FOREIGN STEPMOTHER

It was after we returned from our long summer in China that Cai told me he'd heard from a Wuhan classmate about his daughter, Ting-Ting. According to this friend, Ting-Ting had recently moved to Zhūhâi to live with Wei Ling. She was now only a two-hour boat ride away from us.

"That's fantastic! You should go visit her," I said. With Ting-Ting out of her grandparents' reach, Cai could become reacquainted with her. He hadn't tried to contact her since Wei Ling's parents had refused to let him see Ting-Ting a couple summers ago. I assumed he felt discouraged after that visit and needed a push to try again. I'd been so preoccupied with our wedding in Hong Kong, our banquet in Hidden River, and my chipped self-esteem that I didn't think to ask Cai about contacting Ting-Ting. But now was the perfect time for Cai to make that trip. He could easily go for a weekend or even a day.

"Would that be all right?" he asked.

"What do you mean? Of course it would be. You don't need my permission."

"Thank you." He kissed me quickly on the lips. "I'll call Wei Ling. It's time I see my daughter."

"Do you know how to contact her?"

"My classmate gave me her number. I think he had the same idea."

The following day when I returned from my teaching assistant duties in an undergraduate political theory class, Cai told me about

his conversation with his ex-wife. Ting-Ting was studying at the
school where Wei Ling taught dance. In a month, Ting-Ting would
perform in a school dance concert to celebrate China's National
Day on October 1.

"I'd like to see her perform. Is it okay if I go to Zhūhâi that
weekend?"

As downtrodden as I'd felt when Cai first told me about Ting-
Ting and how he hadn't seen her in two years, I was thrilled that he
finally had the chance to visit her. For a moment, I wondered how
he and Wei Ling would interact with each other. They hadn't seen
one another in years. But then I reminded myself that he was going
to Zhūhâi to visit Ting-Ting, not Wei Ling. "Do you want me to go
with you?" I asked.

Cai looked like he was about to reply, but then paused. "I'd love
for you to meet her. But I think this time—"

"I understand. It's best you see her alone."

He looked puzzled. "How did you know I was going to say that?"

"Well, it has been a long time since you've seen Ting-Ting. Your
first meeting should just be the two of you, not with a foreign stepmother. She'll have plenty of chances to meet me later."

"Thank you. I'll just go for the weekend and stay in a guesthouse
for one night."

"I have friends whose parents divorced at an early age. Just don't
be surprised if Ting-Ting is a little shy with you. When kids don't
see their dads for a long time, they don't always warm up right away.
That's normal."

"It'll be no problem. Ting-Ting is a great kid. We were always
very close when she was a baby."

"But she's bigger now. It's just something to keep in mind."

On the morning of his departure, Cai and I headed down the
mountain to take the train into Kowloon. The boats to Zhūhâi and

Macau left from a ferry pier in Tsim Sha Tsui that was oddly named China Hong Kong City and also served as a shopping mall.

"Have a great time," I told Cai as we approached the gate. The boat terminal resembled an airport's, with a comfortable waiting room and rows of neatly arranged chairs. A neon sign announced the next departure time to Zhūhâi.

"Try to take a few pictures. I'd love to see what Ting-Ting looks like."

"Thank you." He kissed me tenderly on the lips. "Have a good weekend. I'll see you tomorrow back in our room."

I wanted to meet him at China Hong Kong City the following evening, but he insisted I not waste my afternoon. Cai didn't call all weekend, but I didn't expect him to. We didn't own cell phones, and calling Hong Kong from China cost more than calling the United States from Hong Kong with a discounted calling plan. I spent the weekend catching up on my classwork. When Cai turned our doorknob on Sunday evening, I jumped from my desk, where I was leafing through notes for my state and civil society class.

"How'd it go?" I said, beaming.

Cai embraced me and hung his backpack around the back of his desk chair. "It was great. Ting-Ting did an excellent job in her performance."

"That's so good to hear. Was she sad when you left?"

"I think so. I told her I'd come again soon."

"Wonderful. It sounds like everything went really well." We both sat in our desk chairs while Cai fished out a little photo album from his backpack.

"I took these photos and had them developed there. I gave Ting-Ting a copy." He handed me the little paper album, the size of a four-by-six photo. The first photo showed a smiling girl, her hair parted down the middle with little wisps hanging over her forehead. She was missing one top front tooth. Her eyes were narrow like Baba's and her face was round like Mama's. I didn't see Cai in her at all. Maybe she looked like Wei Ling.

But then I turned the page and there stood a petite woman wearing a thin, dark pencil skirt and a cream-colored silk blouse. Her wide doe eyes appeared large on her oval face. I thought Wei Ling looked beautiful, and from what I knew about Chinese standards of beauty—with its penchant for round eyes—she was considered stunning in China, too.

"Ting-Ting's not as cute as before," Cai said matter-of-factly. "But she was really well-behaved."

"She's cute in this photo." I turned the pages of the album, viewing a heavily made-up Ting-Ting in her dance costume: a robin's-egg blue blouse and light pink skirt. In another photo Ting-Ting posed with Wei Ling, both holding up their pointer and middle fingers to form the victory sign.

I wanted to ask Cai so many questions. Did he talk much to Wei Ling? Was their interaction cordial? Did people assume they were a happy family out for a weekend stroll? But I didn't want to appear jealous or insecure, so I simply asked if Wei Ling had been nice to him.

"Yeah. She said she's never found another guy as kind as me."

"Really? What did you say?"

"Nothing. What could I say?" He stood up and took my hands in his, gently pulling me into his embrace. "You're my wife. I wouldn't want it any other way."

"Thank you." I shouldn't have felt insecure. Cai had always made it clear that he didn't regret his divorce from Wei Ling. Still, I couldn't help feeling competitive with his ex-wife. I didn't want to give Cai the trouble that she had during their marriage, arguing at every opportunity and behaving as an individual who was only responsible for herself, not as a partner in a marriage. Yes, I aimed to be the opposite of Wei Ling, to be the type of wife Cai described back in our dorm room the night we got engaged: kind, warm, and soft.

Chapter 17
AMERICA, MY EXOTIC HOME

The flat roads stretched for miles beyond the lightly traveled highway. Gray skies blurred the rising skyscrapers ahead as we drove away from the airport. From inside the car, it looked as if we could be near any big city in China, but Cai and I had just landed in Chicago for winter vacation.

"There, can you see it?" My father pointed to the windshield. "That's the Sears Tower, the tallest building in the world."

Cai nodded and stared off in the distance. Although I'd enjoyed every minute of my year and a half in Hong Kong—minus those three months in China the summer we married—I now longed to introduce Cai to my favorite Chicago attractions: the architecture, the museums, and the wealth of ethnic restaurants. My mother drove while my father continued to point out other landmarks as we approached downtown—the Hancock Building, the Standard Oil Building—proud of Chicago and eager to show it to his new son-in-law.

Once home, my parents ushered us out of the blustery cold and into the comfortable new house they'd bought a year earlier in a newly developed neighborhood just south of the financial district. We climbed the carpeted stairs to the guest room at the front of the two-story wooden house.

"This room only has twin beds," my mom said, "but I pushed them together for you. You're probably tired. If you fall asleep, I'll wake you up for dinner. It's best to get used to the new time zone as soon as possible."

"Thank you," Cai said.

My mom left the room in an awkward silence. I'd never taken a guy home to my parents because there'd never been anyone before.

"*Hěn shūfú.*" It's so comfortable. Cai leaned back into the two pillows on his side of the bed. "America is very nice. I like how everyone drives cars."

That was a relief to hear. I recalled how he had said back in Hong Kong that he didn't want to live in the United States, so I wasn't sure what Cai would think of the excesses here. After all, our parents' homes couldn't be more dissimilar. Mama and Baba shared one bathroom with cement floors and a squatter toilet, while my parents enjoyed four bathrooms, three of them with a shower or tub.

His parents wore plastic slippers over their cold synthetic tile; mine glided in socks or bare feet over hardwood floors or wall-to-wall carpeting. His parents opened their windows in the winter because the outside air felt warmer than the frigid indoor air, but my parents enjoyed the comforts of central heat. I took Cai's interest in cars as a positive sign. Maybe he'd adjust to the United States quicker than I'd expected.

The next morning, I woke to Cai rifling through our suitcase.

"Are you all right?" I stirred, half awake.

"Yes. I'm going to get dressed now."

"It's so early." I couldn't see the clock without my glasses, but the street outside sounded calm and quiet. It couldn't be later than seven. Drowsy with jet lag, I wasn't ready to get up. "Don't you want to go back to bed?"

"I can't. It's so hot I couldn't sleep all night."

I hadn't noticed. After taking a melatonin, I passed out immediately and only woke for several minutes around three in the morning. I had assumed Cai was sleeping then.

"We can close the vent." Putting on my glasses, I climbed onto one of the firm mattresses and reached up to the ceiling. As I closed the vent over his side of the bed, I worried that if he was so bothered by central heat, other things I took for granted—and enjoyed—might cause him similar discomfort. I had just assumed Cai would see the United States through my eyes. But now I realized that way of thinking was both naïve and mistaken.

Of course he would view America through his own eyes, just as I saw China through mine, not his. And as much as I gushed about everything in Hong Kong, after two years he had never warmed up to that city. Even though I knew it was probably futile, I was determined to only show him the positive sides of America so he wouldn't grow disillusioned and not want to return.

For New Year's Eve, my parents brought us to a party down the street. I loved the diversity of their new development and how friendly they were with their neighbors. An African American man and his Caucasian wife lived next door, and on the other side were a Filipina woman and her Caucasian husband. There were also Jewish, Muslim, Buddhist, and Hindu neighbors. The party was held at the home of Steve and Tim, a twentysomething gay couple.

As we entered the din of their new townhouse, I smelled the delicate aroma of fresh caramel. Just beyond the kitchen in a sunken den, an elaborate dessert table greeted us with a tree of homemade profiteroles glistening with cascades of honey in the place of honor in the center. Also on the table were plates of spice cake, mini cheesecakes, and an assortment of holiday cookies. A young man entered the den carrying a tray covered with ramekins of flan draped with fresh caramel. It was dessert heaven. Steve and Tim invited guests to arrive after nine, so we'd all eaten dinner and were now indulging in these homemade delicacies.

"This is very good," Cai said between chews. His plate held a couple of conjoined profiteroles, a mini cheesecake, and a flan. Although his family didn't eat dessert, Cai enjoyed sweets, from Asian pears to the chewy Fig Newton–like pineapple cookies we often bought in Hong Kong.

"They must have spent hours baking." I licked the sticky tips of my forefinger and thumb, hoping no one noticed.

Cai scanned the crowds standing around the dessert table. His face suddenly took on a look of horror, as if he'd spotted someone he didn't want to see. "Are most of these people guy?" Cai asked.

"Guy?"

"You know, *tóngxìngliàn*. Guy." Cai hovered close to me.

"Oh, gay. It's gay, not guy. And, yes, a lot are, but some aren't."

"Are Steve and Tim gay?" He sounded panicked now.

I looked off to the side for a moment, wondering if we were about to embark on a conversation like the one about hotel towels and AIDS during our Hong Kong honeymoon. I took a deep breath while reminding myself that what seemed normal and obvious to me could still appear unfathomable to Cai. "Yes."

"They are?"

Nodding, I wanted to assuage Cai's fears. My father liked to tell the story of when his chemistry students from Beijing had vehemently stated there were no gay people in China. My dad then asked if it was against the law to be gay. Yes, they answered. There you go, my dad replied. That's why no one was coming out there.

I assumed Cai had little exposure to gay men or women. Yet this was the kind of party that I missed when we were in Hong Kong. Now that I was married, I spent my evenings with Cai in our dorm room or when we ventured out two train stops to the Sha Tin mall to eat and rent movies. I was enjoying myself at Steve and Tim's, and didn't want to press Cai about his fear. But I did lead him over to my parents so he could talk to familiar company.

By the time we left Chicago for New York, I could tell that Cai wasn't as thrilled about the United States as he had been on our first night when he basked in the comfort of down pillows and central heat. He had stopped commenting on the newness of the United States: the cars, the comfortable homes, and the enormous restaurant servings.

In fact, he spoke very little when we visited with relatives and former neighbors, and later when we walked down North Michigan Avenue in the crowds of last-minute holiday shoppers. I knew we weren't going to move to Chicago, but I wanted him to like it enough to want to come back to visit with me when we could afford it. Maybe he would take better to New York, our next stop.

Greenwich Village during the wintertime is especially quaint. Narrow streets, lights glowing from brownstones, people braving the winter elements to walk their dogs at all hours of the night. After Cai and I left my parents in Chicago, we flew to New York for a week before returning to Hong Kong. I wanted to show Cai another part of the United States, but our options were limited because we didn't have much cash.

New York worked out since my shirttail relatives—cousins of an uncle by marriage—allowed us to stay in their unoccupied basement apartment in Greenwich Village. They lived in an upstairs unit. Coincidentally, their building sat across the street from where Jin, my crush from Washington, lived when he moved to New York.

I thought New York would be fun for Cai to visit because it was full of people and had a large Chinese population. On our first afternoon in Manhattan, we walked over to Chinatown for a late lunch. Cai picked up a free Chinese newspaper from a small café on Mott Street where we warmed up with bowls of rice noodles and soup. After lunch, we returned to the apartment to rest before dinner. Lounging on the bed as dusk shone in through a few small, upper windows, Cai opened the paper.

"There are so many jobs here," he said in amazement. "Maybe we should move to New York."

"Really?" This was the first time he'd spoken about not returning to China, and while I was excited to hear it, I thought it rash to suggest moving here after a quick glance at a free classified section. We had only arrived that morning. And I knew it wouldn't be easy for Cai to find a job in his field in the United States without patience and hard work. "Are these related to music?"

"No, but it doesn't matter. I can do anything in America."

"Yes, you can find any old job, although it would be a shame if you didn't do something with music. You've worked so hard to get where you are now."

"It's okay. As long as we have each other, everything will be all right."

I admired Cai's idealism, but knew he would feel resentful later on if he gave up his career—and any chances of working with music. But he continued to peruse the New York classifieds as if they were winning lottery-ticket numbers.

"Here's one. Gas station for sale. It's only $85,000." He spoke as though it was a no-brainer for making big bucks. "Where's Queens?"

How in the world would Cai and I run a gas station? "Gas stations are usually dangerous. People hold them up at gunpoint, and we'd have no time off to spend with our kids. I don't even know where Queens is."

"We could get a gun. Doesn't everyone in America have a gun?"

My heart raced. "No way. We're not going to get a gun or use one or work someplace where we'd be an easy target for an armed robbery. Never."

Cai sighed, hurling the paper to the floor.

I needed to calm down before we both became more discouraged. He just didn't understand the way people found jobs in the United States, I reminded myself. It wasn't like China where the government assigned professions and places of employment.

"Don't be discouraged. You haven't started looking for a job in your field. If you could grow up in Hidden River and get a PhD, you can find a great job here. It'll just take some time."

He picked up the paper again. "Here's something. Newspaper journalist. *World Journal.*"

"That sounds better." My voice perked up. "You could even write about music."

"Where's the Bronx?"

"It's another borough, like Manhattan or Queens. There's a zoo and the Yankees baseball team plays there. That's all I know. Is that where the newspaper office is?"

"No, another gas station. This one is only $80,000." He sounded hopeful again about making lots of money.

I closed my eyes and kept silent. Cai seemed so volatile. I was afraid to say anything else that would come across as pessimistic or discouraging. He had to feel overwhelmed by all the choices available to him now, but I couldn't let him make such a huge decision after seeing the city for half an afternoon.

Cai scowled. "It's so dirty here."

"It is an old city. There aren't as many people as in Shanghai or Beijing, but—"

"No, not New York. This apartment. How can people live this way?"

I scanned the room. Nothing struck me as out of the ordinary, especially compared to the dank, roach-infested apartment Cai still kept at the Wuhan Conservatory of Music, where we had stayed on previous trips to China. I could still picture the black soot and gray cobwebs that overwhelmed his place.

"Look at this." He slapped the double bed. "These aren't covers, they're sleeping bags. Newspapers and so much stuff everywhere. I don't like a lot of stuff."

I peered around the apartment and for the first time noticed books scattered on various end tables and in piles on the floor. My parents weren't neat freaks, so the clutter in this apartment didn't faze me. When I thought about it, I realized it was true that Cai didn't own many things. His apartment in Wuhan was bare but for basic furniture like a bed, a table, a couple of chairs, and rudimentary pots and pans.

His parents also didn't own many material goods. I remembered seeing a few curios in a glass cabinet along with that plaster bust of

Mao. But to me, this basement apartment was cozy and charming, occupying a prime piece of real estate on a quiet tree-lined street near New York University. I figured Cai probably preferred the comforts of my parents' new construction, not vintage charm.

Outside the apartment, Cai happily tagged along wherever I wanted to go. His sullen mood from inside the apartment seemed a fleeting digression. Once we started to explore New York, he perked up. Besides visiting Chinatown, we strolled through streets around Wall Street and the calm trails in Central Park, places I thought a first-time visitor would enjoy. On our third day, as we prepared to leave for the Guggenheim on the Upper East Side, Cai made a request.

"Times Square is very famous in China."

I guessed the bright lights and heavy crowds resonated with people in China. "Do you want to go there?"

"Yes." Cai smiled.

We arrived in Times Square that afternoon.

"Let's look over there." Cai pointed to a theater sign reading "Peep Shows $1.00."

Did he know about peep shows? I couldn't imagine such a thing in China. So I followed him to the theater, figuring that he thought it was a feature film at the bargain price of a dollar. Under the marquee, I saw him eye a large photo taped to the inside of the window that showed a buxom blond in a tight, white halter top and matching hot pants, squatting on platform stiletto fuck-me boots. Cai understood the genre.

"Do you want something hot to drink?" he asked, looking away from the theater.

"Sure. There's a coffee shop over there." I pointed across the street.

We crossed the wide avenue, ducking our heads to escape the chill of the wintry wind. Entering the café, I noticed that most of the tables were occupied by men who appeared to be wearing their entire wardrobe. Cai and I found an empty one in front of a window. "What do you want?" he asked.

"Just a small tea, thanks."

Minutes later, he returned with my tea and a coffee for himself. I wrapped my hands around my teacup to regain some warmth. Although I expected him to take the seat next to mine, he placed his steaming cup on the table in front of me and remained standing.

"I want to see the show across the street." He sounded like he was excusing himself to go to the bathroom.

I pictured sleazy old men and even older bodily fluids smeared into the worn, red velvet theater seats. Though I didn't think there was anything wrong with having an interest in sex, I was caught off guard by his request in this seedy area, unfamiliar to us both. Times Square in 1996 still wasn't quite the family-friendly destination it is today.

And when I thought back to the Shanghai Railway Station and how Cai had thwarted the one thing I'd asked for on that trip, I knew I couldn't say no to him now or else I'd be guilty of the same unfairness. For a moment, I even wondered if I should offer to go with him. No, I couldn't imagine feeling comfortable in a peep show. It would be best to wait for him in the warm coffee shop.

Thank goodness I'd taken a book to read on the subway that morning. Besides the women working the cash register, most people in the café were men. I felt safe enough, as it was the middle of the day, but I exhaled in relief when a tourist family entered. I delved into my book, stopping only to reach for my paper teacup. When I looked at my watch, twenty minutes had passed.

Scanning the café, I expected to see Cai approaching my table at any moment. But there was no sign of him. I looked through the hazy window to the crowds outside, hoping I'd spot a tall man with dark straight hair, wearing a navy down jacket and an unofficial Yankees baseball cap bought from a Chinatown hawker. Still no Cai. How long could a peep show take? It's a peep, after all.

Angry with myself for not warning him to watch his wallet, I hoped Cai hadn't been accosted by someone in the theater, someone who caught on that he was a foreigner and unfamiliar with New York. What if he had been robbed and was knocked out cold, sprawled on the floor in the empty, dark theater or in its men's room?

If I left the coffee shop to search for him and we didn't cross paths, he would panic if he returned to the café and couldn't find me. But if he were really in danger, how could I just stay put? As I deliberated what to do, I kept reading the same paragraph of my book over and over. I stared through the front window at the pedestrians crossing the street and couldn't imagine getting up to buy another cup of tea or going to the bathroom lest I lose my seat with its premier view.

Ten, then twenty more minutes passed. Cai and I didn't own cell phones in Hong Kong, and we certainly hadn't bought them for a two-week trip to the United States. Maybe I should head to the theater. If Cai wasn't there, I could ask about him at similar venues. And if those turned up empty, I'd go to the police. I would have to shamefully explain how Cai went off to the peep shows and didn't return. But this was no time for decorum.

Cai had been gone for more than an hour, but it seemed like a whole afternoon. My teacup was completely empty and dry inside. The tourists were long gone. By that time, I didn't even care that I was the only female customer in the café. I just didn't want to lose my husband.

And then I saw him. Crossing the street in a crowd, Cai came into view, black Yankees cap and all. He seemed to be his normal self—walking tall, as if he had traversed this street dozens of times. He didn't appear lost in the slightest. Cai looked at the ground when I met him at the front door. "Sorry."

"I was so worried about you."

"Sorry," he repeated. "I've never seen that before. It was actually very interesting. But some ladies were as fat as a cow."

I tuned him out, not knowing if I should make a big deal about him being gone for so long. That I had worried so much for his safety, that I had felt trapped in my seat. That I had thought about going to the police.

"...and then I went to a bookstore and video store," he continued.

"You know, there are some dangerous people in this area. It's not always safe, even in daylight with many people about."

"It was fine. No one bothered me. I even saw other mainland people in the store."

When we flew back to Hong Kong later that week, Cai seemed to have enjoyed his first visit to the United States, but he never expressed the desire to rush back.

Chapter 18

ANOTHER CHINESE NEW YEAR IN HIDDEN RIVER

I walked ten steps behind Cai, like an ancient Chinese woman hobbling on bound feet. My one-size-too-small black hiking boots had fit better when I tried them on in Hong Kong a week earlier. Cai and I were back in Hidden River to visit his family for Chinese New Year, and my feet hurt so much that even my gentle pace brought pain to my squashed toes. We were on our way to Cai's middle sister's house. Bing-Bing and her husband, Lin, had invited both us and their sister, Fan-Fan, and her husband, Zhao, over for the afternoon, between lunch and dinner. On our way there, we passed a middle-aged man and two younger women at a carnivalesque stall just as the man took aim at a pyramid of rusty tin cans with a pellet gun.

"*Hǎowán.*" That's so fun. Cai smiled his signature wide grin. I didn't respond. I could only think about taking off my boots, resting my feet, and regaining whatever warmth was possible in a city without indoor heat. If I were lucky, the blisters wouldn't have popped yet.

Suddenly Cai's smile disappeared. "What's wrong with you?"

"I'm so cold and my feet hurt."

"Why you always so cold?"

"Because no one here has heat in their homes and I can never warm up. That's why." I'd never snapped like that at Cai, but now I felt relieved that I finally had. Maybe I wouldn't feel so compelled to hide my feelings from now on.

"*What?* What did you just say?" He straightened up before me, his height suddenly menacing.

I guess I shouldn't have blown my cool. "Never mind."

A small group of people gathered around us. Seeing an American woman arguing with a Chinese man in English was probably the most entertainment they'd had since the latest karaoke bar opened over the summer.

"No, not 'Never mind.' You married a Chinese. What did you think China was like? *America?*" he retorted, spitting out the last part in disgust.

"Forget it," I murmured. This was turning into a repeat of the Shanghai Railway Station, only now we were gaining an audience.

"No, I'm not going to forget it. If you're cold, that's your problem. There's nothing I can do." He turned away from me.

"Well, there is." I didn't expect Cai to hear me as the crowds grew denser.

"What?" He faced me again, eyes glassy with rage.

"You could give me some emotional support. You *are* my husband."

With a swift, sweeping motion, Cai stormed off toward his sister's apartment. I didn't know my way back to Mama and Baba's, and wouldn't have left Cai in any case. I would have been afraid to tell Mama and Baba that Cai and I had argued. I didn't doubt their empathy, but they would agonize over it well after Cai and I returned to Hong Kong. I couldn't imagine bringing that on them.

Mama and Baba had spent months of their salaries on our wedding banquet and had gone to great lengths to make sure my family received the best accommodations Hidden River had to offer. So I kept a steady pace behind Cai until we reached his sister Bing-Bing's home. When her husband, Lin, answered the door, Cai put his arm around me and smiled as if we hadn't just entertained dozens with an argument worthy of any Chinese soap opera.

Cai's eldest sister, Fan-Fan, and her husband, Zhao, had already arrived and were seated with Bing-Bing on a tattered sofa in the living room. Even though his sisters were always very pleasant to me, smiling and speaking slowly in Mandarin or with what little English they knew, I still felt like an outsider in their presence. They always seemed to be in the middle of an intense conversation with one another that I felt awkward butting into.

The inside temperature was colder than outside, so we didn't remove our jackets. I nodded shyly to Fan-Fan and Bing-Bing, but before I could join them, Cai spoke up.

"*You méiyǒu dàizi?*" Cai asked Zhao and Lin if they had the videotape.

"*You.*" In unison, they confirmed they had it.

From his man purse, Zhao pulled an unmarked videotape as the three men walked into a bedroom.

"*Wǒ bùhao yisi,*" Cai's middle sister, Bing-Bing, said.

Fan-Fan claimed she, too, was embarrassed.

"*Wèishéme?*" I asked, still standing. Why?

"*Huángsè—*"

All I had to hear was the word "yellow"—analogous to blue movies in the United States—and I knew they had porn. I suddenly felt determined to prove to myself that these movies didn't bother me, even if it meant abandoning my resolve to show Cai's family I wasn't a stereotypically slutty American. I wasn't going to shy away from the movie Cai and his brothers-in-law were about to watch in the bedroom.

"*Wǒ bùyào kàn.*" Fan-Fan said she wasn't going to watch the film. Bing-Bing nodded in agreement.

"*Méi wèntí.*" I replied it wasn't a problem for me, and I followed the guys into the room.

Before the beginning credits stopped rolling, three burly men with long mullets and scraggly facial hair sat in the living room of a Victorian mansion, watching television as they lounged on 1980s dark floral-patterned sofas. A bikini-clad buxom brunette rode up on a motorcycle, peered into the living room window, and motioned them outside with her forefinger.

"You guys are so good," she crooned as they walked out, and then proceeded to unzip the shaggiest guy's pants. Soon all four were outside on the lawn, the bikini thrown aside on the grass like litter. The four of them contorted and groaned like the Japanese woman on Cai's honeymoon pay-per-view movie. The brothers-in-law squatted on the floor, silent and smoking, their eyes glued to the TV as Cai and I sat on the bed, an arm's distance between us.

Suddenly I felt exposed by this woman performing all sorts of acrobatics on the three hairy men. Were the brothers-in-law comparing me to the actress? I felt more uncomfortable than before Zhao had popped the tape into the VCR.

"I'm going back outside," I told Cai in English. He didn't move his eyes from the TV or respond.

Cai and his brothers-in-law emerged thirty minutes later, looking exhausted, as though they'd just finished a grueling all-nighter of mah-jongg. I sat alone on a leather sofa, holding a steaming cup of green tea to keep warm, while Cai's sisters discussed something in the kitchen. Cai carried the tape in a flimsy orange plastic bag.

"*Zǒu ba.*" He patted my shoulder. Since he wanted to leave, I stood up to put my teacup in the kitchen. Bing-Bing broke from her conversation with her sister and, placing a gentle hand on my shoulder, took it from me.

Once we reached the outside, I felt warmer. Walking as quickly as I could in my tight boots and absorbing the pittance of sunlight peeking through the gray clouds above, I regained feeling in my feet, although now my blistery toes smarted against the inside of my boots.

"Why do you have the tape?" I asked.

"I might watch it later."

"What about your parents?"

"They can't work the VCR. Lin or Zhao has to come over and turn it on every time my parents want to watch a movie. The tapes all look the same to them."

I couldn't picture Cai watching the tape, which was more explicit than what he'd watched in Hong Kong, outside his parents' bedroom, even if they were asleep. I found it ironic that as an American, I was supposed to be loose and without morals, yet I seemed more concerned than Cai about Mama and Baba catching him with porn.

It also crossed my mind that if Mama and Baba found the tape or caught Cai watching it, they might think it was mine.

But the tape sat wrapped in its orange plastic bag on a bookshelf in Mama and Baba's living room, along with a few Chinese opera tapes, collecting dust until Cai returned it to Zhao a couple weeks later before we left for Hong Kong.

Chapter 19
THE MYSTERIOUS YOSHIMOTO

The Kai Tak Airport greeting area buzzed with clatter, the singsong staccato of Cantonese a pleasant melody now that I held a better comprehension of the language. A ramp parted the arrivals hall, each side flanked with greeters waiting for loved ones, business associates, or the next fare. When my mom and Budgie appeared at the top of the ramp, scanning the crowds for a familiar face, I waved my hands back and forth. My wild curls stood out amid a field of straight hair.

"Where's Cai?" my mom asked once we stepped off to the side of the arrivals area.

I rolled my eyes. "You'll never guess."

Budgie's eyes narrowed. "In China?"

"No. You won't believe this, but a few days ago he received a letter from Yoshimoto."

Budgie's eyes grew large. He tilted his head to the right, mimicking how Yoshimoto had rested his head on Cai's shoulder at the Wuhan airport the previous summer.

I sighed. "He didn't just ask Cai if he could come for a visit. He *announced* it."

My mom's shoulders dropped. "Yoshimoto is in Hong Kong now?"

"He arrived last night...for the whole week."

Budgie tilted his head once more. "The timing that man has. Is he here for vacation?"

"Pretty much. Cai says he wants them to write a book together about Buddhist and Taoist music, so they're working on that right now."

A look of concern washed over my mom's face. "Will we see Cai at all?"

"Oh, yes. But that means we'll have to see Yoshimoto, too, although I haven't had that honor yet."

"He must have radar to tell when we're coming to visit you," my mom said as we headed out toward the taxi stand.

❧ ☕ ❧

That night, Cai arrived back at our dorm room close to midnight, startling me when he turned on the overhead—and only—light in the room. My mom and Budgie had returned hours earlier to the university guesthouse next door, where Cai had also booked Yoshimoto a room.

"*Ay yo.*" Cai sighed and crouched down onto his side of our futonlike bed.

I sat up. "Are you okay?"

"It's this book," he sighed. "Japanese Father always wakes up so early. He wants me to be there so we can work on it early in the morning."

"You should sleep now."

"But Japanese Father wants me to sleep in his room so we don't waste time. We just finished the introduction and will start chapter one tomorrow."

I didn't move as Cai pulled out a couple pairs of men's bikini underwear from his dresser, along with a T-shirt and a pair of long, brown corduroys. Could Cai not see that Yoshimoto was manipulating him? The guesthouse was all of one hundred yards down the road from our dorm.

I wanted to trust Cai that nothing was going on with Yoshimoto except this scholarly collaboration, but I had a hard time picturing their sleeping arrangements. Budgie and my mom were staying in a double room with two cotlike beds, but as far I knew, Cai had booked Yoshimoto into a single room with one small bed. Was Cai sleeping on the floor? I started to think about the other option, of

Cai sharing a bed with Yoshimoto, but I quickly pushed that idea out of my mind. I couldn't let myself go there.

Instead I recalled Cai's warning back in Suzhou when I voiced displeasure with Professor Xiang from Wuhan. I already knew what Cai's reaction would be if I suggested he spend less time with a professor or questioned Yoshimoto's motives. I also remembered the night the prostitute phoned our hotel room in Wuhan, and how I tried to keep up appearances the next day so I wouldn't ruin my family's visit. With my mom and Budgie now in Hong Kong for a week, I wanted to be able to focus on them, not on a fight or another bizarre development with Cai. So I did what I did best: I kept the peace in my marriage.

Cai stopped packing for a moment. "Japanese Father is very unhappy. Rui was very rude to him in Japan and now they're not speaking."

"What do you mean? Why aren't they speaking?" Rui was the friend from Wuhan who went to Japan to study with Yoshimoto the previous fall.

"You know Japanese Father pays everything for Rui. His apartment, his food, his tuition. But one day Japanese Father went to Rui's apartment and knocked on his door. Rui had just showered and was still in his towel. He opened the door and yelled at Japanese Father for no reason. It's very bad now and Japanese Father's heart is broken."

What? This seemed like something that would happen between kindergartners. "Rui is not the type to scream at someone for no reason," I said. "He wouldn't do that." Rui was the most soft-spoken of all Cai's friends.

"No, it's true. Rui was very rude. Japanese Father can't forgive him after he's done so much for Rui."

Was I missing something? If Rui had raised his voice because he wasn't dressed yet, it still didn't make sense for Yoshimoto to stop speaking to him—and to pull all his financial support. "Is Rui still in Japan?"

"Yes, but he's on his own. Now he has to work and earn his rent and tuition fees himself. It's very bad."

Even that didn't make sense. If Rui wanted to stay in Japan, why would he blow up at Yoshimoto for knocking on his door before he had a chance to get dressed? Or maybe there was another reason. I caught my breath. For Rui to scream like that and forfeit his financial backing, Yoshimoto must have propositioned him or done something else unwanted. Cai probably didn't know the real story since he'd only heard it from Yoshimoto and had immediately taken his side. Before I could think of a diplomatic way of suggesting that Yoshimoto might have made advances toward Rui, Cai changed the subject.

"Japanese Father wants to see you tomorrow, so let's meet for dim sum at the staff canteen. At nine?"

"What about my mom and Budgie?" Surely he hadn't forgotten they'd arrived today.

"Bring them, too. He knows them." Cai disappeared in the bathroom for a minute. When he returned a moment later, he carried his toothbrush and a small bottle of cologne he used in place of deodorant during the warmer months.

Cai zipped his backpack. "I forgot to tell you something. Japanese Father is going to give me a lot of money."

"What do you mean?" I pictured a thousand U.S. dollars as a belated wedding gift.

"He got it from his university and doesn't need it. He wants me to have it for my research."

"How much?"

"Ten million yen."

"*Ten million?*"

Cai shrugged. "He says he already has enough to retire."

"How many yen to the dollar?"

"I think about a hundred." Cai's smile was enormous.

"That's—"

"A lot of money."

Whatever doubts I had regarding Yoshimoto's intentions now skyrocketed like fireworks set off at Chinese New Year. I could feel my legs shake under the covers. The whole thing was too bizarre! Would Cai have to return some unthinkable favor in return? Was that already happening? When Rui refused Yoshimoto's advances, had the professor turned his attentions toward Cai?

But then I remembered Cai's angst at my parents' gay neighbors' New Year's Eve party. I didn't stop to think that many people who act homophobic are in fact afraid that they themselves are gay. Even if this money came with no strings attached, I didn't want Cai to accept it. He and I could earn our own money. But all I could manage to say was, "That's too much money to give to you for no reason."

"You don't understand. Japanese Father says I'm like a son to him. I guess his daughter has enough money. See you tomorrow at dim sum."

As he left, my chest throbbed at the thought of his new sleeping arrangements, whether or not they involved some kind of kinky condition. I wanted to call Janice, but then I'd have to admit that my marriage had problems. She was now living with an Argentine boyfriend in a fancy Wan Chai high-rise with a stunning view of Victoria Harbor and the back of the Hong Kong skyline.

When we were able to catch each other on the phone, I filtered any negative talk of Cai to prove that I had a happy marriage. And for the most part, I *was* happy, as long as we were in Hong Kong and Yoshimoto wasn't visiting. I was afraid that if I told Janice about my concerns about the professor, she would say she'd told me so.

The next morning, the staff canteen hummed with students, staff, and faculty. When my mom, Budgie, and I found Cai and Yoshimoto at a corner table, they were reaching for dumplings in round bamboo steamers. Spotting us, Cai placed his chopsticks on his plate and rose from his chair as we sat down. Yoshimoto looked up demurely but remained seated. He took a dainty bite of his pork dumpling.

Cai was quick to fill our teacups and flag down a waitress, calling out a long list of dumplings, stuffed rice rolls, curried squid, and beef balls. He inquired about my mom and Budgie's flights from Chicago and asked how they found Hong Kong at this time of year. Yoshimoto hardly lifted his head to acknowledge us. He sometimes raised his mouth so it was within earshot of Cai's face, chirping a question or statement, like a baby bird to its mother.

As I stabbed a shrimp dumpling in a bamboo steamer and the insides plopped out of the doughy translucent wrapper, I tried to summon mental images of them composing chapters late at night in the bare-boned guesthouse room. I managed to pick up the ball of shrimp filling with my chopsticks and shove it into my mouth. Next I maneuvered the dumpling wrapper to the safety of my small rice bowl.

Although I felt embarrassed for dropping the dumpling, probably offending Yoshimoto with my clumsy use of chopsticks, he didn't flinch. Yet he seemed as antisocial now as he had in China the previous summer. When Cai received letters from Yoshimoto and relayed his warm greetings to me, I wondered if a different person composed them because he seemed so unfriendly in person.

"Professor Yoshimoto is very tired," Cai said, full of cheer. "We woke at five to work on our book, so he'd like to go back and take a rest. Susan, can you take Mom and Uncle sightseeing?"

I didn't answer. I wished I'd spoken up when Yoshimoto hijacked Cai's time in China over the summer, or just the night before when I learned Yoshimoto planned to give Cai his massive retirement award. Or when Yoshimoto asked Cai to sleep in his guesthouse room. Now as Yoshimoto followed Cai out the front door, I knew things had gotten completely out of control and I had no idea how to speak to Cai about it. I couldn't bear for him to lash out at me or give me the silent treatment as he'd done in China over the summer. I looked at my mom and uncle leaning back in their chairs, sipping tea and reaching for another morsel of *siu mai*, or pork dumpling. I should be able to enjoy myself, too, and not let Yoshimoto get to me.

My mom and Budgie joked about Yoshimoto on our little jaunts around Hong Kong for the rest of the week. We didn't see the professor again except for a quick farewell in the guesthouse lobby the day he flew back to Kyoto. Japanese Father screeched a high-pitched good-bye as he and Cai headed off to the train station.

Chapter 20
AT HOME IN HONG KONG

Shortly after my mom and Budgie flew back to Chicago—and Yoshimoto to Japan—Cai returned to our dorm room one afternoon and announced that Dr. Tsang had offered him a yearlong, postdoctoral fellowship.

I couldn't believe our luck.

Cai would be able to renew his student visa and stay in Hong Kong a year longer than we'd originally thought possible. It seemed like Cai changed his mind every month as to where he wanted to move when he finished his PhD—mostly alternating between Wuhan and Beijing—which meant that we still hadn't decided where we'd settle after graduation. For his postdoc, he'd only be required to go to his campus office half a day, five days a week. At that point there could be no better news than this chance to stay on in Hong Kong for another year.

The next day I delved into my own job search. But as I soon learned, it wasn't easy to find an employer who would sponsor my work visa. With Britain's handover of Hong Kong to China just a year away, many companies had stopped hiring entry-level expats. I found a classified ad for an English editor at a new university in Kowloon, so I applied and was granted an interview and editing test.

I'd never thought about going into publishing, but this job would provide me with both a familiar environment and a challenge to learn a new skill set. A couple weeks after I interviewed, a human resources representative phoned and offered me the position.

No longer students, we rented an apartment on the twenty-fifth floor of a new high-rise development named Sunshine City. In an area called Ma On Shan, the apartment was one of many that rose from reclaimed land in front of a green mountain range across the Tolo Harbour from the Chinese University. Besides the private residential apartments, Ma On Shan was home to a few vertical shopping malls and clusters of government housing blocks with fresh produce and meat markets. I never thought 420 square feet would feel so luxurious, with its two bedrooms, living room, a galley kitchen, and minute bathroom. I looked forward to living off campus, just the two of us, in a place of our own.

Almost as soon as we moved into our apartment, we settled into a comfortable routine. I left home just after dawn to travel ninety minutes to my new office in Kowloon. On most days I found a seat on the top level of a double-decker bus that slowly traveled through the New Territories, passing a monkey forest near the Lion Rock Tunnel.

Once we emerged on the other side of the tunnel, people started disembarking from the bus at various points in Kowloon. We drove by schools and churches, stately colonial mansions, and Sikh-guarded love motels that rented rooms by the hour. Once I made it to my stop, I still had a twenty-minute walk through the narrow streets where Filipina housekeepers waited for grocery stores to open their doors.

Cai left for work after I arrived at my office. His quick bus ride across Tolo Harbour and short walk to his department took just a fraction of the time of my commute. But I didn't complain; I relished my mornings and saw them as a time to enjoy Hong Kong on my own. Since Cai only worked half days, he would stop at the produce market in the basement of our building to buy ingredients for dinner each day. He timed it so that by the time I returned from work, he had dinner on the table, the dishes still hot.

Toward the end of the summer, a couple weeks after we'd settled into our new apartment, Cai put down his chopsticks midway during dinner. "I have some bad news," he said nonchalantly.

"What's wrong?"

"My student visa and passport expire next month. They were only good until the end of my PhD studies, but now that I'm staying for another year, I need to renew both."

I shrugged. "What's so bad about that?" During my graduate student years, I'd renewed my one-year student visa by spending a day at the immigration tower in Wan Chai, leaving just before closing time with a new stamp in my passport for another year. And six months before my passport expired, I headed to the American Consulate to apply for a new one.

"I have to return to China," Cai said.

"You do? Can't you get a new visa and passport here?"

"No. I have to go back."

"For how long?"

"Three or four months," he replied, again matter-of-factly.

"Three or four *months*?" Had he switched the English word "week" for "month" by mistake?

"*Máfan.*" But when he playfully used the Cantonese word for trouble and chuckled, I knew he hadn't misspoken.

"And you have to stay in China *that whole time*?"

"I'll go at the end of this month to apply for the visa, then I can come back here for your birthday next month and stay for a week. But when I return to China to apply for the new passport, I'll have to remain there until it's ready. I'll stay with my parents and spend a little time in Wuhan to visit friends at the Conservatory. I should be back by Christmas."

I didn't celebrate Christmas, so that wasn't an issue for me. But I wished he didn't have to leave. We were finally living like a normal married couple. I wasn't ready for a four-month separation. Luckily I earned enough to pay our rent and utilities. We also had Yoshimoto's money to fall back on if need be, although I felt squeamish when I thought about that. I never mustered the courage to ask Cai to refuse the money. Now I quickly wracked my brain for a solution to our more pressing issue: when I'd next see Cai.

"I can take a week in November and visit you for your birthday," I said.

"That'd be great." Cai reached his hands across the small table and took my hands in his. "Thanks for understanding. Remember, this is *China*."

When Cai left Hong Kong to apply for his visa, I didn't feel overly sad. He'd be back in a week and we'd go out for my twenty-sixth birthday. Those seven days passed quickly. Upon his return, we dined at an elegant Thai restaurant in the Sha Tin mall on the night of my birthday. We shared a small candlelit table and enjoyed minced chicken with basil, beef curry, and a cellophane noodle salad. Cai served me extra helpings of these dishes when he saw I'd eaten most of the food on my plate.

After dinner he led me to Chow Sang Sang—a branch of the same gold store where we bought my wedding ring—so I could pick out a gift. I walked out of the store wearing the yellow gold chain-link bracelet I'd chosen, but my happiness at that moment couldn't blot out Cai's imminent departure the following day. He would be flying back to Wuhan for almost four months. I tried to stay positive and think ahead to when I'd visit him for a week in mid-November.

To make our time apart pass quickly, I met Janice for Indian food one Saturday before she and her Argentine boyfriend left for a week in Cambodia. The next Saturday I sailed by ferry to a barbecue at my British coworker Zara's flat on Lamma Island, a two-hour journey south from my apartment up near the China border.

A couple days after Zara's party, I felt a stinging sensation when I went to the bathroom. I thought nothing of it and figured it would go away on its own.

Within twenty-four hours, I developed an itchy discharge. I almost never sat on toilet seats other than at home, fearful of catching an infection. Perhaps I'd forgotten my golden rule, made contact with Zara's toilet seat, and picked up something from one of her many guests. Or perhaps I'd come down with a yeast infection or urinary tract infection. Even though it had never happened to me before, these things were bound to occur in the heat and humidity of the subtropics.

By Thursday, however, nausea had overwhelmed my appetite and the itchiness intensified. My hopes of it going away on its own had vanished. I thought about over-the-counter creams or pills I could take, but I had no idea what could help. I hadn't seen a doctor since I had arrived in Hong Kong two years earlier. It was now time to find one.

Zara and I went out for teatime every day at work to break up the long days of copyediting English language textbooks. The topics covered a wide range of subjects, including business law, Hong Kong history, environmental science, and nursing. That afternoon, after we ordered red bean ice drinks and found a table in a café, I asked her for a recommendation.

"My doctor is brilliant, but she's out on Lamma."

"That's too far."

Zara sat in silence for a moment. "I could ask a friend who lives near you. She must have a good doctor."

"Could you?" I already felt the itching subside, if for just a moment.

Back in the office, Zara gave me the name of Sally Levy, an internist who practiced in Tsim Sha Tsui, on the tip of the Kowloon Peninsula. I made the next available appointment for two days later.

By the time my appointment came around, I could barely stand without feeling like the itchiness would get worse. Sitting down only provided a temporary respite. And trying to get any work done was proving to be futile. As I sat at my desk, all I could concentrate on was relieving the itching when I thought no one was looking. Everything would be all right as soon as I received some medication.

Dr. Levy appeared to be around fifty years old, her tight salt-and-pepper curls hovering sophisticatedly above her shoulders.

"What can I help you with today?" she asked in a posh British accent.

"I've had this itchy discharge for almost a week. A couple of days ago I started to feel nauseated. It's hard for me to even think about food."

"Let's have a look." She gestured for me to lie back on the examining table.

"Is everything okay?" I asked while she probed me with her gloved fingers.

"Probably just a mild infection, but I'm going to take a culture anyway, which will feel like a Pap test. Before you leave, my nurse will bring in some topical cream to relieve the itching." She took a couple of swabs and then patted my knee. "I'll call you in a few days with the results."

After a day, the itchiness lessened, but the nausea and discharge continued. To feel more comfortable, I went into the bathroom every hour to wipe. While at work several days later, I received a call from Dr. Levy's office.

"The doctor wants you to make another appointment at your earliest convenience," the receptionist said.

"Is everything okay?" I didn't expect to return to her office and figured she could prescribe a medication or tell me to go to Watsons to buy it over the counter.

"It's nothing serious. The doctor just wants to see you."

"Can you tell me what's wrong?"

"I'm sorry. I can't say." She paused. "When can you come in?"

I made another morning appointment for Saturday, three days later. On my way home from work, I sat in my usual seat at the front of the double-decker bus's top level. The bus wound through the narrow streets of northern Kowloon, almost hitting the sides of crumbling pawnshops and grannies ambling across the streets. As we left the densest parts of Kowloon, I suddenly realized why I'd developed these unusual symptoms all at once.

I must be pregnant.

The bus crept toward Lion Rock Tunnel while I leaned back against the worn vinyl bench seat, enjoying the serenity of the mountains ahead and the sun setting next to them. By the time we had entered the calm New Territories, I felt certain. The nausea and recent loss of appetite qualified as symptoms, but what about the itchy discharge? Maybe that was a pregnancy symptom I hadn't learned of through books or movies. Wanting to share the news with Cai, I also knew it was too soon to make the phone call. I'd tell him after I met with Dr. Levy that Saturday.

When the day of my appointment finally arrived, I still felt nauseated and without appetite, but I forced down a bowl of cereal. If I were really pregnant, the baby would need the nutrition. I rode into Tsim Sha Tsui well before my ten o'clock appointment.

Flipping through Chinese gossip magazines at the doctor's office, I glanced up a couple of times after two women returned from the examining rooms, announcing with joy to their companions that they were pregnant. I couldn't wait to get my good news, too.

A nurse finally called my name and led me to the same room where I'd met Dr. Levy the previous Saturday. She pointed to a padded chair as she made to leave. "There's no need to undress."

Moments later, I heard two knocks and Dr. Levy strolled in. She leaned against her desk, not bothering to sit.

"Have you had a lot of sexual partners recently?"

What? Unable to open my mouth, I sat there in silence, my vision suddenly blurry.

"Susan?" She spoke like a strict schoolmarm.

"No."

"Are you sure?"

"Yes. I'm sure." I gripped the sides of the chair, trying to stop my hands from shaking. Something was very wrong if she asked about sexual partners. My mind shut down as I answered Dr. Levy's question like a robot, straightforward and without emotion. "I've been married for a year and a half, and there hasn't been anyone but my husband during that time."

"Well…" She exhaled and put her hand on my shoulder, her eyes turning tender. "Then you're going to have a long talk with your husband. You have trichomoniasis, a sexually transmitted disease common with women who've had many partners."

Too stunned to speak, I sat there, my mouth as open as a panting dog's.

"Your last name is Cai. Is your husband Chinese?"

"Yes, from China." I could barely hear myself speak.

"In Chinese culture, men who are unfaithful often still love their wives. It's not mutually exclusive."

I gazed at her like a lost puppy. Since she worked in Hong Kong, she had probably seen quite a few patients whose husbands had strayed. And I thought back to all those mainland students in grad school who cheated on their spouses. Cai was surely above that, especially after his troubled marriage to Wei Ling. Wouldn't he appreciate a trusting, faithful relationship after going through his divorce?

He couldn't have cheated.

"You need to talk to him. It doesn't mean he doesn't love you."

"But he wouldn't do this. I know him." It was true. I could almost hear our conversation in the dorms two years earlier when he revealed that he knew about my roommate Na Wei and her adulterous relationship. He had seemed too embarrassed to talk about it. No, I reasoned, Cai couldn't have cheated. "Is there any other way I could have gotten it? Like from a toilet seat?"

"I guess that's always possible, but it's usually transmitted sexually. I'm going to give you a prescription that will cause you to feel even more nauseated than you've been. Your husband has to take it, too. I think you should have an HIV test because with diseases like trich, others such as HIV sometime accompany it. I'd recommend your husband get an HIV test, too."

"He's in China now." Tears welled in my eyes. "I won't see him until mid-November." That was still a few weeks away.

She nodded gingerly. "I'll give you a bottle of pills for him. He must finish the whole course. After you complete yours, you need to be retested. Sometimes people need two courses of medication before the parasite is gone. Do you want that HIV test now?"

"Yes," I whispered. This was all too much for me to digest. I just wanted to call Cai so that I could hear him tell me he'd never cheated. Hadn't Dr. Levy claimed it could be contracted in other ways than through sex? I'd know for sure as soon as I heard his voice on the phone. But how to contact him? I didn't even know where he was in China.

"I'll call you on Thursday with the HIV test results," Dr. Levy said before she left the room. "One more thing. If you want to have a baby, you should try soon. I'm afraid if you wait, your uterus will become scarred from this parasite and you'll have a hard time conceiving. Some women become infertile from trich."

I don't remember leaving the building or how I found my way to Nathan Road. It seemed like one minute Dr. Levy was telling me that Cai had cheated and the next minute I was wandering like a zombie, aimlessly roaming Nathan Road, every step a chore. Bus exhaust blew into my face, but I didn't turn the other way. People passed me, chatting animatedly in Cantonese, but nothing sounded familiar. No matter how much I tried to clear my mind, one thought remained: when I really considered it, I wasn't so confident that Cai hadn't cheated. It was a serious kick to the stomach.

For the first time, I felt alone in Hong Kong. It was as if six million people had finally let me in on an inside joke. Was this what people meant by cultural differences? I could handle things like eating sea slugs or using squatter toilets. But a cheating husband was a cultural difference I hadn't bargained on.

Listlessly boarding a double-decker bus to Sunshine City, I hoisted myself up the spiral stairs, collapsed onto the coveted first-row seat, and stared out the window, oblivious to the crowds swarming Nathan Road or to the traffic jam on Waterloo Road. It seemed like ages ago when I'd taken this same bus ride, believing I was pregnant and filled with hope for the future. Even when we reached the calm luxury of Kowloon Tong, I didn't gawk at the love motels or the turbaned Sikh guards out front. None of that held any interest now. All I wanted was to burrow under my comforter.

I slept all afternoon and didn't bother with lunch. When I woke up later on, I thought it must be the next morning. My watch read four thirty. But when I peered out the window, the sun was too high over the horizon for it to be early morning. It was still Saturday afternoon and I still had trich. I needed to call Cai.

He hadn't given me his itinerary in China, and we had only spoken on the phone once since he left Hong Kong, when he went to a post office where he could use a long-distance calling card.

I flipped through my address book until I came to Mama and Baba's number. Theirs was the only phone number I had for Cai in China. After I dialed our long-distance code, I stumbled on China's country code and had to start over. But this time I couldn't even get the long-distance code right. I was in a nightmarish dream where I was trying to dial a number, but couldn't punch in the correct buttons. Finally on my third try, I completed the number. I heard a slow, low-pitched dial tone. On the fourth ring, Cai's father answered.

"*Baba. Nǐ hǎo. Wǒ shi Susan.*"

"*Su Shan, nǐ hǎo, nǐ hǎo.*" I could hear the warmth in Baba's voice even through the static that mingled with our words.

"*Cai Jun zài ma?*" I tried to steady my voice, afraid I'd break into tears.

"*Bùzài. Zuótiān wǎnshàng tā dào Wǔhàn qū.*"

My heart skipped a beat when Baba revealed I'd missed Cai by a day. He'd left for Wuhan the previous night. I asked Baba for the main number at the Wuhan Conservatory. Although Cai's apartment at the Conservatory didn't have a phone, the main switchboard operator must be able to relay a message to him.

"*Tāmen kěnéng guānmén. Xīngqī yī zài kāi.*" He warned that the operator had probably left for the day and wouldn't be back until Monday morning.

"*Xièxiè, Baba.*" Thank you.

In a way I was relieved that I would have to wait two more days to speak with Cai. I needed time to figure out what I would do about my marriage. But one question gnawed at me more than others: Where in the world had I contracted this STD? In the background I suddenly heard a phone ring. Could it be Cai? I willed myself to answer it.

My dad's voice was on the other end. In the chaos of the day, I'd forgotten all about my parents' weekly Saturday evening phone call, which was Saturday morning their time, a cheap time to call overseas. As with Janice, I always relayed positive news to them: Cai's postdoctoral research, my new job, the friends I'd made at work, where I went on the weekends now that Cai was in China. But now my mind froze.

"What's new?" my dad asked.

Should I start divulging this side of my marriage now? I could tell my dad about the STD and admit I'd married the wrong person. Or I could tell my dad about the STD and try to convince him that Cai was probably innocent and that I just needed to get his story and wouldn't be able to do so until Monday, so please don't jump to any conclusions. Or I could just do what I'd always done and say everything was fine.

And in those two seconds, I knew if I told my parents, they wouldn't doubt how I'd contracted the STD. They wouldn't doubt it because I didn't doubt it. Yet if there was even a one percent chance I could have picked it up from a toilet seat, then I owed it to Cai— and to my marriage—to first find out the truth from him. If it were the other way around, I'd certainly want Cai to talk to me before impetuously telling his parents.

Yet part of me desperately wanted to confide in someone. Was Dr. Levy correct? Was infidelity par for the course in Chinese marriages? Or was it just Cai? Until now I thought the strains we'd had in our marriage stemmed from cultural differences. But now I was beginning to consider whether the problems might be due to character, not to culture. What if he didn't love me the way I loved him?

If I told my parents about the STD, they would convince me to leave Cai—and Hong Kong. The last thing I wanted was to suddenly run back to Chicago, advertising my failed marriage and my inability to live abroad. I didn't know what I'd do in Chicago, and living at home after having been married for almost two years seemed like a huge defeat. Besides, I couldn't leave Hong Kong. It was home.

Those two seconds felt like twenty minutes.

"Not much is new," I finally replied, covering my eyes with one hand. "How about you?"

Chapter 21

RED ALERT!

On Monday morning I woke with a lump in my throat, wishing I could turn back the clock to a time before Dr. Levy had given her fateful diagnosis. Today was the day I had to confront Cai. I was usually the first person at work, which for most started at 8:30 a.m. I counted on the Conservatory's operator starting work at eight and felt relieved when she answered on the second ring. It didn't take long for me to explain in Mandarin that I was looking for Cai Jun. She asked if I was his foreign wife.

"Can you please give him a message to call me at home tonight after eight?" Tears pooled in my eyes just thinking about what I'd have to ask Cai that evening.

Later that morning, I tried to concentrate on a manuscript I was editing about new Hong Kong tax laws, but found myself turning the pages without remembering what I had just read. My phone rang, breaking my trance. Without looking at the long number on caller ID, I reached to pick up the receiver.

It was Cai.

I tried to hold my voice steady. Zara and other English speakers surrounding my workspace would understand everything I said in English. And within hearing distance were countless Cantonese coworkers, some of whom also understood Mandarin. There was no way I could speak to Cai about this at work in either language. "I can't talk now, but can you call me tonight at eight?"

"Sure. Actually, can you call me? I'll be at my friend Mr. Chen's. I'll give you his number."

I wrote the phone number on a piece of paper from my recycling pile. After I read it back to Cai and he confirmed it, I folded the paper and placed it in my back pocket.

"I love you." Cai sounded as though he missed me.

"I love you, too," I mumbled. "Sorry, but I have to get back to work." I was afraid I would cry if I didn't hang up right then.

At home that evening, my watch seemed to be stuck between 7:00 p.m. and 7:15 p.m. Nothing to pass the time seemed appealing. I didn't want to eat, read, watch TV, or call a friend. Even flipping through Hong Kong gossip magazines seemed like a chore.

If I had to put money on his response, I still wouldn't know which one to choose. When I quickly looked up trichomoniasis on the Internet at work, I learned it was most often contracted through sexual contact, but some cases involved transmittal through damp towels, bathing suits, or toilet seats. The incubation period was eight to twenty days, which fit Cai's travel timeline. I felt more confused than ever and didn't want to throw away my marriage over a false accusation.

Then something else came to mind. When we traveled to China, Cai was always quick to criticize me for feeling isolated or not adjusting to the cold. My problems were always mine, never his. What if he blamed me for the infection and accused *me* of sleeping around? As much as I wished we could avoid discussing it altogether, I knew I would get sick again if he didn't take the medication.

My watch read 7:50 p.m. I opened the paper with the number Cai gave me and took a few deep breaths. *Relax.* I'd waited this long; I could certainly hang on for another ten minutes.

7:56 p.m. My pulse quickened. I could start dialing in a couple of minutes and maybe stretch out all those numbers to last a couple more minutes. Or maybe he had not arrived at his friend Mr. Chen's place yet.

7:57 p.m. Perhaps the clock in Chen's apartment ran a few

minutes fast. Or perhaps I could act like it was eight and just call a few minutes early.

7:58 p.m. My throat throbbed and I felt like I was going to vomit. To calm myself down, I went over my game plan again. No matter what Cai's reaction was, I would try to work things out. I would explain that I recognized this as a cultural difference, but we had to be faithful from this point on or else our marriage would fail. He would probably view it as a lesson to learn from, not to be repeated.

I lifted my hand, which felt as heavy as an old wok, and started punching Cai's friend's number. I heard static on the other end of the line, followed by a leisurely low-pitched ring tone. Cai answered on the second ring. I could hear the delight in his voice. He recounted his visit with Mama and Baba and described the many lunches and dinners he'd planned with old friends at the Conservatory.

"Cai," I interrupted him. "I need to ask you something." My voice broke. Determined to go on, I cleared my throat and tried to keep a serious tone, not an accusatory one.

"I need to ask you something," I repeated. "I'm sick and have a *xìngbìng*, a sexually transmitted disease. I have to know. Do you have a girlfriend on the side or something?"

"What? Absolutely not! *No.*" Then, all of a sudden, he started crying.

I'd predicted denial, but crying was a surprise. My first thought was that only someone guilty would cry. If he were innocent, I'd imagine he would be sympathetic and soothing to me, not upset. Why then was he denying he had a girlfriend? But then again, he had never cried before, and it caught me off guard. Perhaps he hadn't had an affair on the side, and perhaps my accusation had just upset him. My head spun.

"I would never do that. *Never*," he repeated.

"*Really?*" My voice cracked again. He seemed adamant that he was telling the truth. But if he hadn't cheated, how else could I have gotten it? And what about the incubation period that corresponded to his different trips to China last month? I felt more confused than before I had phoned him.

He sighed sadly and sympathetically. "Of course. *I love you.*"

And that's when my own resolve cracked. "Shh. It's okay," I consoled him gently, quickly forgetting that this was *my* crisis. I couldn't bear to hear him so upset.

"Susan, I'd never do that to you. You know that, don't you?"

My temples felt heavy, like they were about to cave in. Each heartfelt plea of innocence, along with his sobbing and sniffling, tugged at my heart. I didn't want to answer yes because I was no longer convinced of his faithfulness. I also couldn't say no—that I didn't believe him—because the rest of my head was starting to hurt from this conversation, his crying, and my conflicted feelings. So I turned to another matter.

"I have to take a very strong medicine and you have to take it, too, even though men don't get any symptoms. I'll bring it next month. I have to get tested again and will have to take more medicine if it's still there. My doctor said I also need to get an HIV test, just in case."

He started sobbing again.

"If you don't take the medicine"—I struggled to keep from crying myself—"then I'll keep getting infected again and again, no matter how much medicine I take."

"When will you take the AIDS test?" he asked urgently.

"I already did. I'll get the results Thursday."

"*Thursday?* Call me at this number as soon as you return from work that day. I'll be here at six. I'm going to get tested tomorrow for *xìngbìng.*"

His alarm over the HIV test should have told me something, but I was too scared to ask why he flinched at this mention of HIV/AIDS. Was he simply afraid to catch this scary disease, as he'd been on our wedding night with the hotel-issued towels? Or was he genuinely frightened he might have contracted HIV and unwittingly spread it to me?

I should have phrased my question differently, not asking about a girlfriend, but simply another person. But I had been sure I would be able to discern the truth as soon as I asked Cai. It never dawned on me that I should have worded my question another way.

I relayed what Dr. Levy said about getting pregnant soon if we planned to have a baby. Cai wept again, promising me he'd get tested the following day. I hadn't thought about trying to have a baby in the near future, but now with Dr. Levy's warning, this was something else I'd have to consider.

After we hung up, I kept hearing the way Cai cried, "No," followed by sobs. Despite our thirty-minute conversation, I felt more confused than ever and started to question his role in my infection. Maybe I really did contract it from a toilet seat. But what about the peep shows in New York and his flirtatious telephone chat with that prostitute in Wuhan? On the other hand, I was grateful he didn't blame me and accuse me of cheating. This situation had the potential to get ugly and it hadn't. It could have been so much worse.

When I phoned Cai a few days later with my negative HIV test result, he shrieked into the phone. "That's wonderful. I'm so happy." He sounded like I'd just received a hefty promotion. "I was tested for many *xìngbìng*, and they all turned out negative, too."

Remembering the Pap-like swab test, I wondered how the doctor tested Cai. "Was the test very uncomfortable?"

"Not at all! I just peed in a cup."

Maybe Chinese doctors used different testing methods. Or maybe we weren't tested for the same diseases if he peed into a cup and I didn't. Again, I knew I should have been more forthcoming with my questions, but I could only think about holding my marriage—and my peace of mind—together. This was our first crisis, and he'd said everything I wanted to hear. It didn't seem fair to either of us to give up now when I didn't have conclusive proof. Had Cai been in my shoes, I would have been devastated if he left me when I hadn't done anything wrong. So when Cai said he couldn't wait to see me in two weeks, I replied in all honesty that I felt the same.

The moment I spotted Cai at the Wuhan airport, I ran into his arms. He hugged me as if we hadn't seen each other in years. Nothing on Cai's face showed any sign of guilt or wrongdoing. This joyful, loving man was the Cai I'd fallen for two years earlier. Instead of driving straight to Hidden River, he took me to a midrange hotel for the night. Cai held my hand as he opened our room door, as if we were newlyweds. "I wanted us to have some alone time after everything you've been through."

I felt grateful for a night alone with Cai and, as crazy as it sounded, also felt closer to him than ever. But before I could enjoy my time with him, I needed to hand over his medication. "You have to take one of these every day until the bottle is empty. You'll probably feel like you need to throw up."

Silent, as if I'd given him change for bus fare, he packed the bottle away in his overnight bag. I then pulled out a box of condoms. "We have to use these until you finish the medicine and I test negative."

Cai held me tightly. I figured he'd go back to being the old Cai and would treat me as kindly as he had in my dorm room during our tutoring days.

And it seemed very possible that he would. Unlike my last two trips to Hidden River, this week passed without incident. Cai was just as thoughtful as he had been back when we first met, and refrained from going to those marathon card games at his friends' homes. Without knowing anything about my ordeal, Mama had even lightened up about my eating habits.

On my last full day in China, Cai and I stayed at his Wuhan apartment so we wouldn't need to wake up too early for my morning departure the following day. As we strolled down Liberation Road near the Conservatory, Cai stepped into a small bookstore. Ever since the missed opportunity in Shanghai, I cherished any chance to browse through books in China, even if they weren't in English.

"Come here," he beckoned after several minutes. In his hands, he held a Chinese-English Merck Manual. Cai opened it to a page and thumbed down until he found what he was looking for. He pointed to the English and Chinese entry for chlamydia. "Is this what you had?"

"No." I gently took the book from him and flipped through the bulk of the STD section until I got to trichomoniasis. I placed my finger on the passage for trich. "This is it."

Cai slowly brought the book closer, my finger still in place, and read the Chinese. Then he started laughing. "This isn't a sex disease. It's called 'women's disease' in China." He chuckled. "All women get it."

I had never heard anyone in the United States speak of a women's disease apart from urinary tract infections. But even those weren't limited to just women. Perhaps I really had caught it from towels or a toilet seat. If Cai seemed so adamant, I figured he knew something I didn't. I was tested several times over the next two decades and the results were always negative.

If your husband is sweet, be you sweet;
If sorrowful, be you sorrowful.

—Ban Zhao
Instruction for Chinese Women and Girls

Chapter 22

A CHINESE CONCEPTION

Once Cai had returned to Hong Kong—his student visa and passport updated and good for another year—conceiving became my main focus. Remembering Dr. Levy's words after I contracted the STD, I didn't want to lose my opportunity to become pregnant before my uterus became scarred and infertile.

During a lunch break at work, my colleague Zara and I strolled over to a market at a neighboring public housing estate. Sheltered by bamboo poles hung with drying laundry was an outdoor hardware stall that sold red posters decorated with four Chinese characters that people hung around their door frames to bring in good fortune.

"Do you have one for becoming pregnant?" I asked the female shopkeeper in rudimentary Cantonese.

"Yes, over here." She reached up and pulled down a foot-long narrow poster. The vertical characters read 早生贵子. Give birth to a precious son soon. "*Oh m'okay ah?*"

"Okay. *M'goi sai.*" I thanked her and paid the $1.50 while she rolled the banner and secured it with a rubber band. Although I thought the preference for sons silly and outdated, I figured the banner could apply to girls since the 子 character was also found in the word for child.

That evening while Cai cooked dinner, I taped the poster on the left of the inside front door, hoping it would make a difference. We'd only been trying for three months, but even with our upcoming week of spring vacation in San Francisco, I was still determined to get pregnant.

After we ate and I washed the dishes, Cai lounged on the sofa and read a trashy Hong Kong newspaper, one full of blood-splashed color photos of people in car accidents or domestic fights that involved knives and axes. Photos of women in string bikinis covered the back page.

"This article says you can take medicine to have a baby. Some people even get twins." Cai spoke as if he'd just read about the latest digital camera to hit the market and was contemplating buying it. "You should ask your doctor for some."

Normally I would have rejected advice in a tabloid, but by now I was truly anxious that something was wrong with me. Why hadn't our earlier attempts succeeded? Had the STD scarred my uterus so that I wouldn't be able to have children, just as Dr. Levy had warned?

"*I* don't have a problem," Cai reminded me. After all, he had Ting-Ting from his first marriage. When we had first started trying to get pregnant, Cai had told me that it took Wei Ling and him a few years before they conceived Ting-Ting. There was something abnormal about Wei Ling's uterus, he explained. It never occurred to me that Cai might be the one with the problem. Since we weren't having success, something *must* be wrong with me.

The following Saturday, I was back in Dr. Levy's office to ask her about fertility medication. Cai stayed home, enjoying a leisurely morning on his one day off.

"Cai told me he didn't cheat," I said to Dr. Levy as soon as she entered the examining room and closed the door. "I must have gotten it from something else." While I waited for her to reply, I realized it'd been six months since I was diagnosed with the infection. Maybe Dr. Levy had forgotten. But then she looked at me with a pained expression. She remembered.

"Anyway," I continued, trying to shake off her discouraged look, "we've been trying to conceive for several months but nothing's happened. Cai thinks I should take fertility pills."

Glancing at the first page of my chart, Dr. Levy folded her hands together on her desk. "Susan, you're only twenty-six. You're still very young."

I stared at the floor.

"How old is your husband?"

"Thirty-five."

"It could be him."

"But he has a child from his first marriage."

"Things can change over the years. You should try for a full year, and if you still haven't conceived, come back and we'll run some tests. It's too early to worry now." She peered into my eyes as if to say, "All right?"

"Sure."

"You should start taking prenatal vitamins and folic acid, which you can buy over the counter. I'll give you a basal temperature thermometer so you can chart your ovulation. Also, there's no medical evidence behind this, but several of my patients have taken a couple teaspoons of Heinz apple cider vinegar in a cup of warm water every day and have become pregnant."

"*Vinegar?*"

"Yes. Make sure it's in a glass jar. A plastic one won't do. And it needs to be red cider, not white. Don't worry, Susan. You're too young to worry."

I returned home to find Cai reading another Hong Kong newspaper on the couch. He didn't look up. "Did you get the medicine?"

"No. She said we should try for a year. I have a special thermometer to find out when it's a good time. She also suggested drinking apple cider vinegar."

Cai just nodded and continued reading the paper. Since I felt like it would be rash to talk with friends and coworkers about trying to get pregnant, I figured he similarly didn't want to get his hopes up before we had a positive pregnancy test. At twenty-six, I was ready to have a baby.

I was convinced Cai would become more patient and less moody if we had a little boy or girl in our lives. He must still feel incredibly heartbroken over his separation from Ting-Ting. Another child couldn't replace her, but I figured he'd feel more settled—and behave more nicely—with a baby who would act as a steadying presence in our lives.

Chapter 23

SPRING IN SAN FRANCISCO

The cover ad on the free real-estate magazine showed rows of new single-family houses, San Francisco style, built so close to one another that they appeared to be townhouses. Painted in light earth tones, the green-, brown-, peach-, and beige-colored homes came in two- and three-story models. *The Lius, Chens, Zhous, and Zhangs have already moved in*, the caption read. *You could be next.*

Cai picked up the magazine at a rice and noodle shop on Grant Avenue. It was our first full day of a weeklong vacation in San Francisco. He had received a green card after we married and needed to touch down in the United States once a year to keep it. The previous summer we had spent a quick week together in Chicago visiting my family.

"These are so nice." He pointed to the cover sketch. "We should look at them in case we want to move here."

"Really?" Was he serious?

"It's much better than in New York or Chicago. We'll just see these houses. No pressure."

Although this was the first time we'd discussed moving to San Francisco, I decided not to discourage Cai as I had when he'd talked about buying a gas station in New York. Given the choice between moving to China and San Francisco, I knew there was only one answer for me. I'd visited San Francisco twice with my parents in my teens and early twenties and was familiar with the touristy areas.

This new development of 235 homes was in a neighborhood

called Bayview. I'd never heard of it, but the name sounded nice enough. And the price, at $255,000 for a three-bedroom house, seemed like a bargain even in 1997. With our small savings and the $30,000 Cai had earned through a high-interest savings account with the Bank of China, we could make a sizable down payment. But $255,000 was the most we could afford. Cai wanted to keep Yoshimoto's money in reserves to pay bills if we couldn't secure jobs in San Francisco right away.

After a twenty-minute bus ride, Cai and I found ourselves surrounded by modest San Francisco bungalows, their aluminum siding tattered after years of wear, and large one-story factories producing pastries and house paints. At the end of the street we arrived at an open landmass, a third of it covered with cranes and bulldozers. Cai and I walked toward the completed homes and found the model house. We entered the garage, empty but for an older Filipino man seated at a desk in back.

"Good morning." The man stood up to greet us. "I'm Bob. Let me know if I can help you." He sat back down and let us look over the plan of the development.

"Can we see the model?" I asked.

"Sure." He pointed to a door. "You can take the stairs over there."

Cai and I climbed up to the living room on the first floor. The house was long and narrow, about 1,600 square feet, and almost four times the size of our Sunshine City apartment. We entered the eat-in kitchen with tiled counters and peeked into the adjoining den overlooking the small backyard. Once upstairs, we reached an open hallway with built-in linen cabinets and a guest bathroom. At one end of the hall were the master bedroom and bath—and walk-in closet—and at the other end were two guest bedrooms. Cai and I beamed at each other in excitement.

I didn't expect to fall in love with a house in San Francisco. I figured they'd all be old, small, and shabby—at least the ones in our price range. Was this one too good to be true?

Cai chuckled. "It's so light and big. And new. Shall we buy it?"

As I nodded my head yes, I suddenly realized I wanted nothing more than this house—and to get pregnant. I couldn't imagine finding a better deal on a house in San Francisco. And if Cai were to find a job related to Chinese music in the States, it would be in San Francisco. He already knew some former classmates in his field who lived there. We didn't have that luxury in other U.S. cities. If these new houses were really going quickly, I couldn't see the sense in waiting any longer. And buying a house in San Francisco would mean we wouldn't be returning to China.

"We're only here for five more days," I told Bob back in the basement. "We live in Hong Kong and are going back on Saturday. If we're interested, how do we go about reserving a house?"

Bob explained we'd need a $10,000 deposit and should first get preapproval for a mortgage. He suggested that we go to a bank in Chinatown that had financed many people who had already bought into the development.

"Maybe we should call your parents," Cai said on our way to the bus stop. "Would we be able to borrow the deposit from them?"

"Probably." My parents would have no problem sending us the money, but I knew they would think our decision shockingly impulsive. After all, we had no jobs or guaranteed income in San Francisco. I normally would have shied away from such a rash move, but these were special circumstances. We needed to act quickly before Cai changed his mind.

In Chinatown we first stopped at the bank to apply for preapproval. On our way out, we found a phone booth and called Chicago to ask for the $10,000 loan. "Cai and I don't have access to our accounts here but will pay it back as soon as we return to Hong Kong," I reassured my parents, both of whom were on the line. "Can you send it by Friday?"

"You don't have jobs there," my dad said, as I knew he would.

"I know, but Cai has some friends here and they're in the music field. If he can find a job anywhere in the United States, it's in San Francisco. And I'll search for a job on the Internet before we leave Hong Kong."

"When will the house be finished?" my mom asked.

"They say December, but we'll move at the end of February, just after my work contract ends."

My mom agreed to wire the money to the developer. "We're glad you're moving back home," she said. "I could never imagine you living in China with little babies crawling around on those cold, dirty floors." Cai stood next to me, but I didn't relay the last part of that message.

With our preapproval mortgage papers from Bank of America, we signed papers with Bob on Friday and learned that my parents' wire transfer had gone through. That was when it finally hit me.

We'd be leaving Hong Kong in nine months. I hated to go, but I was looking forward to a stable life in San Francisco, free from worries about student visas, expired passports, or time apart from my husband. His green card granted him the right to live and work in the United States. I would be closer to my family, yet still in an area with a large Chinese population. But most importantly, I was saved from a life in China. I was convinced that we were moving forward and things were going to be great.

Chapter 24
A SURPRISE GUEST

The Handover was the event of the summer of 1997. After ruling Hong Kong for a hundred and fifty years, Britain relinquished this last major colony and returned it to China. Suddenly many of the people I knew from Washington, DC, descended upon Hong Kong for the historic occasion. My brother Jonathan flew in for the week and he, Cai, and I roamed the city, hitting parties in the expat community.

At the largest of these parties, I met up with Janice for the first time in months. Our interaction felt a bit forced, but we promised to make plans to see each other soon. Cai and I also took Jonathan to dinners with our mainland friends that week. On June 30, the night of the Handover, the three of us walked side by side along the harbor front in Tsim Sha Tsui, the rain and fog blurring the lit skyline. Maybe due to the weather or perhaps because of Hong Kong's uncertain future, the streets were eerily empty. Without much deliberation, we returned to Sunshine City to watch the midnight ceremony on TV. And just like that, Hong Kong belonged to China. But life in the former colony seemed to carry on as usual, especially when it came to my marriage.

By September I'd still failed to conceive. We'd been trying diligently for nine months and were quickly approaching the one-year mark Dr. Levy had mentioned when I went to see her about fertility medicines the previous winter.

"It's probably because of the stress about the move and finding a job in San Francisco," I mused to Cai one Saturday. "Maybe we should stop trying until after we have jobs and health insurance."

"That's fine." Cai spoke calmly and without the critical jibes about my fertility that he'd lobbed when we'd discussed it before. It was not only a pleasantly unexpected reaction, but it also felt like a heavy weight had been lifted. With all the work we had ahead of us for our move to San Francisco, I was relieved that Cai was okay with putting a temporary hold on trying to conceive. After all, it seemed like the logical thing to do. How would I find a job if I was halfway into a pregnancy?

Out of habit, I continued to use my basal thermometer every morning before I got out of bed, charting my temperature in a little blue booklet included in the thermometer box. On the day in October when the chart showed I'd be most fertile, I suggested we try one more time before putting everything on hold. The next day I woke up and went to work without thinking about our last attempt; I assumed it would fail just like the others.

A month later when I didn't get my period, I also noticed that my clothes stretched tighter over my abdomen even though I had recently experienced a loss of appetite. My chances were slim, but I bought one more home pregnancy test and told Cai about it.

"Do you really think you're pregnant?" he asked, his eyes hopeful.

"I doubt it, but I'll try anyway. It's probably just an irregular period that's causing bloating. My doctor said to take it first thing in the morning, after I've gone hours without peeing, so I'll use it as soon as I wake up tomorrow."

At five the next morning, I couldn't hold it in any longer and crept to the bathroom, the whirring of our bedroom air conditioner buzzing in the stillness of the dawn. I was reaching to retrieve the test from the sink vanity when I heard a knock on the door.

"Are you taking it now?" Cai said from the living room.

"Mmm-hmm." I tore open the plastic wrap. "I'll be out soon."

After I finished, I placed the stick on the sink and washed my hands. When I opened the door, Cai hovered over me, rocking on his heels.

"What does it say?"

"I haven't looked yet. It takes a couple minutes." I turned to reach back into the bathroom and grab it from the sink. Looking down, my heart jumped when I saw a pink plus sign under the clear rectangular window. We were going to have a baby.

Cai gripped my hand. "What does it say?"

My lips pulsed and I fought back tears as I nodded.

"Are you?" Cai whispered.

I nodded again, but before I could answer, Cai screeched and swept me up in his arms, spinning around the small living room while he held me slightly off the ground.

"Thank you," he said. "Thank you so much. *Thank you.*"

Just as I absorbed the fact that I was finally pregnant, my mind raced to what it meant for my predicament with Cai in Hidden River. For one, I would no longer feel so depressed or isolated there. Even if Mama and Baba protested, I would buy a small heater, and if Cai wanted to jaunt off to his friends' homes for marathon card games, I stay warm at Mama and Baba's with the baby, reading and eating what I liked.

And I imagined Mama would no longer concern herself with my eating habits; she would be too busy fussing over the baby. I would appreciate her help with child care when we visited Hidden River, but Cai and I would always keep our baby with us. As I thought about the rosy future, I knew that all my troubles had just been exorcized by a little pink plus.

As much as I wanted to tell everyone I knew, it seemed like a good idea to follow the Jewish custom of not announcing the news to anyone but our parents until I was out of my first trimester. Based on superstition, this tradition also made sense to me from a medical standpoint, as it was common for miscarriages to happen before the end of the first trimester.

"That sounds fine," Cai said.

I hadn't discussed Jewish or American pregnancy and child-rearing practices with Cai before now because I was too focused on just trying to get pregnant. Although not normally superstitious, I worried I might jinx our chances of conceiving if we planned too far ahead. Now I felt grateful that he so readily agreed to wait to share our good news with friends and colleagues.

As I showered and dressed, he cooked breakfast: a large pot of rice congee with red beans accompanied by a platter of sautéed choy sum, which is like a Chinese broccoli.

"You need to eat more now," he said as he took another piece of choy sum in his chopsticks and set it in my rice bowl.

I left for work at seven o'clock, later than usual. It was still too early to phone Mama and Baba, so Cai waited another hour before calling his parents from our apartment. When I returned from work that evening, Cai greeted me at the door, embracing me for what seemed like minutes.

"I'm steaming a fish for dinner. It's good for the health," he said, once he had released his arms.

"What did your parents think of our news?" I knew that they'd be ecstatic but wanted to hear it from Cai.

"My mother cried. She is so happy. Baba, too. They've been waiting for this since they met you in Hidden River those years ago."

Hugging Cai once more, I didn't need to be reminded about that fearful interaction and the conversation with Mama about taking care of our future children in Hidden River. I could almost recall it word for word.

Shuddering at the memory, I reached for our one phone, which rested on a table next to the cheap foam couch our landlord provided.

Cai returned to the kitchen while I called my parents in Chicago. It was still early there, perhaps a little before they would normally wake up, but I didn't want to miss them after they left for work. My mother answered on the second ring.

"Mom?"

"Susan? Is everything all right?" She sounded groggy but not half asleep.

"Yes, yes, everything's fine. Sorry to wake you up, but I wanted to catch you before I'd make you late to work. We have some big news."

"Are you pregnant?" She suddenly sounded wide awake and cheerful.

I laughed. "How did you know?"

"What else could it be? You never call. I was wondering when we would get news like this."

"We've been trying for a while," I said warily. "I'm only five or six weeks, so can you not tell anyone for another two months?"

"Of course." She paused. "That's great timing. We'll be out of school in early June and can come out to help you for the summer. I'm so glad you are moving to the United States."

"We would love for you to help out." I was still getting used to the idea of departing Hong Kong for good, a place I'd never intended to leave so soon. But I knew my mom was right when she said it was best we were moving to the United States. Even though I would have to look for employment in San Francisco while being visibly pregnant, it would be worth the stress.

My parents would be closer and could help out when they weren't teaching. They could even drive to San Francisco for the summer. If we had stayed in Hong Kong, they probably wouldn't have been able to visit more than once a year. The flights were long and exhausting, not to mention expensive. And now that I was pregnant, I felt the need to live closer to my parents, my family.

After my mom and I finished our call, I poked my head into the tiny kitchen and relayed to Cai the news about my parents wanting to stay with us for the summer.

"That's wonderful." He set his ladle on the counter and came out to hug me. "My parents can come help us with the baby after your parents go back to Chicago."

I stood up straight. "Would they want to come to the United States?"

Cai laughed. "Of course. It's their duty as grandparents. They can stay for a year."

"A year?" *A whole year with Mama and Baba?* Somehow I had a difficult time picturing them living with us in San Francisco for a year. I'd never stayed with them for more than six weeks at a time, and never outside Hidden River. Would I go crazy living in the same house with them for a year? I hoped Mama wouldn't continue to harangue me over every little thing I ate. And I couldn't imagine them getting around in a place where they wouldn't be able to read the street signs.

On a practical level, it would be a luxury to have in-house child care. We could never afford to hire a nanny, so our baby would have to go to a day-care facility if Cai's parents couldn't get a U.S. visa. I tried to stay positive about a possible year with my in-laws. Everything would be all right as long as I didn't bend on important issues, like our baby continuing to live with us after Mama and Baba returned to China.

Chapter 25
A GOOD CHINESE WIFE

Cai was turning into the perfect husband. He doted on me at the large Chinese banquets we attended through the Taoist temple where he worked on Sundays, making sure I ate enough and had plenty of nonpork dishes to choose from. I noticed he had stopped watching porn and instead consulted me on movie rental choices. During my weeks of morning sickness, he even suggested I take an expensive taxi ride to and from work. I was touched by that thought but felt fine riding the bus with its scenic route. I knew I would miss my relaxing commute once we left Hong Kong for San Francisco.

But before we moved to California, Cai had to leave Hong Kong for a few months once more. The territory's immigration law forbade mainland students from remaining in Hong Kong to work after they graduated. Dr. Tsang's funding had run out, and he could not afford to keep Cai on for another year. Cai would return to Hidden River while I finished out my work contract.

After a quick phone conversation with Ting-Ting one Saturday, Cai told me that his ex-wife and daughter would be in Hong Kong for a couple days the following month. But Cai wouldn't be there; he would have already returned to China.

"Really? Why are they coming here?"

"Just stopping over after a tour in Thailand."

"Thailand?" In the late 1990s, few mainlanders could travel outside China. Not only was it difficult to obtain visas, but the expenses could amount to a year's salary or more. Everyone I knew from China who had flown abroad did so to study or to visit their children who were students in another country. I'd never heard of mainlanders traveling abroad just to sightsee.

"They're going with a group of teachers from Wei Ling's school."

"Did they want to see you?"

"Wei Ling thought I could see Ting-Ting, but I told her I'd be back in China by then."

"I can take them out to lunch."

He froze. "Really? You'd do that?"

"Of course. She's your daughter." I would have preferred to meet her in Cai's presence, so I could remain in the background. But I was fine meeting them alone. Their visit in January would be my only chance to meet Ting-Ting before we moved.

"What about Wei Ling? You're comfortable meeting her?"

"I've got nothing to worry about, right?"

Cai swatted his hand as if he were brushing away a fly. "Wei Ling was a bad wife, but she'll be kind to you. She's been nice to me since our divorce."

"It should be fine. I can even leave work early if they come during the week. Do you know what day they'll be here?"

"I'm not sure, but I can call Wei Ling back now." Cai embraced me tightly, rocking me slightly in his arms. "You're the best wife."

I closed my eyes briefly, smiling inside. "It's nothing. She's your daughter."

"But you don't have to do this."

"I want to." And I really did. I wanted to meet Ting-Ting. She was my stepdaughter, after all. And I also felt curious about the woman who had left Cai in Wuhan.

Cai called Wei Ling back and they settled on a time and date when I'd get together with her and Ting-Ting. His voice sounded cordial during this discussion, as if he were arranging a meeting at the Taoist temple between a visiting professor and the temple administrator. He often glanced at me and smiled. After ending the call, he turned to me.

"It's all set. They'll be waiting for you at noon three Thursdays from now. Wei Ling said they'll be staying at the old Boundary Street police barracks just above Mong Kok. It's now a guesthouse for mainland travelers."

My mind started racing about where we could go for lunch. One place stood out. "There's a new hotel near the Mong Kok train station. I've had their lunch buffet and it's quite good. It would be nice to take them there."

"Sounds great. They'll be leaving for Zhūhâi late that afternoon. Thank you so much for doing this."

"It's fine. I'm looking forward to it."

"Do you think it would be okay to give Ting-Ting five thousand Hong Kong dollars?"

That was about six hundred U.S. dollars. Living expenses in China had increased since Cai had paid his child support six years earlier, and I figured Wei Ling had spent the 10,000 yuan long ago.

"Of course. And I'll buy her gifts like art supplies and maybe a purse. Something an eight-year-old would like."

Cai hugged me again. "Thank you."

As we embraced in the dusky afternoon, with the waters of Tolo Harbour rippling below, I pictured bonding with Ting-Ting. She'd tell me all about her school, her music and dance lessons, and her favorite books. She'd rattle on about the friends she'd made in Zhūhâi since joining her mother there. I'd ask what she liked best in Thailand and would tell her a little about the trip I took there when I was twenty. She'd be naturally drawn to me.

The next morning, I asked my boss for the afternoon off three Thursdays from then. When I told her the reason, she grinned and said I was a good Chinese wife.

Chapter 26

THE EX-WIFE

The day I was to meet Wei Ling and Ting-Ting, I left work just as my coworkers were heading out for lunch. I rambled through mazelike streets toward the guesthouse where Wei Ling and Ting-Ting were staying. My heart pounded under my two layers of stretchy maternity clothes. While waiting for the light to change on Waterloo Road, I looked at my small baby bump. Would Wei Ling act coldly and selfishly toward me, as she'd treated Cai during their marriage? Would she resent me because I carried her ex-husband's baby?

At the deserted Boundary Street Sports Ground, I found the former Hong Kong Police barracks. The second floor was empty except for an elderly man sitting at a wooden table inspecting a Chinese newspaper. He looked up from his paper when he heard my footsteps.

"Can I help you?" He spoke in fluent English with a distinguished Cantonese accent.

"I'm here to see a woman named Wei Ling."

"Room one-oh-three, third on the left." He pointed toward the hallway in front of us.

"Thank you very much."

The short walk to Room 103 seemed endless. Would Wei Ling even talk to me? Would she begrudge me for marrying her ex-husband? My pulse quickened as I came to an open room with two metal bunk beds. A petite woman sat on the bottom mattress of one bed. I recognized her from Cai's photos. Wei Ling peered up at me with dark almond eyes and smiled warmly. A sudden surge of calmness spread through me. She wasn't mean-spirited or aloof.

"Susan. Come in." Speaking English, Wei Ling sounded kind yet slightly reserved.

I returned her smile and entered the tiny room, squeezing between the two bunk beds, past her knees. On the lower bunk opposite Wei Ling sat a girl with two braided pigtails anchored by red puffballs, her face as round as a moon cake. Ting-Ting's narrow eyes diligently focused on a picture in her coloring book. She looked like the older sister of the girl in the photos Cai had shown me from his first visit with Ting-Ting in Zhūhâi a couple years ago. Wei Ling stood and shook my hand. Turning toward Ting-Ting, she asked her daughter to greet me. Ting-Ting glanced up at me, expressionless, then returned to her coloring.

"Please sit." Wei Ling spoke in English, gesturing to a space next to her. She looked over at my pregnant belly as I sat down. Cai had told Wei Ling we were expecting, but I wasn't sure if Ting-Ting knew. She seemed mature enough to handle news about a new sibling, but I thought it best for Wei Ling to tell her.

"Ting-Ting, say hello to Miss Susan." Wei Ling spoke to her daughter in Mandarin. If I were simply a friend or a visitor, Ting-Ting would call me aunt. But I was her stepmother, and a foreign one at that, so Wei Ling chose the generic *xiǎojiě*, or miss, when she referred to me in front of Ting-Ting.

"*Méi wèntí.*" I assured Wei Ling it wasn't a problem if Ting-Ting didn't warm up to me right away. She barely knew her father, so she couldn't be expected to take to me at once.

Wei Ling clearly preferred to speak in Mandarin because, after my simple remark, she never used English again that day.

"Ting-Ting?" I tried to rouse her from her drawing.

From the corner of her eye, she must have seen me extend a shopping bag toward her because she looked up and begrudgingly smiled before taking it. Ting-Ting reached in and pulled out three wrapped gifts. She tore the red and gold foil paper from the largest item, revealing a Hello Kitty art set: crayons, colored pencils, markers, oil pastels, a small pair of scissors, a lined spiral notebook, a blank notepad, and a pencil sharpener.

She didn't utter a word, but her eyes sparkled with pleasure. Next she opened a thin, long package to find a Little Twin Stars pencil case. When she looked inside the case and found it empty, she tossed it on her bed. Finally, she opened a small, green, shiny vinyl change purse in the shape of Keroppi the frog. Again, she investigated inside but found nothing. Ting-Ting gave her mother the change purse.

"*Ting-Ting?*" Wei Ling spoke in a strict tone of voice.

Ting-Ting looked up at me. "*Xièxiè.*"

"*Bù kèqì.*" You're welcome.

After Ting-Ting packed the art set and pencil case into her backpack, the three of us left the guesthouse and walked down Sai Yee Street. I explained that I was taking them to a buffet at a new hotel near the Mong Kok train station. "*Shénme dōu yǒu.*" I told Wei Ling the hotel buffet had everything. At three and a half months pregnant, I had an appetite that was hearty morning, noon, and night.

We started with the cold appetizer table. The requisite smoked salmon lay in thin slices on a silver tray, tiny capers sprinkled around its periphery. With a pair of small stainless steel tongs, I seized a few slivers of salmon and tried to capture some capers, but only managed a few. I didn't want Wei Ling to see me struggle with a Western serving utensil, so I moved on to the cool sweet-and-sour cucumber salad. I returned to the table with a full plate. Wei Ling hovered over the dessert table, having bypassed the carving stations after she left me at the appetizer table.

As we ate, Wei Ling told me she was tired. "It's hard being a single mom."

"I'm sure, but you're doing a great job." I couldn't imagine what it would be like to be a single mother so far from her family and without a support system, especially as divorce was still a new phenomenon in China. When I decided to meet Wei Ling and Ting-Ting, it had been with the intention of showing Ting-Ting what it would be like to have a stable mother. But now I could see Ting-Ting already had that. Wei Ling appeared to be a tired but hardworking, dedicated mother. She was doing the best she could, and certainly better than I would have done in her situation.

All the time I had been with Cai, I had been trying to be the kind of wife to him that Wei Ling hadn't been. But now that I was getting to know her, I felt confused. Had Cai misrepresented the circumstances of their divorce? Where was the self-centered Wei Ling he'd depicted back in our graduate school days? Or maybe Wei Ling had changed her ways after their divorce. Cai did tell me that Wei Ling claimed she'd never found another guy like him. So perhaps she regretted her past behavior and was making amends.

When I finished paying the waitress, I looked at my watch discreetly. We still had two hours before their ferry departed for Zhūhâi.

"Do you want to go back with us to the guesthouse to get our things?" Wei Ling asked. "Then we can go to the pier if you have time."

"Of course, I would love to." I wasn't ready to say good-bye yet. The afternoon had turned out so unexpectedly well. There was still more I wanted to know about her, and I wished they were staying in Hong Kong longer so we could spend more time together. I felt closer to her than I did to Cai's three sisters in Hubei, whom I'd known for several years.

We made a quick stop at the guesthouse to pick up their luggage and Ting-Ting's backpack. Outside again, the three of us squeezed into the backseat of a red Toyota Crown Comfort taxi. While Ting-Ting worked on her coloring book with the crayons from the Hello Kitty art set, I asked Wei Ling if Ting-Ting knew about her future sibling.

"Yes, she knows." Wei Ling smiled demurely, her eyes warm. As our taxi inched its way down Nathan Road and made a beeline for the shopping mall that housed the ferry pier, Wei Ling reached for her wallet. I motioned for her to put it away and insisted on paying. After protesting a couple more times, she finally relented.

Once we arrived at the gate, Ting-Ting saw their tour group, mostly teachers from their school. She ran up to one of the women, her backpack and puffballed braids swaying back and forth. Wei Ling and I stood with their two pieces of carry-on luggage.

"I think it's almost time for us to board the boat." Wei Ling gently held my wrist. "Thank you so much for lunch and the gifts for Ting-Ting."

"Thank you for meeting me. I had a great time," I said. Then I handed her an envelope with the money Cai wanted to give to Ting-Ting. Without saying a word, Wei Ling gave me a quick hug with her slender arms and gathered her luggage. I accompanied her to the gate to say good-bye.

I hugged Ting-Ting tightly and found myself tearing up a little bit. Just when she seemed to be starting to warm up to me, it was time to part ways. Ting-Ting was a guarded child, and rightfully so. Now I wished I could have spent more time with her. Maybe then I could have gotten through to her more. If only Cai and I could stay in Hong Kong longer.

"Have a good trip home, Ting-Ting. Maybe you can visit us in America some day out," I blurted out.

Ting-Ting looked up at me, beaming. She then faced her mother, her eyes inquisitive.

"That would be nice," Wei Ling said.

Although Cai and I had never discussed Ting-Ting visiting us in San Francisco, it suddenly made perfect sense. I stood at the gate, as we waved to each other once more while they headed toward the ship. Without moving, I daydreamed about my future relationship with Ting-Ting. I would be part stepmother, part best friend. I could help her as she navigated American customs and, at the same time, keep her grounded in her Chinese roots.

I imagined her visiting during summer vacations to spend time with us, which would also give Wei Ling a chance to enjoy some time to herself. And in my naïve fantasyland, Ting-Ting and I would attend Chinese musical and dance performances with her young sibling and catch the latest art film from China when she reached her teens, all while Cai worked hard as a successful academic, returning in the evenings to hear about our day as our family of four or more clamored around the vivacious dinner table. I left the ferry pier full of hope.

Chapter 27

QUIET IN KOWLOON

The streets of Kowloon were quiet on Saturday mornings, compared to the weekday rush of commuter traffic and the noise of schoolchildren chatting fervently with one another. Now, elderly residents hobbled along on their weathered feet, returning from tai chi in one of the tree-lined neighborhood parks. A hunchbacked woman pushed a flat cart piled high with cardboard sheets and crushed drink cans past me as I exited the double-decker Kowloon Motor Bus near St. Teresa's Hospital.

Old and silent, St. Teresa's seemed deserted at this early hour. I found the information desk, staffed by three olive-skinned European nuns who wore habits à la Sally Field in *The Flying Nun*. The nuns' Cantonese was impeccable as they spoke to an elderly Chinese couple.

"Excuse me, can you tell me where I can find the radiology department?" I asked in English when it was my turn.

The nuns didn't answer. The shortest one walked around to the front of the desk and in very broken English asked me to repeat my question.

"Radiology?" I said slowly and ran my hand over the light jacket that cushioned my abdomen from the gentle Hong Kong winter. "Ultrasound?"

She pointed down the hall. "Straight, then left."

"Thank you, I mean, *m'goi sai. M'goi*."

The nun placed her hands together and bowed her head slightly.

I followed the windowless hall and found the radiology department off to the left at the far end, just as the nun had directed. Soon after I checked in with the receptionist, a technician called my name, though I was the only patient in the waiting area.

"When you get in the room, take off all your clothes except your underpants, and button the gown in the front," the female technician said. She opened the door of the examining room and turned on the light. "Are you going to find out the gender today?"

"No. We want it to be a surprise." In China, hospitals weren't allowed to reveal the gender of the baby, but that wasn't the case in unrestricted Hong Kong.

The tech marked a page in my chart and placed it on the desk near the ultrasound machine. Then she left, leaving me in the dungeonlike room. Ten minutes passed before a lanky man in his late thirties entered. He introduced himself as Dr. Leung.

Leung squirted a cool, clear gel on my naked abdomen, dimmed the lights, and started the scan. He typed notes in the computer as he explained to me what he saw. "I see all ten fingers and ten toes. Your baby is very active. Lots of tumbling." He chuckled.

I tried to look at the scratchy gray screen, but couldn't make out head or toes from the image.

"And your baby has three legs," he said, giggling.

"*Three legs?*"

"But one isn't a leg."

"What do you mean?"

"It's something between the legs. Congratulations, Mrs. Cai; you're having a boy!" His eyes beamed back at me through the rays of light flickering from the ultrasound screen.

I didn't share his smile, since Cai and I had decided not to learn the gender in advance and I wasn't particularly thrilled that Dr. Leung had ignored my wishes. But now that I knew, my pregnancy seemed real. Cai and I were truly having a baby, not just a blob on a screen.

When I returned home to Sunshine City, I knew it was still too early to call my parents in Chicago, a time zone a half day behind. I would wait until later to phone and tell them that their first grandchild would be a boy. But Hidden River and Hong Kong shared the same time zone, so I opened my address book and dialed the long number to Mama and Baba's apartment.

"*Wèi?*" Mama answered.

"*Mama, nǐ hǎo.*" No one else with an American accent called them, so it was fairly obvious who I was after my first uttered syllable. Mama yelled out to Cai, who picked up the other phone in their apartment.

"How was your appointment? Is the baby okay?" he asked in Mandarin for the benefit of his mother, still on the line.

"Everything's fine."

"That's great news!"

"Yes. But the doctor did find something," I said.

"What?" Cai asked in a panicked whimper.

"He said the baby has three legs."

"*Huh?*" Cai gasped. Mama didn't reply.

I spoke in my most serious tone. "The third leg isn't really a leg." When they didn't say anything, I couldn't keep up the act and giggled. "It's something else."

Mama shrieked with such force I thought she'd faint.

"*Thank you,*" Cai squealed. "I really wanted a girl, but this is great. Of course it's nice to have a boy." He started crying.

In the background I could still hear Mama screaming, probably telling Baba the good news.

Cai continued to cry and thank me. Mama picked the phone up again. "*Su Shan, xièxiè nǐ, xièxiè nǐ.*" Thank you so much.

I knew Cai and his parents would be happy we were having a boy, but I never dreamed they'd react as if they'd just won the lottery. How would they have responded to news of a girl? Had Cai only said he wanted a daughter because he didn't want to jinx his chances for having a boy? In Chinese culture, only a son of a son counts as a true grandchild, a *sūnzi*. Sons of daughters belonged to their father's family. And daughters belong to their future husband's family. Since Cai was an only son, our baby would be Mama and Baba's only true grandchild. I could only imagine that Mama would resume her bid to care for our baby in Hidden River.

If the husband is angry,
Let not the wife be angry in return,
But meekly yield to him,
And press down her angry feelings.

—Ban Zhao
Instruction for Chinese Women and Girls

Chapter 28

SETTLING INTO SAN FRANCISCO

The house on Newhall Street faced an abandoned warehouse and a chain-locked parking lot. Squeezed between two identical three-story homes, our brown stucco house stood on the border between old and new, between the new development mainly occupied by Chinese families and an old industrial center about to be bulldozed because of the growing housing demand in the landlocked city.

When we first opened the front door and entered our new house, the only furniture inside was a set of twin mattresses that my uncle Budgie had ordered for us as a housewarming gift. Besides being the chief sales agent for the development, Bob also served as caretaker and concierge. He'd let in the delivery crew with the mattresses before we'd arrived in San Francisco. And on our first morning in our new home, he directed us to a mall seven miles out of the city where we could buy new furniture and other household necessities like linens and kitchen supplies.

Although the distance from our house to the mall wasn't great, the whole trip—bus, train, and another bus—took about an hour. Cai and I arrived at the Tanforan shopping center and headed toward Sears. Four hours later, we held receipts for two queen beds and mattresses, two twin bed frames, a sofa bed, a dining room table and chairs, a kitchen table and chairs, a coffee table and end table set, an entertainment center, and a large-screen television on which Cai could watch the free Chinese stations. The furniture wouldn't be delivered for six weeks. The TV and do-it-yourself entertainment center would arrive in a few days.

"Thank goodness Budgie bought us those mattresses," I mused as we left the store. "At least we can sleep on them until our bed arrives."

Since we were to take public transportation home, we only bought as many kitchen and bathroom supplies as we could carry in our arms. Cai managed most of the bags because he didn't want me to overdo it. Pleased with our efficiency, I leaned against a tree in the small patch of grass where we had exited the bus that morning from the Colma BART station. The bus stop sign listed neither times nor frequency of service, but I figured we were to board the return bus here, too.

Cai frowned after we'd been waiting twenty minutes. "I'm not sure it's coming. It should have been here by now."

"Maybe it doesn't run so often at this time of day? It's not quite rush hour. We probably need to wait a little longer."

But as the minutes ticked on, I, too, wondered if the bus had stopped running or if it didn't come to this stop in the afternoon. Maybe there was another stop for the return trip. I wished I had asked the driver that morning.

Cai's lips turned down and his eyes tightened in serious concentration, yet his gaze was distant. After ten more minutes of silence, a taxi parked near our patch of land. The driver left the car and rushed away before I could catch his attention. Cai didn't seem to notice the taxi; he barely wavered from his zombielike state.

If the driver didn't come back in ten minutes, I would walk back to the mall and call a cab. I imagined myself weaving through the shiny metallic cars, sparkling in the sun like Christmas tree ornaments, while Cai remained in his comatose stance. But then a man came out of the Sears exit. Please let it be the cab driver, I prayed. He continued in our direction and soon enough I saw that it was indeed the driver.

I waddled to the taxi. "Are you free?"

"Where are you going?" the middle-aged man asked.

"Just to the Colma BART station."

"Hop in."

Cai snapped out of his daze and entered the car after me, loading our bags between us in the backseat. Once we arrived at the BART station, the rest of our trip would be easy.

Inside the Colma station, I glanced up at a red-lettered screen hanging above the platform. My pulse quickened when I saw that the next San Francisco–bound train would arrive in twenty minutes. Maybe Cai wouldn't notice it, and the train would come well ahead of schedule. But then I saw Cai eyeing the sign.

"*Ay yo*. This is terrible." Before I could say something to calm his worries, he turned his face away. Sure it was frustrating that the train ran infrequently after we had stood waiting for a bus that never arrived, but certainly Cai had waited for trains or buses in China.

I thought I heard a whimpering sound. The other people on the platform weren't close to us, so it had to be coming from Cai. But he was still turned away from me and I couldn't see his face. With his head lowered and his shoulders drooped, it looked like he was crying. That couldn't be right. Cai would never cry over a delayed train.

But then I heard sobbing sounds.

"*Cai?*"

Turning around, he had tears pouring from his eyes.

"Oh my God," I gasped. "What's wrong?"

"It's not convenient here." He sobbed. "It's not like Hong Kong."

"It's okay," I said, patting his shoulder. He still held most of our bags. "We haven't been here for twenty-four hours and don't know our way around yet. It's normal to feel disoriented when you move to a new place. But it will take longer than a day to adjust."

Cai turned away and continued to cry, his profile visible to me. I thought back to Cai's first day in the United States, when we'd arrived at my parents' home two years earlier. Back then, I had assumed that Cai would see the United States through my eyes, but I soon realized that he would form his own opinions, just as I had about China. And while I, too, now felt frustrated that the public transportation wasn't as convenient as in Hong Kong, or even China for that matter, I knew we would adjust soon enough. I just had to remember to stay optimistic.

"I don't know how long I can stay in America." Cai sounded so hopeless.

Don't jump to conclusions. I wanted to take him by the shoulders and plead with him. After everything we'd purchased that day, plus the huge expense of the house itself, he couldn't be serious about leaving and moving back to China. Even so, it worried me to hear him talk this way now that I was well into my second trimester. I wanted nothing more than to put down roots. Besides, I'd never wanted to live in China in the first place, so Cai's talk about returning there put knots in my stomach.

"We'll get a car soon and none of this will matter. You've been waiting for the chance to learn to drive and own a car. Why don't we look for a car first thing tomorrow?" My grandmother had generously promised to buy us a car, and Cai had seemed excited by the prospect of owning a new automobile, his own car, in America.

He remained silent.

"And once you get a job," I said, trying to remain calm, "you'll feel better about being here. I know there's a great job just waiting for you." I smiled when he looked at me, his eyes still red and puffy. Even though I tried to paint a bright picture, I knew, as I had back in New York when Cai perused the classifieds in the Chinese newspaper, that he wouldn't find a decent job overnight. It would take time and patience and networking with other academics or musicians.

Cai didn't speak until after the train arrived. I needed for him to adjust to San Francisco soon. With no health insurance and no jobs, I didn't want the added stress of Cai talking about leaving this all behind to move back to China. It reminded me of when my older brother, Danny, first left home and started running away from his school. My parents argued about him so much that I thought it might break our family apart. I craved stability at home and knew how to keep the peace. Just like back then, I silently vowed to do everything in my power to ensure Cai's happiness in the United States. I hoped he'd feel more confident once we bought a car and figured out our way around the Bay Area.

As efficient as we were in buying furniture for our house, finding a car and a job for Cai was surprisingly (and thankfully) even easier. We entered the Honda dealership on Van Ness Avenue on our second morning in San Francisco and drove out with a new four-door, metallic green 1998 Civic that afternoon. To celebrate, we made our way to a Chinese restaurant in the Richmond district for an early dinner. Cai picked up a free Chinese paper in the entryway and carefully read the job ads while we waited for our food.

"I can do this job." He sounded as upbeat as he had when we'd purchased the car a few hours earlier.

"What's it for?"

He read the brief job description for a city reporter in the Chinese-language *World Journal*, the same newspaper he'd read in New York on our first visit to the United States. The person in this position would cover events in city government, new initiatives in social services, and happenings in the Chinese community. The salary amounted to $20,000, and the benefits included health insurance, a 401(k) retirement plan, and paid vacation days. Although the salary was low, it sounded like the perfect introductory job for Cai.

That night we decided to stroll around our new housing development. Outside, we met the woman who lived just east of us. She spoke Cantonese-accented Mandarin and introduced herself as Mrs. Chang. Like most people in our development, Mrs. Chang and her family had moved from Chinatown. She, her husband, and their daughter, Tiffany, shared the house with Mr. Chang's parents. Originally from Guangdong province, the Changs had lived in the United States for more than ten years.

"When are you due?" she asked me in almost perfect English.

"Early July." I patted my ever-expanding belly.

"Where are you going to deliver?"

"Probably San Francisco General. But if I find a job before then and get insurance, I might go to another hospital."

"My daughter, Tiffany, was born at General. We were very happy there."

I smiled. "That's so good to know."

"Enjoy your walk." She smiled kindly. "Welcome to the neighborhood."

The following week, I drove Cai to the newspaper's office south of the city. I offered to wait in the car while he sat for his interview because I thought it would be good for Cai's self-assurance if he handled it on his own. I also was confident that the manager would be drawn to Cai's outgoing personality and academic background. There was no reason for him not to receive an offer, but if he didn't, I feared he would grow even more cynical than he had in the subway station. Since then, his spirits had been higher, but that outburst on the platform had come from out of the blue so it could happen again without warning.

Half an hour later, Cai appeared back in the parking lot with a grin that advertised his success well before he reached me. I screeched when Cai finally got to the car and told me the good news.

"Did you ever think we would move to San Francisco, buy new furniture and a new car, and you would find a job all in a week?" I asked ecstatically. "And now we'll have health insurance."

He looked away. "That doesn't start until I've worked here six months."

"We'll have had the baby by then." I paused. "It's okay. I'll call the hospital to see about paying out of pocket. Something will work out. I'll look for a job, too." Near the end of my fifth month of pregnancy, I still held out hope of finding a job in the next month while I could hide my bulge.

Cai didn't reply. Coming from a country where the government

provided everything—health care, education, housing, and retirement pensions—the concept of health insurance was foreign to him.
He'd never received medical care in the United States and didn't
fully comprehend the many expenditures, insurance or no insurance. I couldn't let Cai turn down the job and keep looking just
because he wouldn't be eligible for health insurance until the end of
the summer, especially when it was something he seemed eager to
pursue. I hadn't bothered to ask him about promotion opportunities,
and I suspected he didn't mention them during the interview.

I viewed this job as a way for Cai to integrate into San Francisco
and into the Chinese community. Maybe he'd make a successful
career out of it, or maybe it would provide him with the right con-
nections to people involved with Chinese music. I would be the one
to apply for any job that provided health insurance.

"My first assignment is tomorrow." Cai looked at me with
anticipation. "Can you go with me? I'm afraid my English isn't
good enough."

"No problem. Do you have the address?"

He showed me a piece of paper with the time and location of a
lunch event at a new recycling plant. "I have to return to the office
afterward and type the article on their computer. They said they'll
give me a digital camera tomorrow night to use in the future."

For the first time since we had arrived in San Francisco, Cai
sounded enthusiastic. For now, I was happy to drive him to his
assignments and interpret if he didn't understand the English
speakers. I could also take him to the newspaper building after his
interviews so he could type and submit his articles. But as soon as
I started interviewing and, with any hope, found my own job, Cai
would have to work on his own. That meant he would need to learn
to drive and to improve his English.

We enjoyed the recycling luncheon and attended a press conference the following day at a Chinatown community center. On both
occasions, I drove Cai to the newspaper office around three in the
afternoon and returned when he phoned me after filing his articles.

When he hadn't called me by eight on his first night, I dialed the newspaper's main number. Cai answered.

"Cai? Is everything okay?"

"I'm sorry I haven't called." His voice sounded depleted of energy. "I'm still typing. The software is a little difficult. I'll call you when I'm finished."

Of course. I should have realized Cai wasn't proficient with computers. He'd written his dissertation by hand, as well as his books and articles. Either the universities or the publishers typeset his writing, but he himself never typed his work. I closed my eyes in the hope that he wouldn't let this latest frustration dampen his feelings about the job and living in America.

Sitting at our kitchen table one weekend, I skimmed the newspaper before concentrating on the job ads. In the arts and entertainment section, a blurb leaped out at me. *Concert, Chinatown, traditional Chinese instruments, Saturday.* I read the paragraph a couple of times, digesting each sentence. It sounded perfect for Cai, encompassing his interests and background in Chinese music. I brought the paper to Cai, who was in the living room watching the Chinese news on our new wide-screen television.

Cai slowly read the English blurb and then shrugged, as if he didn't understand why I'd bother him. During the month he'd been working at the *World Journal*, his spirits hadn't improved, even after he'd received his driver's license. To me, this concert was just what he needed: meeting other Chinese musicians, perhaps even learning about jobs in the Chinese music community and, at the very least, attending something familiar. Going to this concert had to beat pouting at home.

Every night before Cai returned from the newspaper office, I lay in bed, unable to sleep until he pulled into the garage. And every night when I asked about work, he replied the same way—he didn't know how long he could continue to work at the paper. Cai was burning out.

"What about asking your boss if you could cover this concert for the paper? You could write an article about it. Then on the side you can ask these musicians about jobs."

"That's a good idea." His eyes sparkled with a ray of hope. "I'll ask my boss tomorrow."

The following Saturday, Cai drove us to Chinatown and parked in the garage opposite the Holiday Inn. We entered the Chinese Culture Center in the hotel's basement and found the small concert room. The conductor, a middle-aged Chinese woman, stood in front of a dozen musicians, wearing a simple, red, long-sleeved *qípáo*.

Some of the music seemed familiar from CDs Cai had played in our Hong Kong dorm room. I even thought back to our early days together, when we practiced reading his Taoist music paper aloud. I recognized the two-string *erhu*, the table harp *guzheng*, and the round guitarlike *pipa*. After ten minutes, I saw that Cai's eyes were closed and his hands were swaying slightly in front of himself, as though he were conducting the concert. We had found the right people for Cai to meet.

At the end of the concert, I led Cai toward the conductor, but he didn't speak. I figured he was just shy, so I introduced him, stressing his background at the Wuhan Conservatory of Music and, more recently, the Chinese University of Hong Kong. The conductor's eyes lit up at the mention of Wuhan.

"I studied at the Central Conservatory." From my observations, Chinese conservatory alums seemed to have an affinity with one another, regardless of where they studied. "I'm Wang Yuhan."

I stood back as Cai and Yuhan spoke in Mandarin like they were old friends. I felt a thrill that I hadn't experienced since we had arrived in San Francisco. Meeting Yuhan was even more momentous than purchasing furniture for our house in one day or buying a car. When Yuhan mentioned she needed a male emcee for a Chinese concert at the stately Herbst Theatre, I almost accepted before Cai did.

On our way home, Cai and I rehashed his conversation with
Yuhan. A few hours later, I drove him to the newspaper office so he
could type his article and upload a few photos. Before he left the car,
I touched his sleeve. "If you want to quit your job, maybe now is the
time. You can focus on getting into the Chinese music community.
Yuhan seems like a great contact." Although I didn't say it, I also
thought she was the ticket to his happiness in the United States.

"How will we pay our mortgage? How will we eat?"

"I've been getting interviews and should find something soon."
Even if it took me a few more weeks to find a job, we had savings to
pay the bills for several more months. And if worse came to worst,
I could look for a job after the baby was born. My parents could
probably lend us some money for a couple of months. I was willing
to do anything so Cai would feel settled in San Francisco. For the
next three days, Cai spoke on the phone with Yuhan before he left
for work each afternoon.

"I can't live this way," he said on the fourth night around 1:00
a.m. "It's not good for the family."

"Cai, you don't have to justify it. If you kept your newspaper
job, how would you be able to handle more work in the music
community? I really think this concert with Yuhan could lead to
more contacts."

He smiled softly. "Thank you for your support. I'll quit the
paper tomorrow."

Cai could finally do something in his field. And he wouldn't
come home every night from the newspaper office past midnight.
Of course, I didn't know that midnight would soon seem quite early
for his nightly returns.

Chapter 29

AT HOME IN AMERICA

The Silver Avenue Family Health Center stood at the end of the San Bruno business district near our house. The clinic was housed in a shabby cement box of a building that would have fit perfectly in the middle of China. I started receiving prenatal care at this outpost of the San Francisco Department of Public Health soon after we moved to California.

I arrived at the clinic for my monthly checkup and sat on a tattered floral sofa until a nurse's aide led me past the waiting room doors to an open corridor where she took my blood pressure and weight. She marked these down in my chart and led me to a private room. Several minutes later, a registered nurse knocked on the door. I would see this nurse and others like her for all my appointments until I went into labor.

"When the time comes for you to deliver," the nurse said, "you'll go to San Francisco General and will be attended by residents at UCSF. I suggest you and your husband take a tour and a class at the hospital. They're held every month."

Without jobs, neither Cai nor I had health insurance. My mother had made some phone calls before we left Hong Kong to see about purchasing insurance in California. But because I was pregnant, I had a preexisting condition that even private insurance policies would not cover. I felt lucky that the San Francisco Department of Public Health would allow me to receive prenatal care. They charged according to each patient's salary. Since I had no salary, I didn't have to pay. I still held out hope that I would find a job that provided immediate health-care insurance before I was due to deliver in early July.

At my April appointment, I finished with the registered nurse and moved on to a cubicle where I met with a lactation consultant and a social worker. These services were included in my free health care. When the Silver Avenue social worker reviewed the financial documents I had brought as requested on my first visit, she announced I could receive WIC, the social program to provide food and nutrition education to low-income women, infants, and children.

I looked at her askance. "But we own a house and a car, and our bank account isn't exactly—"

"Your assets don't matter. You and your husband don't have an income, so you qualify."

I wasn't ashamed to receive free health care, and now public assistance in the form of free food coupons, but I felt unworthy of it because we possessed all those assets. Shouldn't someone in more need use the coupons?

When I arrived home, Cai had other ideas. "You should take it," he said. "We got free food in China all the time when I was young. It's a waste if you don't use it."

"I guess you're right. The coupons are already written out to me."

Later that week, I phoned San Francisco General to sign up for a one-day prenatal class at the hospital that Saturday. We joined a dozen other couples, visiting the labor and delivery areas and meeting with a prenatal nurse who showed a frighteningly graphic video of several women giving birth. I had to turn my head at one point and noticed Cai doing the same. The nurse also talked to us about breast-feeding and cloth versus paper diapers. At the end of the class, she passed out vouchers for a ten-dollar infant car seat we could pick up in a storeroom down the hall.

Since Cai and I had spent the day talking about childbirth, when we returned home that afternoon I mustered up the courage to ask

Cai about a bris for our baby boy. Even though my family wasn't observant, we adhered to basic Jewish traditions, including circumcising baby boys in a *brit milah* ceremony. Most males in China weren't circumcised, so this custom was new to Cai both as a medical procedure and as a religious custom. I was certain he would reject my idea right away.

"In the Jewish tradition, baby boys have a circumcision ceremony." Careful not to preach, I explained the tradition and why Jewish people subscribe to it.

"Do you want that for our baby?" he asked genially.

"It would make my dad very happy."

"That's fine with me. I respect old traditions. If only people in China cared about traditional Chinese culture—"

As Cai delved into the moral decline of the mainland Chinese, I happily wondered why I had ever hesitated to broach this subject with him.

Later that month, I found a job ad in the newspaper for an editorial assistant in the UCSF development office. The position requirements included a few years of copyediting and experience working at a university. I figured the benefits at UCSF, a state university, would be fairly comprehensive.

"It only pays $30,000?" Cai asked when I returned home.

"Yes, but the benefits are good. We could get health insurance right away."

"I know, but $30,000 isn't much."

It's a lot more than you were making at the newspaper, I wanted to say. But I couldn't pick a fight with Cai. He was still going through an adjustment period and I wanted to remain sensitive to that. It couldn't be easy for Cai, and every time I pictured the tables turned, I felt thankful we weren't living in China. I would do my best to help Cai acclimate to the United States, even if it meant holding my tongue. So I said, "I'll get my foot in the door and then look for a better job in a year."

I hadn't revealed my pregnancy until after I was offered the job. Erin, my new boss, wasn't thrilled to learn that I would need to take off unpaid time later that summer, but I was determined not to let my pregnancy get in the way of providing for my family. We could pay our mortgage, and we had health insurance that would cover my delivery and the many well-baby visits to come.

Chapter 30
THE NEW ARRIVAL

On the day of the summer solstice, I lay on the sofa with a sharp pain in my abdomen. Still two weeks from my due date, I wondered if feeling sick was a typical symptom that occurred during the end of a pregnancy. Or perhaps I was coming down with a stomach bug. Maybe it was the beginning of appendicitis. I tried not to think about that. Cai cooked me a light chicken soup with vermicelli and cubed tofu, one of my favorite dishes. He hoped it would settle my stomach.

After a bowl of soup and a long rest that afternoon, I told Cai that I couldn't imagine how women worked for the last two weeks of their pregnancy if they felt this achy. We agreed that I would call my doctor the next morning if these symptoms remained.

When I woke at 5:00 a.m. to go to the bathroom, my water broke. I rustled Cai out of sleep and called my new obstetrician, a Hong Kong–born man named Dr. Kwan, whom I had only seen once. Since Cai's English wasn't completely fluent, especially when it came to medical terminology, I choose Kwan, who could speak Cantonese. He had privileges at California Pacific Medical Center, the premier obstetrics hospital in San Francisco, which was where he would deliver my baby. For a pediatrician, he recommended a kind man named Dr. Kwok, who was also Cantonese.

Dr. Kwan insisted we head to the hospital at once. Because my water had broken, he said it was imperative that I deliver within twenty-four hours, as I was now prone to infection. From my hospital room, I phoned my parents in Oregon. They had planned a leisurely drive from Chicago and hadn't figured I would go into labor two weeks early. Just a couple days ago they had phoned from Portland, where they had gone to spend the weekend with some friends.

"Guess what? I'm in the hospital," I told my mom just as she and my dad were sitting down to a casual breakfast in their friends' kitchen.

"Is everything okay?"

"Things couldn't be better. My water broke and I'm in labor. The doctors think I'll have the baby by early evening."

"Oh my God." My mom sounded panicked. "We'll leave right away. But I don't think we'll make it before later this evening. It's at least a nine-hour drive."

"Don't worry. The baby won't go anywhere. Just drive safely." Truth be told, when I'd imagined the day of my delivery, I had only pictured Cai in the room with the medical staff and me. I was grateful my parents would spend the summer with us in San Francisco, but for the actual delivery, I wanted it to be as private as possible. If they arrived after the baby was born, that was fine with me.

Then I called my boss, Erin.

"I'm on the table now, in labor. Sorry I can't come to work today."

She laughed and wished me a good delivery. I would be back in six to eight weeks, and the office had already hired a temp to fill in for me.

By early afternoon, the pain was so severe it felt like I was about to be split in half. When the anesthesiologist left my room an hour later, my legs felt cool and heavy. The pain had disappeared completely.

The next time the nurse checked me, around 2:30 p.m., she announced I was dilated ten centimeters. "Susan, it's time to call Dr. Kwan."

Cai and I had talked about videoing the birth and agreed he wouldn't start filming until our baby was born. As the nurse uncovered her instruments and opened the sterile packages, Cai readied his video camera and placed it on a table next to my bed. Dr. Kwan popped in to say hello before leaving to scrub in.

Moments later Kwan stood in position, spaceship shield guarding his face. Cai remained on my right, helping me to count as I pushed, with the nurse doing the same on my left. When we were finished with the second round of counting, Cai stepped away from the bed, collapsing onto a chair.

"I'm so tired." He panted. "I need a break."

I almost had to laugh. If only he knew.

Less than an hour later, at 3:53 p.m., our son Jacob arrived, skinny and screaming. Cai started filming after Dr. Kwan expertly cut three loops of umbilical cord from around Jake's neck. The nurse wrapped Jake in a warm blanket and placed a pink-and-blue hat on his tiny head while Cai continued to film our baby's every move. I had never seen Cai more in awe. It was the happiest day of my life, the happiest day of our marriage.

The nurse handed Jake to me, encouraging early breast-feeding. I saw Jake's pink face for the first time and looked for Cai's features in him, but he didn't look Asian at all. Instead, he reminded me of a photo I'd seen of myself as a newborn; we had the same round nose and peaceful expression. Cai thanked me over and over just as he had the morning we learned I was pregnant.

Five hours later, my parents entered the room where I'd been placed after my delivery. My mom and dad hovered around Jake's bassinet as he rested peacefully, swaddled in a hospital blanket, his eyes squinting under the dull ceiling light. Just before 10:00 p.m., my parents and Cai returned to the house on Newhall Street to give me a chance to sleep. But I was afraid Jake would stop breathing (he was so tiny!) and couldn't bear to take my eyes off him. I barely slept that night.

The morning I was to leave the hospital with Jake, my obstetrician entered the room minutes after Cai arrived.

"Today's the big day." Dr. Kwan checked my stitches while Cai stood next to Jake's bassinet. Jake slept swaddled in a blue, white, and pink hospital blanket and a new matching knit hat. "Everything looks great. You can leave as soon as you complete the discharge paperwork."

"Thank you, Doctor." Cai spoke in English as he shook Kwan's hand.

Kwan faced us with his hands in his suit pants pockets. "You probably know about the Chinese traditions for women after child-birth, but they're old-fashioned and not based on medical evidence. It's completely fine to take a shower and wash your hair now."

"I don't know what you're talking about." I glanced at Cai. He stared at the opposite wall with a blank face.

"Oh, I see," Dr. Kwan continued. "Well, in ancient China, when water was unsanitary and dangerous for women in the early days after childbirth, they stopped bathing for a month until their immune systems grew stronger. Some Chinese people today continue this tradition. But like I said, it's all based on ancient conditions. Our water is clean and safe. I'll see you in six weeks." He patted my knees through my blankets.

All through my pregnancy, Cai had never spoken of Chinese prenatal rituals. I ate whatever I wanted and certainly showered every day. And as for postpartum customs, we'd only spoken of the Jewish bris, the tradition of circumcision. Once Dr. Kwan left, I slowly stood up and grabbed the clean clothes I had packed the morning of Jake's birth. I headed toward the bathroom.

"Where are you going?" Cai asked urgently.

"To take a shower."

"You shouldn't do that."

"What do you mean?"

"You shouldn't take a bath for a month after you have a baby. It's bad for the health."

What? "Didn't you just hear Dr. Kwan say—?"

He rolled his eyes. "He doesn't know anything."

"But that's based on old-fashioned ideas. It's—"

"Bad for your health. You should get dressed. American parents will be here soon."

I glanced at Jake, who continued to sleep peacefully. My heart filled with love every time I looked at him, every time I nursed him, changed his diaper, or held him. I didn't want to argue with Cai now and spoil this special time. But this custom seemed old-fashioned, just as Dr. Kwan had suggested. And to me it sounded sexist. How could Cai ask me to refrain from taking a shower for a *month* when I was still bleeding from Jake's delivery?

I thought back to the humiliating time he had commanded me to bathe in his dirty Wuhan apartment. If Cai really thought women were dirty and smelly, why would he go along with this ancient and restrictive postpartum custom? I felt like crying when I thought about caring for my new baby in dirty clothes and with unwashed hair. Trying to hold myself together, I knew I would be able to shower and shampoo my hair once we returned home, when Cai wasn't watching over me.

Chapter 31

THE NEIGHBORS

We hadn't been home from the hospital for more than a day when Cai lifted Jake from my mom's hands. She had been cradling him in the living room after dinner.

"Susan, we should visit the neighbors now." When Cai spoke of our "neighbors," he meant the Changs next door. We barely knew our other next-door neighbors, a Cantonese family of four generations who kept to themselves.

"Do you think it's okay to take Jake out?" I asked. The sun had already set and the late June temperatures nipped like a chilly day in Chicago.

"Yes. It's polite to introduce them to Jake."

Reaching for the front baby carrier, I fiddled with the straps. It was my first time using it. Cai placed Jake in his car seat and gently took the straps from my hands. Instead of helping me put it on, he loosened the straps and secured them over his oversized DePaul sweatshirt, a gift from my parents.

"Cai, I wanted to carry Jake."

He snorted as he picked up Jake and placed him into the front carrier. "You can't walk down the stairs with Jake. It's not safe."

"What?" I glared at him. "I carry him up and downstairs every morning and night."

"We have carpet inside." Cai spoke slowly like a wise sage. "The neighbors will worry you'll fall carrying Jake. You just went through a hard time. It's time for you to regain your strength."

My parents were in the same room, so I acquiesced and followed Cai down the steep front steps to the Changs' house next door.

Soon after Cai rang the doorbell, Old Mrs. Chang peered at us through the front metal security door, something most of our neighbors installed upon moving in. I'd somehow talked Cai into purchasing a security system instead of an ugly front grille. Old Mrs. Chang ushered us inside, imploring us to take a seat on the leather living room sofa.

Clapping her hands twice, Old Mrs. Chang held them out to Cai, as if preparing to receive a dish at the dinner table. Cai took Jake out of the carrier and offered him to the elderly woman, whose bowed legs rocked back and forth as she waddled to the adjacent love seat.

Young Mrs. Chang joined us and sat in an oversized chair next to me. "How was your delivery? Was it painful? When I had Tiffany, it was *awful*."

We drifted into labor-and-delivery war stories while Cai conversed in Mandarin with Old Mrs. Chang. Young Mrs. Chang had just entered her nineteenth hour of labor, starting the play-by-play of her second epidural, when she jerked her head toward her mother-in-law as Old Mrs. Chang offered another bit of wisdom.

"Of course, no showers or hair washing for a month, and no cold drinks. The coldness will suck out her calcium and your baby won't grow." Old Mrs. Chang sat perfectly upright, looking like a Taoist nun at a temple high in the mountains among the clouds.

"Ma, don't forget pig feet soup. That will bring her milk in." Young Mrs. Chang then looked over at Cai as if I were invisible.

Cai's eyes lit up when she mentioned milk. "What are the ingredients for the soup?" He squinted in concentration.

There was no way I was going to eat pig feet soup. Cai was probably feigning interest to be polite. He knew I didn't eat pork and that my milk supply wasn't a problem. Already I was walking around with wet spots on my blue nightgown from forgetting to change a nursing pad or two. What would I do with more milk?

As Old Mrs. Chang handed Jake back to Cai, Young Mrs. Chang rattled off more dishes to increase milk and nutrition. "And be sure to give her plenty of eggs." Suddenly the thought of eggs churned my stomach.

"Fish head soup also has lots of nutrition. You can cook it with dates and it's delicious," she added.

Why was I never included in conversations that centered around me and no one else? When Mama discussed my eating habits with Cai, or when he spoke with the Suzhou temple staff about my adjustment to China, no one stopped to ask what I thought. This discussion about my postpartum diet reminded me of those times in China when I felt like I had no control over matters that only pertained to me.

Was this a weird cultural difference that viewed non-Chinese people as incapable of making certain decisions for themselves? I wanted to wave my hands back and forth to see if I was in fact invisible to Cai and the Changs. But then Cai turned to me. "I'll go to the store tomorrow to buy these things for you. Especially the eggs."

"Oh, and don't forget to keep his belly button covered," the old lady interjected. "If it's exposed to air, he could get very sick."

What? These customs sounded like voodoo. I longed to return to the time when Dr. Kwan warned me about these practices, called *mǎnyuè* in Mandarin. If only I had had the sense to ask him to explain to Cai that we didn't need to follow these rules! I wished I hadn't assumed Cai was on the same page as Dr. Kwan before he left the room. Biting my lip, I forced a smile. I didn't want to create a rift with our neighbors. We already had one set that didn't speak to us, so I wanted to keep a good rapport with the Changs.

Perhaps they would awkwardly confess they hadn't eaten dinner yet and invite us, which was the polite thing to do. That would give us an excuse to leave. We would thank them for the invitation but decline because we'd already eaten. The minutes passed, and no such invitation seemed forthcoming as Cai asked more about the traditions of *mǎnyuè*. The Mrs. Changs warned about taking Jake out during the first month and advised Cai of more home remedies for protecting my calcium and stimulating my milk.

When we returned home, my parents were still reading in the living room.

"How'd it go?" my mom asked. Cai took Jake out of the carrier and handed him to me, then wandered off to the kitchen.

"Terrible. They couldn't stop talking about all these horrible things to eat to increase milk, conserve calcium, and regain strength. And the worst thing"—I lowered my voice to a whisper—"is that Cai is going along with it."

"Sounds like witchcraft, but I suppose Chinese people have been doing this for thousands of years and find value in it. You should just do what you want."

"I'm trying to, but Cai already said he would go to the store tomorrow to brew me up a strange soup to increase my milk."

"Increase your milk? Can't he see you have plenty?"

The next day at breakfast, I wasn't surprised when Cai announced he was heading to a Chinese grocery after he finished eating.

"I'm going to cook you traditional Chinese food for new mothers," he said, sounding every bit the doting husband. "Like what the neighbors told us last night."

"I won't eat pig feet soup."

Cai promptly scowled, his face punctuated by his trademark eyebrow furrow and tightened lips. "You need to eat special food or else your milk won't be enough. This is a sensitive time and you need more strength."

"But I have enough milk. It leaks all the time." I looked down at my bowl of cornflakes. "And I'm not weak."

My parents sat at the table with us, their eyes focused on the morning San Francisco newspaper as if they didn't understand English. Cai mopped up the last of his eggs with a piece of toast and shoved it into his mouth. He pushed his chair out from the table, the screeching sound piercing my ears.

"I'm going now."

When Cai returned from the grocery store, he carried bags containing a fish head the size of a cantaloupe, a package of smoky dates, two dozen eggs, blocks of tofu, a basket of tomatoes, and two packages of ground pork, along with replenishments of green onion, ginger root, and garlic. Then he got to work in the kitchen, chopping, mincing, and dicing. He sautéed, boiled, and simmered. The water in the rice cooker bubbled, escaping around the sides and through the tiny steam hole on the cover.

Just after noon, Cai entered the living room, wiped his sweaty brow with his hand, and smiled at his latest culinary achievement. Despite his frustrations about living in the United States, cooking brought him calmness, reminding me of our early months together in Hong Kong. "Lunch is ready."

Carrying Jake in his car seat, I followed my parents to the kitchen table and sat down to a normal meal for us: three entrees and a soup. Succulent tofu sautéed in soy sauce, ginger, garlic, green onion, ground pork, and frozen peas; Cai's signature egg and tomato scramble; pork and egg fried rice; and a large glass bowl with a fish head peeking out of the cloudy light broth, its eyes engaged in a stare-off with me.

Thankful Cai had bypassed the pig feet and opted for the less repulsive fish head soup, I spooned a few ladles into my rice bowl. Small brownish-red dates fell to the bottom after breaking the surface of the broth. Crunchy lotus seeds, a staple Cai stocked in the kitchen cabinet, dove toward the dates.

I dipped a Chinese soup spoon into my bowl and brought it up to my lips. The dates tasted as if Cai had moments ago lifted them from a charcoal campfire. I didn't mind a subtle smokiness, like in cheese or turkey sausage, but this harsh smokiness crushed the flavors of the other ingredients in the soup. I took another spoonful and stopped breathing through my nose.

More thirsty than hungry, what I really wanted was another glass of the lemonade my mother had hand-squeezed that morning while Cai was at the grocery store. I could almost taste the cool, tart beverage. I tried one more spoonful of soup, but I couldn't muster another sip. Cai saw me place my spoon on the plastic placemat shaped like a watermelon slice.

"Why aren't you eating?" His words interrupted my daydream of lemons, sugar, and ice. "You need to eat."

"Those dishes have pork and eggs."

"So? Just take the pork out. When did you stop eating eggs?"

"I don't feel like eggs. And when I eat food cooked with pork, I can still taste it even if I pick around it."

"*Máfan.*" I didn't know if he meant I was troublesome or if he was referring to my picky eating habits, but I couldn't gather the strength to argue, especially in front of my parents who were still acting like everything was normal. I always was uncomfortable bickering with Cai, but especially in front of my mom and dad. After all, they had not only given up their summer to help us with household chores like laundry and cleaning, but had also purchased most of Jake's clothes and baby supplies.

Most of all, I didn't want to argue with Cai because I thought, for Jake's sake, we should behave civilly to one another. Although he couldn't understand what we said, Jake would be able to sense distress if we fought. But my worries about Jake being distressed vanished after we finished lunch and Cai walked into the living room to watch television. As we cleared the dishes from the kitchen table, I unleashed a rant my parents had never before heard from me, while rocking Jake in his car seat.

"I can't believe he's being so difficult. I'm the one who just had a baby, not him. I just want to eat what I want, not some god-awful fish head soup with those disgusting smoked dates. I never thought I'd be stuck in China after we left Hong Kong."

My mom stopped placing dishes on the kitchen counter. "Have you talked to Cai about this?"

"What's the point? He's listening to the neighbors over me. If they say I need to eat pig feet, he asks how many. We never talked about these postpartum customs before Jake was born. I wish I had had some warning."

Even though Cai was in the other room, supposedly watching Chinese television, I didn't lower my voice. I wanted him to hear my anger. Since coming home from the hospital, I felt like my emotions were more volatile than ever. Every night I cried tears of joy just looking at Jake. Now I felt a rage burning inside like a hundred red firecrackers. I didn't know it at the time, but after each of my pregnancies, I would come down with the baby blues, a dramatic shift in emotions after giving birth and suddenly losing all the new hormones my body had built up over nine months.

"Calm down. Do you want to talk to him in front of us, or alone?"

"I don't want to talk to him at all. Every time I try to speak with him nicely about something he doesn't want to do, he yells at me or gives me the silent treatment. I don't want to fight. I just want to do whatever will make my life—and Jake's—peaceful."

My dad placed a stack of rice bowls in the sink. "He probably feels so isolated here. You've had tremendous life changes these few months: a move across the world, a new house, new jobs, and now a baby. Each of these things can be difficult to adjust to, but put them all together, and no one could make a smooth transition."

"I've told him that many times, but he just doesn't listen. He hasn't even tried to find a good job."

"Dad is right," my mom said. "You are going through incredible changes. Even if Cai doesn't acknowledge it, I'm sure he's trying in his own way. He's become involved in the Chinese music community and he's learned to drive. He can find his way around the whole Bay Area now and has made new friends. Those aren't insignificant achievements. He's probably upset he hasn't been able to provide for the family. I know you don't care about that, but many men do."

It felt good to vent to my parents and to know it was normal to feel frustrated. I didn't want them to tell me to leave Cai, and I didn't want that myself. But I wished Cai would act more like an equal spouse instead of a surly housemate. From three years of marriage, I could look back and see that there were two Cais: the one who was happy in Hong Kong, and the one in China who gave me the silent treatment and took his professors' sides when they made me feel uncomfortable.

What my mom said about feeling helpless about not supporting the family could be true to some extent, but that hadn't been the reason for his bad behavior in China. But my parents were correct about Cai—and me—experiencing many life changes all at once. Maybe I was overreacting. Who could complain about a comfortable house in San Francisco, a job that gave me excellent health benefits, a beautiful, healthy new baby, and a caring mother and father?

After I returned to the living room with Jake, the doorbell rang. We weren't expecting company so I was still dressed in my blue cotton nightgown, my postpartum costume de rigueur. I placed Jake in his car seat and pulled on a long burgundy sweater. When I peered through the peephole, two unrecognizable Chinese women and a Chinese man stared back at me. I turned toward the sofa where Cai sat reading a Chinese newspaper. "I think your friends are here."

Cai opened the door and greeted these friends I'd never met, his eyes and smile illuminating the dusky room. He introduced them to my parents and me. "This is Miss Chen Xiaohong, Miss Liu Bingying, and Mr. Liao Gang."

After Cai emceed for Yuhan's performance, he signed up for a few more shows. His deep voice, movie-star looks, and tall stature made him a sought-after emcee in the Bay Area. He rarely got paid for these performances, and when he did, it was an honorarium of fifty or a hundred dollars. But he was making a name for himself and I hoped he'd eventually find paying jobs in the field. These were friends he had met in the Chinese music community.

Mr. Liao handed Cai a shopping bag while Miss Chen sashayed into the living room on her long, thin flamingo legs. She carried a cardboard egg flat, the type found in produce markets, holding thirty-six light brown eggs. I led her into the kitchen, where she gently placed it on the tiled kitchen counter.

"For you." She was pretty with shining hair and almond eyes that delicately tilted up.

"Thank you." What else could I say? No one had ever brought me three dozen eggs before.

Back in the living room, Miss Liu lifted Jake out of his car seat without asking. She held him up and his shirt bottom separated from his pants, exposing his midriff, taped umbilical cord and all. Liu turned to me with a grave look on her face. "*Ay yo*. You have to cover his belly button. He could get sick."

Cai's friends visited for about thirty minutes. After they left, I pulled out two outfits with matching hats from the bag Liao had brought. A slit down the seat of each pair of pants rendered them useless to us. I knew from my trips to China that these pants would expose Jake's diaper in back. In China, even in the 1990s, it wasn't the custom to use disposable diapers, so parents trained their children much earlier with pants like these. Young children could just sit and squat, relieving themselves where they pleased. I tucked Jake's new pants under a few baby blankets on the high shelf in one of the guest closets, never to be used.

Chapter 32

TRYING TRADITIONS

On Jake's eighth day, my parents and I prepared for his bris. For the special occasion, my mom's eighty-two-year-old mother, Adeline, had flown in the previous day. My parents' friends Larry and Judy lived an hour or so north in Sonoma County and had driven down as well. They had introduced my parents to each other thirty years earlier.

My grandmother peeked out of our living room window after a rotund man stepped from a brown sedan out front, his salt-and-pepper beard hanging to the bottom of his torso. She turned to me. "Where did your father *find* him?"

"He asked around the Jewish delis. This guy is supposedly the Elvis of mohels." I stared through the white curtains, just enough to take a longer glance at the stranger who was about to perform Jake's bris.

Stepping inside, his protruding belly entering first, the mohel nodded a quick greeting to me under his black hat and headed toward my father, who had been looking forward to this milestone for his first grandchild. The mohel stood in the dining room, explaining the ceremony to us. Cai, who had seemed calm all morning, nodded his head as if he understood the mohel.

After speaking English exclusively with me for three years, Cai's Chinese accent had whittled down to just enough to reveal he wasn't a native speaker. But he didn't always understand what others said in English, especially in a new context. And no matter how willing Cai had been to go along with the bris, I wondered if he really grasped what it would entail.

We leaned against a wall, standing in a line, while Larry cradled Jake in his arms. The mohel set up his instruments and placed a cup of kosher red wine on the dining room table. He chanted a prayer and then instructed Larry to pass Jake to my father and then down the line until he reached Cai and me. We carried Jake to the mohel, who placed him on a blanket on our naked dining room table. Dipping his right pinky into the wine, the mohel rested this finger in Jake's mouth to give him a taste of wine—and to numb the oncoming pain.

My dad and Larry walked toward the table, standing behind the mohel while Judy, my mom, grandmother, and I gathered against the wall, choosing not to look. Cai, aware Jake's foreskin was about to be cut, hovered between the women and the men. I thought it best if he stood back with me. But when I saw how Cai's face beamed with pride in his son, I remained silent.

I didn't know the mohel had clipped Jake's foreskin until a piercing scream filled the room. I looked toward the table and saw him place another wine-dipped pinky in Jake's mouth to ease the pain. My grandmother sighed in relief as the mohel dressed Jake's affected area with Neosporin and gauze, encasing it in his diaper.

"You can give him a little Tylenol," he told us as he finished zipping Jake's sleeper, his voice overpowering Jake's whimpers. "Change the dressings every time you change his diaper. Dab a little Neosporin on a fresh piece of gauze. He'll probably sleep for the rest of the afternoon." The mohel handed Jake to me.

But Cai's face, a moment ago calm and relaxed, now transformed back into the look he wore months earlier in the Colma BART station. Tears flowed from his eyes, as if he were lost in a foreign country with no friends or family and longed to be in a familiar place. I'd had these same feelings in Hidden River, but this was different. My unhappiness hadn't involved our newborn child. I understood that Jake's pain was only temporary and that the bris was important to my father and to our traditions. I also grasped how foreign this concept was for Cai. Jake would be fine, but I knew that I needed to attend to Cai before he descended into another funk.

My mom was engaged in a conversation with Larry and Judy, while my dad and grandma spoke with the mohel. No one else seemed to notice that Cai was crying, so I tried to soothe him before it blew up into a bigger deal. "It'll be okay. Jake only felt the pain for a second. See, he's not crying now."

Cai shook his head like a child refusing his parents' orders. "It hurt him. He cried so much. We're never doing this to another baby."

I lightly stroked Jake's wisps of baby hair. But then Cai pulled Jake from me and marched into the den. Hunched over like a weeping willow, Cai cradled Jake in his arms. I saw Cai's pursed lips and closed eyes, and knew enough to give him space. Back in the living room, my mom interrupted her conversation with Judy. "Where is Cai?"

"He's in the den with Jake. He seems pretty upset about the bris."

"I'm sorry. I know it's such an unfamiliar idea."

"Jake is sleeping and seems fine. When we see Dr. Kwok next week, he'll check to see that it's healing properly." I was confident Jake would be fine but still worried about Cai.

Just then Cai stormed by, his eyes focused on the floor as if he'd had a quarrel with someone. I checked the den to see if anyone was there. It was empty except for Jake, sleeping soundly in his car seat. When I turned back toward Cai, he had already stomped upstairs. I wanted to reassure him again that Jake was no longer in pain, but from experience, I knew he needed time to settle down on his own.

Later that evening, Mr. Huang, a friend of Cai's from Wuhan who now lived in San Francisco, stopped by. Cai ushered him into the kitchen and introduced him to lox and bagels, including how to spread the cream cheese and where to place the tomatoes and onions. He'd calmed down, and thankfully, Jake didn't cry again that day.

Chapter 33

A PARENTAL INVASION

Halfway into my parents' stay that summer, Cai and I applied for tourist visas for Mama and Baba. Cai gleamed at the prospect of his parents living with us for a year, but I half hoped that their visa application would be denied. I was ashamed to feel that way, but I worried that their presence might drive Cai further into home-sickness, reminding him of what he'd left in China: the food, the conversations, the culture. If Cai's parents suggested we all move back to China and I refused, would Mama really want to leave San Francisco without Jake after bonding with him for a year?

One evening my parents and I huddled around Cai in the kitchen while he dialed his parents' number in Hidden River. Jake slept soundly in his car seat. We knew that Mama and Baba had just returned from their visa interview at the U.S. Embassy in Beijing. Cai greeted his parents on the phone but remained silent for minutes as his parents spoke. Was it unsuccessful and were they trying to lessen Cai's disappointment? I would need to start looking for a day care that could take Jake at the end of the summer.

Suddenly Cai laughed out loud and pumped his fist in the air. Mama and Baba would be coming to San Francisco instead!

My parents cheered like fans at a basketball championship game.

"This is great," my mom said to me. "Jake will get to know his other grandparents and won't have to go to day care for another year."

With a forced smile, I hugged Cai after he got off the phone. But his laughter was contagious, and I soon chided myself for ever having hoped Mama and Baba wouldn't be able to come. My mother was right. No one would love and care for Jake as much as his other set of doting grandparents.

I returned to work a couple weeks before my parents drove back to Chicago. There was a two-week gap between their departure and Mama and Baba's arrival. Cai would be responsible for taking care of Jake during that time. After he had quit his newspaper job, Cai became involved with a group that was organizing a Chinese concert for the following spring. They always met in the late afternoon or at night.

On Cai's first day alone with Jake, I returned home to find Cai disheveled and exhausted, his eyes bloodshot. He excused himself to take a shower, grabbing a handful of almonds on his way upstairs. "I haven't eaten all day."

"Cai, you can bring Jake in the bathroom while you shower. I do it all the time. And there's no reason you can't eat while you're looking after Jake."

It had been a difficult day for me, too, returning to a job I didn't love and leaving my baby home when all I wanted was to stay with him. I cried when I pumped milk twice that day in a kitchen galley that didn't lock. My boss shunned personal phone calls, so I could only call home for a minute when she and the rest of the office left for lunch. When I came home at six the next day, Cai dashed upstairs for his shower. Again, he hadn't eaten that day.

"*Méiyǒu yìsi*," Cai lamented that evening as we watched Chinese TV after a quick dinner of instant noodles.

"What has no meaning?"

"This." He looked around the room. "This life. Staying home all day, not working, not having friends—"

"But you've made many friends here. More than I have. And you have the rest of your life to work, so you should enjoy this time with Jake. Many dads wish they could stay home with their kids, but they can't because their jobs aren't flexible. You're lucky you have this time now."

"In China, friends come over every night for talking and chatting. It's so *rènào* there, but here there's no meaning. It's so quiet in the house. The friends here aren't even good."

I tried to remain supportive, all while digesting what he had just said about there being no meaning in our house. I felt sad and frustrated that Cai found no meaning in staying home with Jake when that was all I wanted to do. As a new mother, I didn't want to leave my home or my baby for eleven hours a day, so this arrangement wasn't easy on me, either. But instead of voicing my feelings, I said, "If they're such bad friends, why do you drive a hundred miles every night to see them?"

Cai ignored my question and repeated, "I don't know how long I can stay here."

"Your parents will be here in two weeks. Once they arrive, you'll feel more at home." But a larger question loomed in my mind. What would happen after they left a year later?

When your mother-in-law sits
You should respectfully stand;
Obey quickly her commands.

—Ban Zhao
Instruction for Chinese Women and Girls

Chapter 34
BATTLING THE TIGER MOTHER

On the day Mama and Baba were to arrive in San Francisco, I woke early to track their flight on our erratic dial-up Internet connection. Cai and I sat down for breakfast while Jake rested contentedly in his car seat on the floor next to us. I dug into my bowl of cornflakes as Cai sipped coffee and buttered a bagel.

"I'm going to a party at Chen Xiaohong's in San Jose tonight, but I won't have to leave until five," he said.

Tonight? "What about your parents?"

And what's so important about Chen Xiaohong's house? I wanted to add. Chen Xiaohong was the woman who'd brought me three dozen eggs after Jake was born.

"My parents will be okay." He laughed. "They'll be tired. Xiaohong is hosting this party so we can discuss plans for Chinese music activities in the Bay Area."

The purpose of the meeting sounded reasonable. "But what about dinner? I don't think Mama and Baba will like the food I make."

"I'll cook dinner before I leave. Then they can take a rest."

We arrived at San Francisco International Airport an hour before their plane was to land. The arrivals hall at the international terminal teemed with anxious family members waiting for loved ones to clear customs. I stood with Jake, his car seat secured in his stroller, while

Cai paced the narrow passageway in front of the doors separating the arrivals hall from customs.

When passengers started trickling through the security doors, Cai and I stood at attention. His mouth twitched in nervous excitement, and my hands gripped the handles on Jake's stroller. After what seemed like hours, Mama and Baba strolled through the security doors. They didn't look like peasants fresh off the boat. Their heads held high, they appeared to be seasoned travelers, full of confidence.

"*Yan.*" Mama screamed when she spotted Cai.

He ran to Mama, taking her carry-on and placing an arm around her shoulder.

"*Nǐ hǎo, nǐ hǎo.*" Baba bobbed up and down. He peered into the stroller at a quiet, wide-eyed Jake, and giggled.

Mama greeted me with a smile and then looked at Jake. "*Ay yo. Tā zhēn tīnghuà.*" He's so obedient.

Cai took the giant suitcase from Baba as we made our way to the garage. The five of us piled into our Civic, Mama in the back with Jake and me, and Baba up front with Cai. Driving up Highway 101, Cai wove through the dense Saturday afternoon traffic while Mama gushed over Jake, laughing happily. Baba marveled at how well Cai navigated the streets and steered our car. We exited at Paul Avenue, turning onto San Bruno Avenue, where I pointed out the Chinese barbecue shops, a dim sum restaurant, and a Chinese grocery.

At home, Cai set about dicing and chopping garlic, ginger, green onion, and tofu before heating the oil in our wok. Mama and Baba oohed and aahed as I showed them their room and the hall bathroom they would use for the next year.

We sat down to a late lunch of sautéed tofu and minced pork, canned sardines and black soy beans swimming in oil, stir-fried tofu and green onion, and chicken and tomato soup. That's when Cai broke the news to Mama and Baba about his party that evening.

"You won't be here for dinner?" Mama sounded disappointed.

"I'll eat at the party. You're tired and should go to bed first."

Mama and Baba nodded and started in on a second can of sardines.

The next morning, they found me in the kitchen as I finished nursing Jake, sitting in the calming sun. Mama pulled up a chair next to me, while Baba made himself a cup of tea from our hot water thermos.

"Is Yan still sleeping?"

"Yes. He came home pretty late, but he should be up soon."

"When did he get home?

"A little after two." I didn't mean to be a tattletale, but they asked and I didn't see a reason to protect Cai. After all, these were his parents and he had left them on their first night away from China.

Mama and Baba looked at one another. "That's too late." Mama pouted.

I shrugged, secretly glad she was on my side. "It's normal for him. His friends live an hour away."

In Hidden River, Mama and Baba ate noodle soup for breakfast, so while Cai slept, I showed them our noodles, garlic, green onion, ginger, and leftover dishes from lunch and dinner, which they'd use as a soup base. Baba set to work on their breakfast while Mama burped Jake.

Two hours later, Cai strolled downstairs while his parents and I were watching Chinese television and Jake was sleeping in his car seat. Mama stood to greet Cai. "You should come home earlier."

"*Bùyàojǐn.*" Cai brushed her off, saying it didn't matter, and headed toward the kitchen. He might not have thought it was important, but I was grateful for Mama's reprimand. At least I wasn't the only one uncomfortable with him staying out until the early morning. It's true I had encouraged Cai to meet people in the Chinese music community and knew these late meetings were crucial for networking. But I hadn't planned for him to be out almost every night, and certainly not that late.

Once I took the job at UCSF, we were able to afford cell phones. So now Cai had a way of contacting me from the car. I worried less about him wandering around the Bay Area by himself. But I wondered how these late-night excursions would affect Jake. When Jake was older, would his dad ever be home at night?

During the week, I left the house at seven in the morning to catch the bus downtown. Cai's day, on the other hand, often didn't begin until six in the evening when he picked me up at the Sixteenth or the Twenty-Fourth Street BART station. Later at night, after dinner, he would drive down to San Jose, Mountainview, or another city in the South Bay, often traveling a hundred miles round-trip.

But no matter when Cai left the house, Mama always greeted me the same when I returned home.

"*Tā bù chī.*" Mama's eyes would bulge, telling me that Jake didn't eat that day.

"Well, he nurses all night and his diapers are always soaked in the morning. Are they dry during the day?"

"No, they're wet."

"Then he's eating plenty."

"He should eat more during the day. It's not enough to just eat at night."

That's crazy. If he ate thirty ounces at night, why shouldn't he eat less during the day? But arguing with Mama seemed futile. Every day we clashed over the same issue. I cringed when Mama came running into the living room when I came up from the garage. It was hard enough to be away from Jake all day. I just wanted to spend time with my baby and felt worn down by Mama's unrelenting angst. But there was nowhere to escape. Cai and Baba disappeared with Jake into the kitchen as soon as Mama started haranguing me.

I also clashed with Cai's parents over Jake's clothing. One day after work, I peeled three layers off Jake's small body, leaving on his cotton onesie. Perspiration covered his forehead and his hair was so sweaty that he looked like he'd just come from a bath. Baba usually was calm and comfortable living in the periphery, but he rushed up to me. "It's cold outside. He needs all those clothes."

"I know, but it's hot inside." I pointed toward the thermostat, which controlled the central heat in our house.

"He'll freeze with just one layer."

But it wasn't cold inside. I didn't know how else I could explain central heat and how the outside temperature could be 50 degrees and the inside 72 degrees. Cai stood by, mute as a stone statute.

"I'll call the doctor and see what he says." I picked up the phone and dialed Kwok's number, which I knew by heart after making Jake's many well-baby appointments. The pediatrician kept evening office hours a couple nights a week, and luckily that night was one of them.

"Sorry to bother you, Dr. Kwok, but I have a question about clothing Jake. He's five months old, about seventeen pounds, and we keep our house at seventy-two degrees. How many layers should he wear indoors?"

"If you have central heat, a diaper and T-shirt are enough when he's awake. At night he can wear a medium-weight sleeper. Make sure he's not too hot."

I thanked Dr. Kwok and relayed his message to my in-laws and Cai after hanging up.

"*What?*" Baba violently pulled down his collar and revealed a thick sweater I hadn't noticed before. Under that he showed a thermal undershirt. "If I wear all these layers, there's no way Jake can wear just a diaper and T-shirt."

I stared at Baba's layers. How did he not pass out in all those clothes? He wore the same clothes here with central heat as he did in Hidden River without as much as a space heater. Could he really not tell the difference?

Baba lovingly replaced Jake's layers and rocked him in his arms as if he were protecting him from a life of destitution. There was no point in picking a battle with Baba, the only semblance of calmness in this anxious household. I would wait to undress Jake after bringing him upstairs for bed a couple of hours later. Just as when Cai admonished me not to take a shower for a month after Jake's birth, I pretended to agree but would do as I wished once I put Jake to bed.

If my in-laws' protests about Jake's eating and clothing weren't stressful enough, his sleeping habits capped the trifecta of cultural child care differences I endured with them. Mama and Baba arrived in San Francisco a couple weeks shy of Jake's third month, before he'd developed a regular sleeping pattern. Jake enjoyed catnaps in his car seat throughout the day and longer stretches of sleep in the confined quarters of his bassinet at night.

During Jake's fourth and fifth months, when he should have learned to soothe himself to sleep and use his crib during the day, Mama and Baba played cards or watched Chinese soap operas as they rocked Jake to sleep in his car seat. When Jake outgrew the car seat as a bed, Mama or Baba cradled him in their arms until he dozed off. Because of this, at around five months, he started having difficulty falling asleep.

One rare evening when Cai didn't go out, I brought Jake upstairs a little before 8:00 p.m., the time he usually started to wind down. Jake thrashed about and couldn't seem to settle himself to sleep. I brought him back downstairs where Cai and his parents sat mesmerized before a Chinese nighttime soap opera, thinking that he must not be tired yet.

The loud voices from the television didn't help Jake calm down. He cried and arched his back when I held him in my arms. Mama stood before me and clapped her hands twice. She then held them out in front of her, waiting for me to hand Jake over.

I shook my head. "It's okay. I'll just bring him upstairs again. He needs to learn to sleep in his crib." But when I put him in his crib, his screams filled the house, sending Cai sprinting up to our bedroom.

"What's wrong with Jake?" Cai yelped.

"Nothing's wrong. I'm just trying to get him to sleep in his crib."

Cai cradled Jake in his long arms, swaying like a hammock in the wind. He bent his head over Jake, his lips pursed and eyes closed like a meditating monk.

"I think we need to let him fall asleep on his own," I said. "This isn't a good habit."

Continuing to rock Jake in rhythmic motions, Cai ignored me. If he wasn't going to speak to me, I wasn't going to argue with him. Fighting about this wouldn't help Jake sleep any faster. So I left Cai to calm Jake, joining Mama and Baba back downstairs. I knew that I'd have to get Jake to sleep on his own, especially because Cai often wasn't home when Jake went to bed. I would start sleep training when Cai was at one of his meetings.

Ten minutes later, Cai vaulted downstairs like a victorious hero, finding Mama and Baba engrossed in another mainland soap opera. All three of them watched the show as I strained my eyes to read by the light of the only floor lamp.

Just then I heard a shrill cry from above.

Cai and his parents, eyes glued to the TV, didn't look up as I climbed the stairs.

I spent the rest of the night lying in bed, trying to nurse Jake to sleep. Every time it seemed like I could creep away to join the family downstairs, Jake stirred and began crying again. I ended up falling asleep next to him and didn't wake up until my alarm clock sounded the next morning.

The next evening, I came home to find that Mama had dressed Jake in four layers. Before I had walked two steps toward the kitchen, she started in on Jake's failure to eat. I knew I couldn't convince her that Jake was perfectly healthy, so I simply smiled and made my way to the kitchen where Cai was feeding Jake in the high chair. During dinner later, I told Cai and his parents that I thought we should let Jake cry when we put him to bed at night so he could learn to fall asleep on his own.

"It's not going to hurt him," I said. "He'll be fine."

"Jake will get sick!" Mama interjected. "He can't cry."

"That's not true." *Stay calm*, I told myself. Me getting upset wouldn't lessen Mama's hysteria. "All babies cry. You had four and I'm sure they cried."

Mama's eyes bulged and her lips pursed like Cai's did when he got upset. She glared at me as if I'd just sentenced Jake to a life of hard labor, not to a comfortable crib in a quiet part of the house, away from the blasting television spewing overdramatized dialogue from Chinese soap operas. Sometimes I wondered how Mama had raised four kids, many of them without Baba's help since he was stationed to teach in another village during the last half of the 1960s.

"She's right," Cai jumped in. "Jake shouldn't cry."

Are you kidding me? First I couldn't put my own baby to sleep the way I thought best and now Cai was defending his *mother*. What had happened to the supportive husband back in Hidden River who told his mother to stop badgering me about my eating habits and about raising our baby while we lived elsewhere?

Never one to be overly patriotic, I suddenly felt like screaming that we were in America, not central China. I knew that Mama and Baba, and even Cai, worked hard to take care of Jake and that their ideas of how to raise a baby were voiced with Jake's best interests in mind. But for a moment I wanted to remind them that none of us would be able to live in this house if it weren't for me. I exhaled slowly, trying to stay rational.

"He's my baby," I said slowly and softly. "I want him to be able to sleep on his own."

"Jake is my baby, too," Cai spat. "Grandmothers, mothers, they're all the same. If my mother doesn't want Jake to cry, he won't cry."

If your mother is the same as me, you should have married her. Mama and Baba stood in silence, staring at the linoleum floor. I wished they would stand up for me just once.

Interactions like these began to make me feel more like a lowly daughter-in-law in a Chinese backwater town where I had no rights and no say. I desperately needed to redirect my role at home, but trouble continued to greet me every time I walked in the front door after work, even after Mama and Baba had lived with us for a few months. Mama never stopped lamenting Jake's poor eating habits, which seemed to contradict his 80th and 90th percentiles for height and weight.

After Jake turned six months old, he started to eat rice cereal and jarred pureed baby food. He still nursed throughout the night and woke with a diaper so saturated that most mornings, I found glistening crystals in the fat folds in his groin.

The only thing that saved me from going out of my mind was my parents' upcoming visit during their spring vacation in mid-March. Only a little while longer, and there would be people in the house who would stand up for me unconditionally and be on my side.

Chapter 35
A LETTER FROM YOSHIMOTO

Soon after the Chinese New Year, which we celebrated with a large dinner at home, Cai greeted me with "Great news!" as I walked through the door after work.

Had he found a job? Although he continued working with his friends to produce the grand concert for later that spring, he had also been talking about looking for a full-time job. Mama had started pestering me to find one for him so I sent out a few inquiries to community colleges for teaching jobs, even though they were positions for which Cai had shown little interest. Now I felt hopeful. Maybe one of these had come through.

Cai's eyes glowed for the first time in months. I could barely stand the wait.

"Japanese Father is coming to visit!"

"When?" My voice simultaneously squealed and cracked. Coming to visit meant staying with us. Yet as unappealing as it sounded to me, what could I do? Yoshimoto had given Cai all that money. I was fairly sure Cai had told Mama and Baba about the money, but for them that amount seemed no different from the $13,000 my grandmother had given us to buy a car. Both Yoshimoto's money and my grandmother's gift were more than anyone in Cai's family would see in a lifetime. For once, I was happy to have a full-time job so my interaction with Yoshimoto would be minimal.

"Next month. I just got his letter."

"When next month?"

"Let me see." Smiling, he took two sheets of tissue-thin writing paper from the dining room table and skimmed black ink-brushed Chinese characters until he found the dates. "It's the fourteenth through the twenty-first."

My stomach turned over. Leave it to Yoshimoto to plan his trip the very week my parents were scheduled to visit. I never imagined that Cai would tell Yoshimoto when my family planned to visit—so Japanese Father could schedule his trips to see Cai at the same time—but later I did wonder about that. Had it been a simple coincidence, or had Cai requested Yoshimoto's presence to avoid spending time with my family?

Cai's smile quickly turned to a frown. "What's wrong with you? You have that face again."

I have that face? "My parents are coming that week. I told you a month ago." They only had one week of spring vacation.

"That's okay. We have enough room."

"We do? Mama and Baba are in one room, and my parents will be in another. Where will Japanese Father sleep?"

"Can American parents sleep on the living room sofa bed?"

My parents would be willing to do that and would be polite to the professor, just as they had been in China and in Hong Kong. *Yoshimoto's radar strikes again*, I imagined my mom saying when I told her the news. They wouldn't complain, but I wasn't sure I could remain so composed.

🍵 ☕ 🍵

On the day of Japanese Father's arrival, around the same time I was looking forward to my parents' impending visit, I returned home after work to find Mama, Baba, Yoshimoto, and Cai at the kitchen table, their chopsticks lazily strewn across their bowls. Jake sat in his high chair, an empty jar of baby food on his tray. Uncharacteristically Mama didn't bombard me with Jake's failure to eat or drink milk during the day.

I smiled at Yoshimoto. "Nice to see you again."

He looked at me and squeaked something unintelligible while Cai stood up from his chair. "I'm so sorry. Japanese Father was hungry, so we just ate some congee. I'll heat yours up now."

"No worries. I'm going to change my clothes." I took Jake and headed upstairs. *This is going to be a long week if the man barely speaks to me.*

I placed Jake on my bedroom floor while I changed into a pair of sweatpants and a T-shirt. When we returned to the kitchen, Yoshimoto and Cai were headed toward the dining room.

"Japanese Father is very tired. I'm going to show him to his room now. I'll heat your dinner up in a couple minutes."

Mama and Baba remained seated at the kitchen table, Mama clapping her hands twice and extending them toward me, which was Chinese sign language for "I want to hold your baby." I heated some congee and ate it with salty sardines and black bean sauce, pickled Sichuan radishes, and a dish of leftover ground beef and frozen vegetables.

"Your parents are coming tomorrow?" Mama asked.

"Yes, in the afternoon. Cai's going to pick them up at the airport around two." I had been counting down the days to their arrival and was thrilled it was less than twenty-four hours away. It was a busy time at work, so I couldn't take vacation days while my parents were in town. Still, it would be a treat to spend time at night and on the weekends with people who would neither pester me about Jake's eating habits nor ignore me.

The next morning when I stepped into the upstairs hallway to take Jake downstairs, I noticed the light in Yoshimoto's room peeping under the bottom of his door. By the time I left the house, he had yet to emerge.

When I returned home after work, my parents greeted me as I walked in. "We waited to eat with you," my mom said as we walked into the kitchen.

"Japanese Father was hungry, so I cooked him dinner first," Cai said apologetically.

On Yoshimoto's fourth morning, my phone rang at work. I was surprised to hear Cai's voice, since he didn't normally phone me at work. I usually snuck in a call to check on Jake during my morning breast-milk-pumping break. Although I used to call home from my desk when my boss left for lunch, I now would use my lunch hour to get out of the office for a while, too, to walk or window-shop with coworkers. These outside jaunts became the only time when I felt like I lived a normal life in San Francisco. For an hour I could leave behind both an unsatisfying job and a stressful family life.

"You'll never guess where we are!" Cai shouted on his cell phone above what sounded like gusty wind.

"Where?"

"Calistoga! Japanese Father wanted to enjoy the hot springs. It's beautiful here." Something muffled in the background, but then Cai came back. "Don't wait up for us tonight. We'll be back late."

Before I could reply, the call dropped. Cai and I had never spent a weekend away, had never gone on a day trip, just the two of us, and had never visited a resort area. How dare he jaunt off to Calistoga with that man!

When Yoshimoto left San Francisco a few days later, he had spoken a total of two sentences to me. A couple years later, I would relay my thoughts to a friend back in Hong Kong. Via email we would discuss Yoshimoto's bizarre behavior. My friend reminded me that people in Japan do not touch one another in public. They would bow instead of shaking hands. So when Yoshimoto rested his head on Cai's shoulder at the Wuhan airport, my friend thought that crossed a boundary. Too afraid to learn the truth, and confident that Cai wouldn't tell me anyway, I never asked him what went on between the two of them in China, Hong Kong, or Calistoga.

Chapter 36

"WHY DO YOU NEED MOTHER'S DAY?"

Families in China didn't celebrate Mother's Day, or Father's Day for that matter. When I told Mama about the holiday, she seemed baffled by the concept. "What do you do for Mother's Day?" she asked, her eyes bright and curious.

"Most families go to a restaurant. Kids buy their mothers gifts like candy or flowers or make something for them at school."

Cai understood the importance of this celebration and planned a special outing for my first Mother's Day. He thought it would be nice for the five of us to drive down to Palo Alto. We would walk around the gardenlike Stanford campus and have an early dinner at a nearby Chinese restaurant. Mama and Baba preferred to cook their own meals and couldn't believe the exorbitant prices in San Francisco for simple Chinese barbecue. So we rarely went out to eat. But when Cai described the sprawling Stanford campus, Mama's eyes lit up in delight. She wanted to go.

Before we left in the early afternoon, Mama and Cai put together a light lunch. Jake sat in his high chair between Mama and me. I alternated between feeding baby food to Jake and digging into my own lunch of dried tofu and green onion, a chicken-based noodle soup, and the ubiquitous canned sardines. Mama fished a noodle from her rice bowl and cut it into inch-long pieces with her chopsticks. Just then, she picked up one piece and held it close to Jake's face. I put my hand up to stop her from placing the noodle in his mouth.

"No." My hand met the chopsticks in midair. "He's too young to eat noodles."

Ever since Jake was several months old, Mama had wanted to feed him table food. I had read too many articles about food allergies and how babies shouldn't eat table food until their first birthday. Thanks to my experience with Mama in Hidden River, I knew that I needed to set strict boundaries with her when it came to Jake's feeding. If I acquiesced to soft foods like rice or ground beef, I feared Mama and Baba and even Cai would stretch that to prohibited foods like eggs, tofu, and noodles. Even Dr. Kwok had recommended that we wait on table food until Jake turned one. With noodles came the added worry that Jake might choke.

Mama scrunched her eyes and nose. "Yan ate noodles when he was three months old."

"But Jake's doctor wants him to wait until he can chew better." And Yan was a baby during the Great Leap Forward, when forty-five million died of starvation. If we were living under those conditions, I would have done anything to feed my baby, too. But we were fortunate in the United States to have enough age-appropriate food for Jake.

Something else bothered me while we sat at the table eating lunch. While I processed acknowledgment letters and toiled in the filing room at work, I wondered if Mama and Baba were secretly exposing Jake to allergens. Or was today the first time they had tried to feed him table food?

I hated being separated from Jake during the day, and now I had an added worry. If Jake had an allergic reaction when I was at work and Cai was out, would Mama and Baba know what to do about it? The food on the table suddenly seemed unappetizing, so I placed my chopsticks next to my rice bowl and leaned back in my chair.

Cai slammed his fist on the table. "What are you doing?" he shouted in English to spare his parents from our argument, but his meaning was decipherable in any language.

I cringed at his violent outburst, but for once felt relieved we had an audience. Now Mama and Baba could see their son's despicable behavior. In response to Cai, I shrugged and said, "I'm not hungry anymore."

"You always want your way, Susan." He then placed his chopsticks next to his bowl. "My mom raised four kids in China. We were poor and had little to eat, but she did a great job."

"I know. I'm not saying she didn't. I just don't want Jake to develop food allergies. Dr. Kwok said—"

"I don't care what Dr. Kwok said." Cai pushed his chair back and stood up. "We're not going to Stanford today." He stormed out of the kitchen.

Mama and Baba continued eating, as if it were a normal meal and a friendly conversation. When Mama finished her rice, she looked at me like a child anxious to open her birthday presents. "What time are we going to Stanford?"

"We're not," I whispered in Mandarin, trying to hold back my tears as I handed Jake his sippy cup of water. I could tell that neither of them would go after Cai to reprimand him for his unacceptable outburst. They didn't need to understand English to comprehend what had just happened. Their way of coping was to dish out more soup and slurp it from their grease-coated rice bowls. If my child had just acted that way toward the mother of my grandson, I would have run after him and put him in his place, no matter what his age. For some reason, Mama and Baba didn't parent that way. I wondered if they had ever disciplined their precious son.

Cai came downstairs an hour later and told his parents that he had a meeting to attend in Union City. He didn't look at me. Neither parent questioned why he was going to a meeting when we had planned to spend the afternoon at Stanford. I held Jake tightly, willing Cai to leave the house. Part of me wished he would never come back.

The next day, I spent an hour emailing my parents about my dreadful Mother's Day. I relayed the argument over what to feed Jake and how Cai had stormed out of the kitchen, calling off our trip to Stanford. I told them how Mama and Baba just sat there without chiding Cai, and how they had a couple of chances to speak with him but never did. It was the first time I had complained about Cai since the time my hormones were out of whack after Jake was born.

With this Mother's Day account, I started a habit of emailing my parents first thing in the morning from my office. Between Cai and his mother, I always had something to gripe about: Jake's feeding and clothing, Cai's despair over not working, and his regular late nights out. Many times when I wrote these emails, I would look up at the clock on my screen and see that I'd spent more than an hour writing to my parents. My problems at home were starting to affect my job and my family's livelihood.

Chapter 37

PEACE AT LAST

My parents drove out from Chicago to help us for another summer, relieving Mama and Baba after they left San Francisco to return to Hidden River. Although I had dreaded Mama's daily barrages about Jake's eating habits, when faced with their departure, I felt sad to see them leave. I realized, perhaps too late to enjoy it, that I appreciated Mama and Baba's company.

We'd spent all those evenings bickering about our differences over Jake's diet, sleep habits, and how many layers of clothes to dress him in, but I'd also grown to appreciate their companionship when Cai went out at night and on weekend mornings when he slept in. Baba was a quiet ally and Mama spoke to me more than anyone else in our house except when my parents visited.

I knew I'd miss our nightly routine of watching the news from Beijing, followed by a nighttime soap before I took Jake upstairs. Mama and Baba could have applied for green cards to stay longer, but they preferred to return to their friends and family in Hidden River.

My mom drove all seven of us to the airport the morning of Mama and Baba's departure. It was a good thing my parents had a minivan that could fit us all. Once Cai had checked his parents' bags and received their boarding passes, he smiled and joked around with his father about the long flight and ensuing jet lag. Mama dabbed her eyes with a gray handkerchief she kept up her sleeve.

"It's okay, Mama," I said to her gently. "We'll send you photos of Jake." I made no mention of visiting Baba and her in Hidden

River. She also didn't say anything about it, nor did she bring up her earlier offers to care for Jake in Hidden River. I figured (admittedly with some relief) that perhaps we had finished that chapter of our lives and she had realized Jake's future was with us in San Francisco. Hopefully her silence was an acknowledgment of that. And to my knowledge, she and Baba had never tried to persuade Cai to return to China. Mama sniffled and blinked her eyes energetically to whisk away the tears forming in them.

"Mama, thank you for all your help. Cai and I are so happy you could stay with us and take care of Jake."

"*Mo shi, mo shi,*" Mama said in her local dialect. It's nothing, think nothing of it.

"Of course it's something. Thank you." I wasn't used to hugging or kissing Mama and Baba and didn't know if I should start now, but seeing Mama this upset made me want to embrace her and comfort her. My parents stood awkwardly off to the side, my mom holding on to the handle of Jake's stroller, the same stroller Mama and Baba had pushed Jake in for almost a year.

It was as if this simple gesture of holding onto Jake's stroller signified a change in regime, with my parents taking over Jake's care while I was at work. Although I was grateful my parents were able to help us with Jake for the whole summer, I felt a tear in my heart thinking about what Mama and Baba must be going through at that moment.

Cai looked at his watch. "You should probably go to your gate now," he told his parents in Mandarin. He then turned toward mine and repeated it in English.

My mom hugged Cai's mom good-bye and said a few thank-yous and good-byes in Mandarin. *Xièxiè, zàijiàn.* Since my mom hugged Mama, I followed suit, grasping her padded shoulders in my arms. I felt a tight squeeze and held back my tears. Although I didn't regret standing up for what I thought was best for Jake, in the end I wished our evenings hadn't been defined by those differences. Was Mama feeling the same?

My mother then hugged Baba good-bye, so I let go of Mama and embraced him, too. We'd never so much as shaken hands. Baba smiled when I let go, but I could tell from his sad eyes that this good-bye was not easy for them. I didn't know it then, but this farewell was the last time I would see them.

For the first few days after Mama and Baba had left, the house seemed empty, even though it contained four adults and an energetic one-year-old. Cai went on with his evening meetings and daytime shopping trips to the Chinese grocery in the Richmond district. He had resumed his porn viewing in San Francisco, so sometimes he would stop at a South of Market adult video store before heading home after his nighttime meetings. Before I knew it, my parents, who had been with us for more than two months, headed back to Chicago. Suddenly we found ourselves alone, just the three of us.

Chapter 38

TO DAY CARE OR
NOT TO DAY CARE?

My employer kept a list of licensed home day cares in the Bay Area, so after Mama and Baba returned to China, I requested names of caregivers near our house and near my office. Before my parents returned to Chicago, my mom thought it would make for a smooth transition if we secured a day-care provider while they were still in town. They could take Jake there for a week before starting on their drive back to Chicago. One Sunday I asked Cai if he wanted to join us on our first home day-care visit.

"No, you and Mom can go." Although I wanted this decision to be a joint one, I figured Cai trusted my judgment to find a suitable caregiver for Jake.

At the first day care, located in the basement of a house several blocks from our place, I spotted a long stream of ants marching single file from one side of the room to the other. My mom and I looked at each other and politely told the woman in charge that we had just started our search and would get back to her if we were interested.

The following weekend my mom, Jake, and I visited another day care near our house, on a quiet side street off Bayshore Boulevard. A porch with high walls was attached to the back of the basement facility. Laura, the owner, was a thirtysomething woman who had started the day care after being unable to find satisfactory care for her daughter. I was drawn to Laura's kind and bubbly personality, but thought we should still look at other day cares.

"The place is kind of small and a little dark," I told my mom as we started on our walk home.

"But the back porch lets in sunlight, unlike that first place. And it's a secure area for the kids to play in," my mom replied.

I still wanted to see other places, so one day after work, my mom met me near my office to check out a Russian-run home day care. The facility was spread out over three colorful rooms, each with bins overflowing with toys and musical instruments. Four providers cared for a group of twenty kids.

"We bring in a music teacher once a week," Katya, the owner, told us. "Then we have a gymnastics teacher another day each week."

"I'll talk to my husband, but I'm sure we'll get back to you soon." I imagined Jake learning to walk in this facility, surrounded by stimulating colors and nurturing caregivers. Although I had liked Laura, I was more drawn to the Russian day care for its planned activities and spacious rooms.

When we arrived home, Cai was finishing the last preparations for a four-course dinner. He still cooked most evenings when he was home. I couldn't wait to tell him that I'd found the perfect day care for Jake. But before I could finish describing the weekly music class, he interrupted me.

"I just talked to the neighbors. They know a Chinese day care near San Bruno Avenue." He sounded as if he had made a final decision and my input was cosmetic.

"Is it licensed?" I knew the Changs, who Cai still referred to as "the neighbors," sent their daughter to an unlicensed place. Unlicensed facilities, they explained, were cheaper. These day cares didn't receive government-funded food stipends and the teachers didn't need to pass CPR or other first-aid classes every year. They weren't inspected by the city, and there was no restriction on the teacher-to-student ratio. I would never consider sending Jake to an unlicensed day care.

"Yes, it's *licensed*." He spit out the last word.

"Does the woman speak Mandarin?"

"I think so." Cai reached for a newspaper; he was finished with this conversation. Even though I wasn't thrilled with the way Cai had told me about this day care, I did like the idea of Jake continuing to hear Mandarin during the day. If it were really licensed, it could be a good fit for him.

"What do you know about her?" I asked.

He looked up from the paper. "The neighbors' friends send their kids there. They say it's a little cold in the winter."

"Why is it cold?"

"I guess the basement doesn't have heat."

"That doesn't sound good. I don't want Jake to be cold all winter."

"It doesn't get that cold here. We can just put more clothes on him."

I supposed we couldn't lose anything by just looking at the day care. "Do you have her number? I'll call to make an appointment."

"I'll call." He continued reading the paper.

The following week, Cai, my parents, and I walked with Jake in his stroller to Mrs. Lim's house on the other side of San Bruno. When we rang the doorbell, a girl no older than five answered.

I peered over her head, expecting to encounter Mrs. Lim. But all I saw was a younger boy wandering to the front door.

"Is Mrs. Lim here?"

"Yes." The girl opened the door.

We followed her to the back, through the basement, and found ourselves in a dark room where several kids sat in front of a TV. The open back door led to a spacious yard. Mrs. Lim came in from the outside, while a middle-aged man stood before several preschool-aged children riding tricycles on naked concrete surrounded by shrubbery sprouting like patches of fur on a mangy dog.

Mrs. Lim nodded her head and shook my hand like a limp fish. She spoke to Cai in Cantonese.

I tapped Cai's shoulder as Mrs. Lim led us outside. "Does she speak English or Mandarin?"

"I'll ask."

The setting sun cast a red stream of light on a small puddle near some of the shrubbery. Three industrial-sized paint buckets stood near a layer of wooden planks covering a hole in the cement. Several nails sprouted from the wood, their points facing the sky. As the tricyclists neared the planks, I winced, hoping the kids wouldn't stumble on a stray rock and fly onto the boards, nails and all.

My mom peeked into the buckets while Cai held Jake and questioned Mrs. Lim in halting Cantonese. When he walked closer to me, I asked again if she spoke English or Mandarin.

"I don't think so."

"Well, can you find out? It'll be hard for me to communicate with her if she doesn't." Cai nodded quickly without looking at me, and I instantly regretted even asking that. There was no way we'd send Jake here.

After our tour, we reemerged on the street and headed home.

"She seemed very nice," my dad volunteered. Cai nodded proudly, as if Mrs. Lim were his star protégé.

I glanced at my mom, who rolled her eyes. Back at home, Cai slumped onto the sofa, turned on the television, and mumbled something about how we had found Jake a suitable day care.

"I'm not sure about her," I said. "She doesn't speak English or Mandarin. What if there's an emergency and she can't communicate with me? Or if I'm running late and she doesn't understand what I'm staying?"

"She could call me and I'll call you."

"But you're always out and might not get the call right away. I think it's too risky." It wasn't just the thought of leaving Jake in this woman's care that brought a lump to my throat. How could Cai think about sending his son to such a place? And why couldn't Cai and I discuss this matter like two responsible adults? His tired eyes showed a look of finality: he had made his decision and wanted Jake to go to this day care.

Even with my parents in close proximity, I felt afraid to speak to Cai about something I knew he wouldn't agree with. I had thought talking to him would become easier after we had Jake, but if anything, it had become more difficult. I felt nauseous thinking about Jake spending his days in an environment so unsafe.

Later that evening, Cai left to meet his friends at a restaurant in the Sunset district. As I sat down with my parents and Jake to eat Cai's home-cooked leftovers, my mom broke some news about the day care.

"Those paint buckets were filled halfway with water. There's a drowning waiting to happen."

My appetite vanished. "Jake can't go there. Did you see those nails in the wooden boards? And why did those kids answer the door when Mrs. Lim was outside with her husband?"

My dad remained silent. He never liked to argue. I had always admired this quality, but now I wasn't so sure. My dad probably still thought Mrs. Lim was a nice woman, but Jake's well-being was my priority. I couldn't sit back in silence this time.

"I just don't know how to tell Cai we can't send Jake there. Despite my protests, Cai thinks the decision—his decision—is final. When I asked about the language barrier, he said he could be the go-between. That's never going to work." I slumped into my chair.

My mom's eyes focused on something in the distance, then back at me. "Do you want to have a family discussion? Then Cai might not be so quick to discount your opinion. There's no way Jake can go there."

"That would be great. I hate not being able to talk to him on my own."

"I know." My mom nodded in empathy. "He's still getting adjusted to life here. It's only been a little over a year. That's a short time in the long run."

I hoped what she said was true, and remembered what it felt like being isolated in Hidden River. Even though he hadn't been supportive of me in China, I would be supportive of him in San Francisco. For Jake's sake, I needed Cai to acclimate. I would do whatever I could to see that happen. But first I had to convince Cai that we couldn't send Jake to Mrs. Lim's.

The next day, while my mom baked lasagna, I joined Cai in the living room where he soaked up the evening news rebroadcast from Beijing. "Cai, my parents have some concerns about Mrs. Lim and want to discuss it with us."

He nodded as if I'd just told him I was running to the store to pick up a gallon of milk.

"I think they want to talk about it before dinner." Just then, my parents entered from the kitchen.

My mom reiterated what I'd told Cai: she and my dad had some reservations. The paint buckets, the nails, the hole in the cement, the language, the children planted in front of the television.

Cai's brow furrowed. "Susan lets Jake watch TV all the time."

Yes, I sometimes watched TV while holding Jake, but Mama and Baba camped out in front of the TV day and night with Jake every day for almost a year. I wasn't going to pay for Jake to spend yet another year in front of the television. Afraid I'd blow up if I opened my mouth, I remained silent.

"It's not just the TV." My mom's voice remained even and calm. "We'd be so worried about Jake if he goes there."

Cai looked back at the stoic news anchor and muttered something about looking for another day care.

My heart trembled and I could feel my face flush. We didn't need to start from scratch. "But we've already visited other places. There's Laura on Crane Street or the Russian one near my work."

Cai's eyes remained focused on the television. "I don't care."

"But I want you to help make the decision. We're both Jake's parents." I should have just made the choice myself, but I needed to prove to myself that we could still make a joint decision.

"I liked the Chinese woman," Cai said, pouting.

"I know, but we don't feel comfortable sending Jake there. Do you want to visit Laura's or the Russian place?"

"I have no interest in that."

"Well, then where do you want Jake to go?" Pulling teeth had to be easier than getting a decision from this man.

"I don't want him going to the Russian's."

"Laura's it is, then," I responded with a finality that surprised even me. Although frustrated that Cai based his decision on such an arbitrary reason, I was more relieved that Jake would be in safe hands. And although my first choice had been the Russian place, I liked and trusted Laura. So I called her the next day to reserve a place at her day care starting in early September. I wasn't taking any chances that Cai might change his mind.

When the husband goes out,
The wife should respectfully ask how far he must walk.
If by the middle of the night
He has not returned home,
She may not sleep, but must still wait for him.

—Ban Zhao
Instruction for Chinese Women and Girls

Chapter 39

INDIAN SUMMER

An Indian summer came to San Francisco in early October. I settled into my morning routine of dropping Jake off at Laura's day care, then driving up through the foggy hills of Twin Peaks to Inner Sunset and searching for a parking place along the southern perimeter of Golden Gate Park. We'd bought a used car that summer after I started a new job administering a neuroscience research center on the UCSF campus.

With both sets of parents back in their respective homes, Cai's days still remained free except for Saturday, when he taught piano at a world music center. He had stumbled upon this center in Chinatown and quickly accepted their offer to teach very part time. He continued to spend his nights out with friends, singing karaoke or simply chatting, as he described it, until the early hours of the next morning.

One evening when Cai was out with his friends, Jake was inconsolable. No matter how I tried to soothe him—rocking him in my arms like Mama and Baba had done or resting with him on our bed—he cried and thrashed. We were both exhausted. Just as I thought about throwing my hands up and letting Jake cry it out in the crib he never used, I heard the garage door open. Cai could help. He still had a way of cradling Jake that calmed him and lulled him to sleep.

I carried Jake downstairs, eager to pass him off to Cai. But when Cai opened the door to the living room, he jumped back as his eyes landed on us.

"*Ay yo*. You scared me."

"Sorry, but Jake isn't going to sleep and I'm so tired. Can you try rocking him?"

Cai looked away from me, his lips tightening together. "If Jake is so troublesome, I'll just send him to China to live with my parents. It's better there anyway. And cheaper."

I felt a jolt up my spine. Is that what he really wanted after standing up to his mother years earlier when she suggested the same thing? Or was he just saying this to hurt me? No matter the reason, I had to put an end to this discussion. "We are not sending Jake to China. I just asked for help this one time. He's your son, too."

He sighed deeply. "I've been here for almost two years, and now I know what American wives are like. I also know what Chinese wives are like. And then there's *you*." He spat out that last word.

"I just asked for help this one time."

"You didn't leave your country and your family for a life like this. No meaning, no anything here."

"I thought you had a wife and son here."

Anger swelled up in his eyes. "You're so lucky I don't hit you."

Speechless and shaking, I fled upstairs with Jake, too afraid to look back at Cai. How had I gotten myself (and now Jake, too!) into such a mess? No one had ever threatened me like that before. I desperately wanted to talk to Cai about it, to figure out why he was so unhappy and held so much resentment toward me. But I was too exhausted to muster up the energy that would take. All I could think about was crawling into bed with Jake at my side and blocking it out. So I did and prayed things would be back to "normal" in the morning.

After that night, I never asked Cai for help again. I couldn't bear to give him any scrap of a reason to take Jake back to China. His threat to hit me had a lingering sting, like a sharp slap to the face. Cai and I barely spoke to one another in the weeks to come. I couldn't remember the last time we'd been intimate. I still attributed our problems to the changes in our lives.

Cai was right that it was difficult for him to adjust to living in the United States. But when I compared the way he'd treated me in China to the way I gave him carte blanche in America, it made me furious. And since I wasn't accustomed to voicing anger, I reminded myself instead that we had only been a family of three for one month since my parents left San Francisco. I owed it to Jake to try harder.

One rare night when Cai didn't go out, the three of us sat down to dinner. Serving a spoonful of sautéed tofu into his rice bowl, Cai rehashed his karaoke session from the previous night.

"And then this guy asked me if he could sing a song with Xiaohong." He laughed as he mentioned her name.

I stabbed a piece of *kŭ guā* with my chopsticks, placing the ridged vegetable on my tongue and feeling the bitterness seep into my taste buds. When I didn't reply, he must have felt an explanation was needed.

"This guy thought I was *with* Xiaohong." He gazed at the ceiling, grinning as if remembering a tender moment. "So I said, of course you can sing with her. We're not together."

What could I say? There's always a reason people think couples are together—usually it's because the two people are acting like it somehow. I wasn't sure I wanted to learn the details, and besides, I couldn't imagine he'd ever confess to anything other than friendship.

I thought back to when Xiaohong brought me the flat of eggs after Jake was born. Willowy with long, wavy hair, Xiaohong was divorced with a child who still lived in Beijing with his father. I'd met her type before in China: flirty, witty, and full of confidence. She was as outgoing as I was reserved, and I could see how anyone would be taken in by her charm. Yet it was intimidating.

To the best of my knowledge, Xiaohong didn't work, but lived with her mother and brother in a San Jose McMansion. When Cai went out at night, he sometimes drove to Xiaohong's place to meet his group of friends. According to Cai, he and his friends either ate and talked at her house or went to a restaurant. She sang in most of the performances Cai emceed.

Since I had met Cai, he'd never divulged any information about his previous relationships, except with Wei Ling. So I doubted he would suddenly reveal an affair with Xiaohong this way. I figured they were just friends and that he probably just relayed this story to show me how important he was in the Chinese community. At least that's what I told myself.

Chapter 40
THE PLAN

In early December when I read an invitation in my work mailbox, I immediately began to conjure up excuses to skip the office holiday party in two weeks. *No significant others.* Cai hadn't stayed alone with Jake since before his parents moved in with us more than a year earlier. And after his threat to ship Jake off to China, I felt like I couldn't ask for help again. I needed to prove I was the best person to raise my son.

Then I had a thought. My parents. I knew it was an extreme idea, but Cai and I had never hired a babysitter, and with his volatile behavior, this wasn't the time to suggest that a stranger come to our home to care for Jake.

That evening, after Cai left for San Jose, I phoned my parents in Chicago. My mom didn't even question it or ask why Cai couldn't stay with Jake. We both understood why. Since my parents were scheduled to visit London over their winter break, they wanted to see Jake before they left, and that weekend was as good a time as any. My mom immediately agreed to my plan.

I simply told Cai that my parents were going to visit us for a weekend before they flew to London. He never opposed their visits and was always willing to let them stay with us. I steadied my voice as I tried to casually mention that I'd be going to my office holiday party for a few hours the Friday my parents would be in town. He nodded without commenting.

They arrived Thursday night, after finishing their morning

classes. While the five of us sat in the living room, Cai announced that he didn't have plans the following night. "There's no gathering tomorrow."

My first thought was that I hadn't needed to ask my parents to come out to San Francisco after all. Yet upon reflection, I realized that it was a good thing they were here. Now Cai would be able to see how easy it would be for me to go out once in a while.

I returned home from work around six on Friday so I could see Jake before I left for the restaurant. When it was time for me to head back out, my mom held Jake and walked with me to the door leading down to the garage.

"Have a good time," my mother said.

But as I opened the door and started downstairs, Jake's screams echoed through the walls. He still cried when I dropped him off at day care, but usually he stopped minutes after I left to go outside. I drove to McCormick & Kuleto's assuming the same would happen this time. But just to be sure, I paused outside the restaurant and called home on my cell phone. As my mom answered, I heard Jake wailing in the background.

"He's still crying?" I gasped.

"Yes, but don't worry. I'm trying to get him to go to sleep."

"How's Cai doing?"

"Well, you know… Just have a good time and don't worry."

"Is he really upset?"

"He'll be okay."

I didn't know whom I should worry about more: Cai or Jake. I hadn't expected Jake to cry so much when I left. Although I had always been there when he went to sleep at night, he was used to me leaving for work each morning and should know that I would eventually come home. Still, his cries tugged at my heart in a way that was more distressing than when I left him at day care. I could barely muster up an appetite.

During the soup course, I checked my watch, only half listening to my coworkers' stories that erupted in laughter every few minutes.

While waiting for the main course, my colleague Anna turned to me, asking if something was wrong.

"I don't know. Jake has been crying since I left, and Cai gets really upset when that happens."

"Why's he crying?"

"He's not used to me being away at night. I always put him to bed." As I explained to her and another colleague how I'd asked my parents to fly out to watch him that night, it sounded as outlandish to me as it did to them. But it also felt good to talk about my bizarre family life. In the past I would have kept this inside, yet after hearing Jake's screams that evening I didn't see the point in protecting Cai anymore.

"Sounds like you need to get out more." Anna lived near me and was raising her daughter, May, on her own, although her mother and sister often helped out on nights and weekends. She enjoyed more freedom than I did.

The interval between the main course and dessert dragged. I fidgeted in my chair, wondering if Jake was still crying. If I called home and woke him up, my parents would have to start soothing him all over again. Maybe I should just forgo dessert and leave. It was becoming increasingly difficult to join the table's conversation.

Cai's brooding face kept creeping into my mind, sucking away all my energy like a parasite. The waiter passed out dishes of tiramisu, but I had no desire to eat another bite. When the waitress took coffee orders, I stood to leave. I said a hurried good-bye to my coworkers and rushed out the door. I couldn't get home fast enough.

The living room lights were visible from the street, but dimmed. I pulled into the garage and expected to hear Jake's cries when I opened the door leading to the first floor. Instead, an eerie stillness hung in the air. I found the living room empty, the rest of the floor silenced in darkness. When I reached the master bedroom, I first noticed Jake asleep in the middle of the bed. My eyes then shot to Cai, standing at the foot of the bed, glaring at me with hatred like I had never seen before. He walked briskly past me to the bathroom and shut the door with a definitive slam. Fortunately Jake didn't stir. Once Cai finished in the bathroom, he undressed and got into bed as if I were invisible.

"Cai, why are you so mad? You knew I was going out. Besides, my parents were here to help. You didn't even have to stay home tonight."

He neither replied nor turned his head. Was he really not speaking to me because I went to one work-related dinner? I couldn't even keep track of the times he had left me alone with Jake at night. It probably numbered in the hundreds. I quivered to think what he would say when he started talking to me again.

That question remained unanswered the next morning when he refused to look at me before leaving the house to teach piano. At breakfast I told my mom about Cai's latest antics.

She put her teacup down before taking her next sip. "Let's go somewhere nice for lunch today. You don't deserve this."

My mom drove, and my dad sat next to her in the front seat while Jake and I rode in the middle section of their minivan. As we crossed the Bay Bridge to Berkeley, I stared out the window, still wondering why Cai was so angry. Going to a work function was not a break in our marriage vows.

Under the warm December sun, we strolled down Shattuck Boulevard in Berkeley, stopping in front of a bakery to buy Jake a muffin. My dad entered the shop as my mom and I waited with Jake in his stroller on the sidewalk.

My mom turned to me. "Susan, you don't have to put up with this."

I looked away from my mother as I felt my eyes tear up. All I could think about what how exhausted I had become. It wasn't just from working during the week or trying to get Jake to sleep each night. I was also tired from missing Jake during the day and wishing I could spend more time with him in a positive light. In some ways I felt more like a guardian than a parent to him. Most of all, I was spent from trying to keep the peace in my family and to help Cai adjust to America.

My mom reached out to gently pat my shoulder. "There's another way, you know."

I turned my head to look at her this time. "What do you mean?"

"Have you ever thought of leaving him?" Her serious tone of voice masked the anxiety in her eyes.

I almost choked. A kaleidoscope of pictures flashed through my mind: meeting Cai in our dorm, marrying him in Hong Kong, buying our first house, racing to the hospital to deliver Jake. They were all things that made me fall—and stay—in love with him. How could I just leave someone who had been through all that with me? But the images soon changed, and what came into view were the Shanghai Railway Station, freezing winters in Hidden River, our first day in San Francisco, and the night Cai threatened to hit me.

"Actually, I've been hoping he'd leave and just go back to China." Although I had never expressed those feelings out loud, it now felt good to tell my mother. It felt reassuring to know that my mom would support me unconditionally. She no longer seemed to be holding on to the illusion that Cai just needed time to adjust to San Francisco.

We both noticed my dad exiting the bakery. As he reached us, my mom told me again to think about it. "You don't deserve this."

Later that afternoon, after we'd returned home, I played with Jake on the living room floor while my parents read on the sofa. My heart raced when I heard the garage door open. My mom turned to me without speaking. The air felt as tense as if we were waiting defenseless for an intruder to enter the house.

I heard footsteps on the stairs that led up from the garage. My father concentrated on a journal article and my mom went back to her book. I, too, tried to act normal, building a tower with colorful soft blocks Jake had received for his birthday.

With each of Cai's steps up the staircase, my heart seemed to thump faster. The door gently opened. Cai stepped out and he nodded at my parents, but he didn't so much as a look in my direction. As Cai headed toward the kitchen, Jake toddled after him, but Cai didn't slow down. My mom glanced at me again and rolled her eyes.

Jake wandered back to the living room where we resumed knocking over block towers. It seemed like Cai remained in the kitchen for hours. When he finally reemerged, he headed toward the stairs leading to the second floor. My mother stood up and quickly uttered his name. He turned back to look at her.

"I don't know why you're ignoring Susan. You certainly have no problem going out whenever you wish. Can't she go out for a work dinner and not worry about coming home to this?"

Cai stared at my mother in disbelief for a moment. He then quickly turned and stormed upstairs. I was so grateful to my mother for speaking up, for doing something I wish I had had the nerve to do years ago. Without uttering a word to my parents, I followed Cai upstairs. I found him in our bedroom, seated on the edge of the bed, seething with rage.

"She shouldn't have said that to me," he said. There was no explanation for his silent treatment since I returned from my work dinner the previous night. Instead, he continued to stew about what my mother had said. "No one has ever spoken that way to me."

Are you serious? I wanted to scream at him. *No one?* Inside I could feel the same anger bubbling, but mine was only directed at Cai, not my mother. And, to be honest, my rage was directed at myself as well. Why had I been so frightened to speak out all these years? Starting with the events surrounding Jake's birth, I'd confided in my parents about cultural problems with Cai. And after my disastrous first Mother's Day, I had complained to my parents again. Instead of telling them, I should have spoken directly to Cai. I'd done none of us any favors by tiptoeing around him. But how would I change now? I felt afraid he'd either yell at me or continue to give me the silent treatment.

I just wished I knew why Cai was acting this way. And after all these years, I wondered if perhaps our cultural differences were not at the root of our problems, but rather irreconcilable differences that had nothing to do with culture. With nothing else to say and my mind in a jumble, I silently crept out of the room and downstairs to the refuge of my parents and of Jake.

Cai appeared downstairs an hour later, quickly announcing that he was leaving for a meeting in the South Bay.

Two months later would mark our second year in San Francisco. Cai seemed more distant than ever, staying home all day while I worked and leaving at night after I returned home from day care with Jake. During my lonely nights when I felt like a single mother, I stopped centering my hopes on Cai suddenly adjusting to life in the United States. Instead, I realized I needed professional help.

Chapter 41

A STORM IS BREWING

With the new year, I knew it was time to work on my marriage. If things didn't change soon, I couldn't imagine that my relationship with Cai would improve. Most of all, I owed it to Jake to try to fix the problems in our family. He was now eighteen months old and if he didn't understand the tension brewing at home now, he would soon. To reverse our misfortunes, I would need to start speaking out. And I had to see if Cai could change, too.

Growing up, I thought people who went to therapy were either all mentally ill or, if they weren't, others would view them that way. Even though I had friends who went to therapists, I still thought of therapy as something shameful. It was definitely a matter that you kept secret. But after four months without parents or in-laws, my relationship with Cai hadn't improved. If anything, it was growing more contentious. I couldn't fix these issues on my own and knew it was time to see a therapist myself.

On my first day back at work after the long New Year's weekend, I flipped through a booklet listing health-care providers in my insurance network. I found a few psychologists, one of whom worked near an affiliate UCSF hospital that I could easily reach by a free shuttle. I called her and made an appointment for later that week during lunchtime. It would be easy to duck out for an hour and a half in the middle of the day.

I arrived on time for my first appointment with Nancy, a blond middle-aged woman with a reserved disposition. As I sat on the couch in her warm, living-room-like office, I wondered why I hadn't started therapy years ago.

Nancy took a chair opposite me and held a legal pad. "I'd like you to use this first session to tell me your background and why you're here. I might not speak much because I want to hear your story."

Lightly clearing my throat, my hands on my knees, I chronicled my quick courtship to Cai. I told her about our years in Hong Kong and how his personality changed when we traveled to China. I spoke of my frustrations with his inability to adapt to San Francisco and how for almost a year I had supported five people on a secretary's salary. When the timer rang, Nancy hadn't said a word. She stood up and escorted me to the lobby. "I'll see you next week, Susan. Good work today."

I floated to the shuttle stop like a balloon whose weight had been cut. It had been years since I had felt so hopeful. Therapy wasn't such a bad thing after all. In fact, next Thursday couldn't come soon enough. Nancy would help me figure out ways to cope with Cai's moods. We would role-play to come up with the best ways for me to build my confidence and communicate better with Cai. Maybe she would even give me her cell phone number so I could check in after I tried one of our exercises.

By the time I picked up Jake at Laura's day care that evening, Cai had left to go out with friends. I didn't mind because I wasn't ready to tell him about Nancy quite yet. If he knew I was going to a therapist, I was sure he'd say something demeaning and would use it against me as proof that I was a crazy, unfit mother. But once I regained my confidence and worked out a plan with Nancy, I would tell him everything and try to get him to go with me to couples counseling.

The phone rang as I brought Jake upstairs for bed that evening. An unknown woman's voice asked for Cai. She spoke English with a thick mainland accent.

"He's not home. Can I take a message?" I reached for a pen and a piece of paper on my bedside table.

"Just tell him Pan Mihui called. He has my number." She sounded young and confident, yet still demure. Something about her insouciance made me think that she wasn't just a casual acquaintance, but I shut it out of my mind because I didn't want to ruin the positive outlook I'd gained since my session with Nancy that afternoon.

I tried to soothe Jake to sleep and ended up dozing off myself. Hours later, I awoke when Cai strolled into the bedroom, turning on the bathroom light near my side of the bed.

"Someone called for you tonight."

"Who was it?" He turned and stopped before entering the bathroom. Jake stirred next to me.

"Pan Mihui or Pammy Hui. Something like that."

I could hear Cai sigh and could see the frustration and anger on his face. "Why did she call here?" he asked.

How would I know? He was the one who knew her, not me. I remained silent and thought he would explain who she was. But he didn't. The only woman he mentioned on a regular basis was Xiaohong, the woman who brought me three dozen eggs after Jake's birth. Pammy was a new name to me.

"*Hěn máfan.*" He mumbled that something was troublesome as he stepped into the bathroom. It was clear that her call threatened him in some way. But I was afraid to probe further because ultimately I didn't want to know the truth about this woman and whatever she was to my husband—and to have to choose what to do about it. I wanted to save my marriage, so I didn't ask why he felt so angry she had called. He wouldn't have told me anyway.

Cai must have spoken with her because I never heard from Pammy again.

The day after I first met with my therapist, Cai stayed home and cooked his standard, Chinese three-course meal. It was hot out of the wok when I returned home with Jake. He never inquired about my day or if anything special happened. It wasn't something I ever heard Mama or Baba ask one another, so I chalked it up to another cultural difference. Nonetheless, with my new resolve to restore my marriage, I asked, "How was your day?"

Throwing the dishrag onto the counter, he groaned as if I had just suggested he donate bone marrow.

"Cai, what's wrong?"

"I don't know. Every day is the same. Stay at home, do nothing, cook dinner, watch TV, go to sleep. There's no meaning here."

Here we go again. But I kept my composure, taking a deep breath. "You usually go out with your friends, so it's not like you're home every—"

"You know what I mean. There's no meaning here. It's so different from China."

I'd heard his soliloquy so many times I could finish his sentences. In China, friends come over every day, people chat and sing together, everything is so *rènào,* so loud and exciting.

"If you hate it here so much, why don't you go to China and see if you want to move back?" I spoke slowly and steadily, hopeful that he would listen to me like a reasonable adult. I wanted him to think about his words, to understand the weight they placed on me. It was too unsettling for me to hear this veiled threat every few weeks. Besides, I felt fairly confident that he wouldn't take me up on this offer. If he really wanted to go to back to China, he would have done it long ago. "Before you make any decisions, go back and look for a job and see if that's really what you want."

His eyes widened as if I had threatened divorce. "But what about you and Jake?"

"We'll cross that bridge later. Your happiness is most important. If you really like it back in China, if you find a job at a conservatory that you like, then we can see where we are and can decide later."

"That's no way for a family to live." He continued to mope, putting the last dish on the table for dinner. We ate in silence, Cai never once looking at me. Compared to the other times when he grew angry or gave me the silent treatment, I could tell that this time was different, that he was just frustrated with life in California. I hoped to learn some coping skills the next time I saw my therapist, Nancy.

After dinner, Cai retreated to the living room to listen to a local Mandarin radio talk show. He stayed in that evening and watched Chinese television after the radio show finished. I brought Jake upstairs to start his bedtime routine, changing him and settling him into the middle of our bed. He hadn't slept in his crib in over a year, yet it remained next to our bed, untouched. Soon Jake started to cry. I rubbed his back like I did most nights to soothe him to sleep, but he continued to wail. Next I picked him up, pacing the room to calm him, but that didn't work either. Jake's screams became louder and more piercing. Just as I turned toward the door, Cai burst into the room.

"What's going on in here? Why isn't he sleeping?"

"Cai, this happens every night. He needs to learn to sleep on his own."

"He shouldn't be crying like this." Cai took Jake from me, but Jake only cried harder and louder.

I stood back, half wishing Cai would volunteer to lie with Jake for three hours. The other half of me hoped Cai would let Jake cry it out so he could learn to soothe himself to sleep. It was no wonder we were all exhausted.

"Jake! Stop crying!" Cai started screaming, competing with Jake's piercing cries. When Jake thrashed his head as if reaching back to lie on the bed, Cai stormed down the hallway to the empty guest room where Mama and Baba, and at other times my parents, had slept for many months.

"*Stop crying. No one likes you when you cry,*" Cai yelled. I raced after him and before I could get to him, Cai kicked the guest room door open, placed Jake on the carpet inside the room, came out, and slammed the door shut, closing Jake off from the light in the hallway. Jake's screams intensified.

"Cai, what are you doing? He's only a year and a half." I ran past Cai to open the door gently so I wouldn't hit Jake if he was too close to it. When I reached him, I cradled him in my arms, sick with grief. Cai had started to retreat downstairs, mumbling that Jake shouldn't cry. I huddled with Jake on my side of the bed, hoping Cai would go out and never return.

🍵 🍵 🍵

My next session with Nancy couldn't come soon enough. As I sat down for our second session, she asked me to continue from where I'd left off the previous week. I concluded my monologue of frustration over Cai's view of his future in the United States. I also voiced my worries over his violent rant from the previous week.

Nancy leaned back in her chair and placed her legal pad on the desk next to her. "Thanks for sharing your story, Susan. I know it must have been difficult. But I believe if you put yourself in Cai's shoes, you might see a different perspective. Try to think of how he feels, alone and lost in a new country."

A lump formed in my throat. If she continued to speak, I didn't hear it. All I could think about was what she had said. What in my story showed I hadn't been thinking about Cai for the last five years? Had she heard me during the two hours I recounted my story, or was it Cai whom she was concerned about? I was so taken aback by her response that I sat in shock, speechless, while a familiar fury simmered inside. When I left Nancy's office at the end of our session, it was for the last time. There was no way I'd go back.

The next time Cai stayed home, he barely spoke when I came back from day care with Jake. During dinner, he said, "The concert tour check came today." He looked down at his lap. "It was only five hundred dollars."

Five hundred? For a year and a half of driving a hundred miles at least four days a week, often more. I quickly calculated that this check probably only covered his meals for a few of those months. Cai already seemed upset about it. If I added my frustration, I worried he would crawl into a deeper depression.

"That's okay. You didn't expect it to be a moneymaker. It was more for the experience, you know?"

"It's impossible to make money here. Xiaohong's brother is moving back to China. He says it's so easy to make money there now."

What could I say to that? It was true; China was *the* place to make money nowadays, especially as the Internet boom started to fizzle in the Bay Area. China was just opening up to foreign investors, and for the first time since the 1940s, people outside the government were able to make unlimited amounts of money. I was at a loss as to what I could say to Cai to calm him. I still believed that money wasn't the answer to our problems, but I knew he wouldn't feel any better hearing that from me. It was time to ask about seeking professional help.

"Cai, maybe we should go for couples counseling. I think you might feel better talking to—"

"I'm not talking to anyone." He scowled. "Chinese people don't do that."

"But—"

"No. *I* don't have any problems." He pushed his chair out, as he had on Mother's Day, and stormed into the living room. Jake didn't seem perturbed by Cai's rant, yet I knew there would soon be a day when he would understand what was going on. And it would most certainly affect his behavior. I took Jake from his high chair and held him tightly for comfort, while the Mandarin radio show drowned out the silence from the living room.

Chapter 42
A "CASUAL" VISIT TO CHINA

After my failed attempt to start therapy and to get Cai to see a couples' counselor, I felt too discouraged to look for another psychologist. Would he or she also tell me to look at my problems through Cai's eyes? If I heard another reaction like that, I worried that I would start to believe it was true. I'd been in this dysfunctional relationship for five years and could no longer tell what about it was normal and what was unacceptable.

I needed to hear that I was correct in feeling that something was terribly amiss in my marriage. Which meant that something good did come from my two appointments with Nancy: I was now ready to discuss my problems with friends. Doug and Anna, the coworkers I sat with at my work holiday party, let me vent during hour-long lunch breaks across the street at the student union. I grew to look forward to these powwows.

Cai called me at work one morning with excitement and energy in his voice that I hadn't heard in months. At first I had thought he had found a full-time job, but it soon became apparent he was calling for a different reason.

"I just talked to a travel agent and found a cheap flight to China. I think we should go this spring to visit my family."

I suddenly felt dizzy and grabbed the chair's armrest with my free hand. "Really?"

We hadn't spoken about visiting Mama and Baba in Hidden River, but the idea had lodged in the back of my mind since we'd decided to move to San Francisco. Now that we had Jake, it frightened me to think about taking him to China. What would I do if Jake got sick there? Hidden River wasn't Beijing or Shanghai with English-speaking physicians and nurses. Cai didn't know many English medical terms, nor did I know many Chinese ones.

And of course there was Mama's offer to raise Jake until he was old enough to attend elementary school—and Cai's threat to carry out these wishes. When I thought about going to Hidden River with Jake, I felt like throwing up.

"It's only one thousand dollars for each of us, and Jake can go for free because he's not two yet," Cai said. "Once he's two, we have to buy a ticket. So we need to go before June. I'm thinking April."

Excuses of how I could stall him flew through my mind. There was no way I could let Jake go to China. I closed my eyes and took a breath.

"Well, don't book anything yet. My boss is going to Europe in a few days, so he's busy preparing for that. I'll try to ask before he leaves, but if not, I might not be able to ask until he returns in a couple of weeks."

Miraculously, Cai agreed to wait. I now had at most three weeks to get myself—and Jake—out of going to China. Once my boss returned in the middle of March, I would no longer have a reason to hold off buying plane tickets to China. I couldn't concentrate on work, which was becoming commonplace. I spent an hour each morning emailing my parents about Cai, and only answered my work emails and took care of one or two tasks before breaking for lunch. And for that hour, I would talk to coworkers like Doug and Anna. By the time we returned from lunch, I felt too daunted by the pile of work in front of me and figured it wouldn't make much difference if I tackled it the next day.

This had been going on since just after I met with Nancy the therapist for the second time. Cai consumed my every moment. Now with this China trip on the horizon, I sat in front of my computer agonizing about being trapped in Hidden River for a few years if

Cai and his parents refused to let Jake return to the United States. After all, I would never leave Jake behind in China. Memories of feeling isolated and depressed in Hidden River started to flood my mind until I couldn't read the words on my screen.

At home that evening, Cai's enthusiasm from the morning had evaporated and his usual pessimism had returned in full force.

"Xiaohong's brother paid five hundred a month for day care in San Jose before he moved back. It's much cheaper to raise the baby in China. It's not even five hundred a year."

How could I reply to that? We had already had this discussion, and I knew costs were cheaper in China. But I had to say something. Silence, I'd come to learn, equaled compliance.

"Jake is in a small day care, which seems to be good for him."

"Some grandparents take care of their grandchildren. Then it's really cheap."

There was no way Jake would live with Mama and Baba. I didn't know how I could get Cai to understand this. He seemed to understand back in Hidden River when Mama had first brought it up, but that had changed somewhere over the years. It was futile to engage further in this conversation. "I'm going to heat the leftovers now."

As usual, Cai wasn't talkative that evening. So once I dropped the topic, he didn't revisit it that night.

Back at work the next morning, I emailed my parents for more than an hour, relaying what Cai had said about it being cheaper for Mama and Baba to raise Jake in China. I hated being paranoid for thinking Cai would want to keep Jake in China, but given his unhappiness, I couldn't put it past him. My mom wrote back right away, mirroring my concerns.

Over lunch in a student union café, I also told my coworker Doug about my conversation with Cai the previous night. When I mentioned how Cai wanted us to travel to China in April, Doug put his hand up in midchew.

"Susan," he said a moment later. "My friend's brother went

through the same thing, but he actually lost his daughter in China. I think you should talk to my friend Aimee. She works in neurology."

I agreed immediately, partly because Doug was willing to go to the trouble of asking his friend to talk to me and partly because I wanted to hear from someone who knew what could happen in my situation.

The next morning I heard a knock at my open door. Aimee Chan stood before me with a reserved smile. She looked to be about my age and carried her wallet and ID card in one hand. "Do you have a minute?"

"Yes, of course. Come in."

She squeezed into the empty chair in my tight office, her long hair swinging to one side. I closed the door as she sat down.

"Doug said you're thinking about going to China with your husband and baby." She pushed her oval glasses up the small bridge of her nose. "My niece is there now and I'm not sure we'll ever see her again."

I sat forward in my chair, facing Aimee as she recounted her story. Born and raised in San Francisco, Aimee's older brother, Tim, had turned twenty-nine several years earlier and wanted to marry. With no prospects in America, he sought a wife in his parents' ancestral home back in southern China.

"Tim visited our relatives there and met a shy girl named Mei. They fell in love, and Mei moved to the United States a few months later to marry Tim.

"When my niece, Katherine, was born a year later, she became the star of the family. Mei never found a job and lounged around at home while my parents took care of Katherine. So when Mei wanted to bring Katherine back to China to visit her family, Tim thought it would do Mei some good." Aimee sniffled as tears welled in her eyes. "Tim drove them to the airport on his day off and told Mei he'd meet her in two weeks at the SFO international terminal."

Aimee sniffled again, so I handed her a tissue from the box on my desk. She slid it under her wire-framed glasses.

"But when Tim went to the airport, Mei and Katherine weren't there. He worried they'd missed their flight, which originated in Hong Kong. So he phoned Mei's parents in China when he arrived home. That's when he learned Mei didn't want to return to San Francisco."

"How old was Katherine then?"

Aimee sniffled. "She wasn't two yet. We were planning a big birthday party for her the week after she was supposed to return. I'd already bought her a new dress and doll." Sobbing, she couldn't continue.

I reached for more tissues, this time for both of us. Katherine had been in China for a year now and Tim had only seen her once, during his annual two-week vacation.

"Why couldn't he just take Katherine back with him?" It seemed like that two-week vacation would have been a perfect time to bring Katherine home.

"Who in Mei's town would side with Tim? The laws there favor Chinese citizens, not Americans."

"Katherine and Tim are United States citizens, so can't our government help?"

"Thousands of kids are kidnapped to other countries every year. Our case is just one of many. We're not famous and we're not rich, so we haven't been able to get anyone to help us."

I rubbed my hands over my face, frightened for Aimee's family and for myself. Although her story seemed shocking, I knew it wasn't uncommon for Chinese spouses to take their children back to China. I just assumed the U.S. government would do more to help children who were kidnapped to other countries. But now I could see that didn't happen.

Aimee glanced at her pink Hello Kitty watch. "I'm sorry, but I have to get back to work."

"I understand. Thank you so much for sharing your story with me. I know it's hard to talk about it." She had given me more to think—and worry—about.

After she opened the door, she turned back to me. "Don't do it, Susan. Don't go."

For the family's prosperity,
There are very good rules;
Women should zealously learn them.
Of these, to follow peace
Is of the first importance.
Obedience in all things is the next.

—Ban Zhao
Instruction for Chinese Women and Girls

Chapter 43
NOW OR NEVER

If Aimee's brother thought he had a good marriage and this had happened to him, I would be delusional to think it wouldn't happen to me. Cai had already said he wanted to send Jake to live with his parents. Aimee was right—I couldn't go to China or let Cai take Jake there.

How to tell Cai was another issue. When I thought about how he would react, I felt sick to my stomach.

That evening, Cai greeted me with a rare smile.

"I bought *niángāo* today. Your favorite." *Niángāo* is a gooey, sweet cake made from glutinous rice that people eat on Chinese New Year. I had quickly fallen in love with it while we lived in Hong Kong.

It was unusual for Cai to make something special for me, especially these last couple years. He barely spoke to me, and he certainly didn't touch me anymore. So this gesture naturally seemed suspicious. He really must want to go to China, I thought.

After setting the table and carrying the dishes he had just whipped up in the wok, I sat down with Jake and Cai, hoping for a peaceful dinner, one in which he didn't scowl or storm out of the kitchen. Miraculously, Cai continued to act upbeat. For the first time in months, he looked happy.

"I got a job today."

"*You did?* What is it?" This was the news I'd been waiting to hear for almost two years, and I hadn't even known he'd applied for one. I sat on the edge of my chair, waiting to hear more. The news would be even better if he announced that we wouldn't be able to go to China now.

"Well, you know that Chinese radio show I sometimes listen to?"

I nodded. When Cai stayed home in the evenings, he still tuned in to the local Mandarin radio program where listeners called in to speak about politics, the arts, China, or current affairs.

"I'm going to host a radio show." He beamed with pride as he helped himself to a round of ground beef and *kǔ guā*, canned sardines, and dried tofu with scallions.

"Cai, I'm so proud of you. This is great!" After all this time, he had finally found a job commensurate with his qualifications. Maybe he would finally feel more settled in San Francisco. This job could be the turning point for his depression, the job that would bring back the old Cai from when we met in Hong Kong.

I could picture it clearly: Cai would become well-known in the Bay Area, and wherever he went in the mainland Chinese community, people would know his voice. He'd be offered other speaking engagements, like the emcee jobs he'd been doing, but for more pay. Without knowing more details, I thought it sounded like the perfect job. All my former resolutions started to fade away. After all we'd been through, I couldn't give up on him now that he'd found a job he seemed interested in and qualified for.

"I didn't tell you about it because I wanted it to be a surprise if I got it. Today I went to talk to the producers, and they liked my deep voice and background in China and here."

"That's wonderful! See, it just took some time to find the right job." I leaned back in my chair before helping myself to more tofu and green onions. Although the Chinese dishes we ate at home had long ago started to taste the same, tonight they seemed novel.

In a flash, Cai's smile disappeared and his eyes darted south, staring into his rice bowl. "It's just a part-time job. Six to eight, Monday through Thursday. I start tomorrow."

"That's okay. It could lead to something with more hours. You never know unless you try." He might feel discouraged about the lack of hours, but I still saw it as a wonderful opportunity and a giant step through the door.

Cai shrugged and lifted his rice bowl to his lips, shoveling the remains into his mouth to finish dinner and this conversation. For the rest of the night, he stared at the TV, watching the evening news from China.

The next morning, I raced to my office to email my parents about this change in events.

Cai found a job hosting a radio show. With this exposure to the Chinese community, I think he'll regain confidence. He starts tonight, but said he can still take off two or three weeks to go to China in the spring. I wonder if I should just go with him. It might be more difficult for him to go in the future, if he gets more jobs and becomes more well-known in the Bay Area. This could be Jake's only chance to see Mama and Baba for years. In the worst case, if Cai and his parents want to keep Jake in China, I can take our passports and some Chinese yuan and find a taxi near his parents' *danwei*. I could leave when everyone's sleeping and take Jake to Wuhan by taxi, even though it's a two-hour drive. Then we could get on a flight to Shanghai or Beijing and from there use my credit card to buy tickets to the U.S. or Hong Kong.

My mom replied an hour later.

Great news about Cai's job, but I'll worry about you if you think you'll need an escape route. That sounds very frightening. Maybe you should look into the rights you'd have in China if they did try to keep Jake there. The State Department would know. So would a lawyer specializing in international custody law.

Though she had a point about the escape route, I wanted to see how Cai would behave once he started his radio job. If this position finally helped him adjust to San Francisco, I didn't want to say anything that would bring him back to his depressed state. I could always call an international law expert if need be.

That evening, I arrived home with Jake just as Cai's show started. I flipped on the radio and listened as he cohosted with another man from China. Cai handled the callers with diplomacy, not cutting them off when their time was up, but suggesting they call back another day when there was more time to chat. I thought he sounded like a natural, as if he had been doing this for years. I couldn't wait to congratulate him when he arrived home.

A little after ten, I heard Cai drive into the garage. Jake had fallen asleep in our bed moments earlier.

I greeted him at the top of the garage stairs. "You did a great job tonight."

"It was okay." He walked past me, holding the black plastic bag synonymous with porn rentals.

"I thought it was wonderful."

Walking up the stairs to our bedroom, he stopped and turned back toward me. "It was just a bunch of crazies calling. What's so wonderful about that?" He faced forward and continued upstairs.

When he slammed the bathroom door, Jake woke up, screaming. Cai rushed out of the bathroom, and before I could enter the bedroom from the hallway, he grabbed Jake. Storming into the hall, he held Jake over the ledge at the top of the stairs, an exposed space with nothing to break Jake's fall but the carpeting a floor below.

"*Stop crying!*" Cai screamed. Without speaking, I secured my hands around Jake's upper body.

"Please let me have Jake." Trembling, I tried to speak slowly and softly to show Cai I had a solid grasp. He brought Jake closer to him, away from the danger of dropping him down a flight of stairs. Once Jake was on our side of the ledge, I felt Cai's hold on Jake lessen. The next thing I knew, Cai was walking into the bedroom, his head slumped in defeat. Within seconds, he returned with the black plastic bag and headed downstairs.

I phoned the international law expert the next morning.

It was my boss's last day at work before his two-week speaking trip to Europe. To make sure he had everything he needed before his trip, I checked in with him moments after he walked past my door. He handed me a list of contact numbers where I could reach him in an emergency and said email would suffice for less urgent matters. As my boss went over his itinerary, I barely listened. My thoughts drifted to the phone call I would make when I left his office.

Back at my computer, I searched the Internet for "international custody law" and "California." Hundreds of sites appeared, including a listing for a law professor specializing in this field at the University of California, Davis. I closed my office door and dialed the long-distance number. I felt my stomach drop when a receptionist answered the phone. My pulse quickened as I asked for a professor listed on the website.

"And the purpose of your call?"

"I'd like some information about custody laws for American children in China."

"Please hold."

A woman answered the phone, introducing herself as the professor.

"I'm sorry to bother you, but I'm an American citizen married to a Chinese national. My husband wants us to visit China in a couple months with our twenty-month-old son. He has threatened to send our son to live with his parents in China, so I wanted to know my rights if they decided to keep our son there. Is there any law that would protect me and guarantee my son's safe return to the United States?"

A second passed. I thought I heard her typing in the background.

"What's your name?"

"Susan."

"Thanks, Susan. Well, there's something called the United Nations Hague Convention on the Civil Aspects of International Child Abduction. When a child born in Country A travels to Country B and one parent wants to keep the child in Country B, the

Hague Convention stipulates that the child must return to Country A. It's often a long-winded process to hear a Hague case, but the law theoretically protects the child from remaining in Country B."

I sighed, relieved. "Thank you. That's what I wanted to know."

"Wait. I'm not finished."

"I don't understand."

"China hasn't signed the Hague Convention."

My stomach fell. "You mean I wouldn't have any rights in China?"

"You got it. I'm sorry, Susan. When's your trip?"

"My husband wants to go in April."

"If you worry he'll try to keep your son there, just tell him that you and your son won't go. That's the only way to avoid a problem."

Tears streamed down my cheeks. "I can't tell him that."

"What do you mean you can't tell him?"

"He hates it here." I sobbed, trying to hold back more tears. "This trip means so much to him. If I tell him Jake and I won't go, it'll be the end of my marriage."

"I see. You're really scared, aren't you?"

"Uh-huh."

"Can I be blunt here?" But before I answered, she continued. "Why are you married to this guy?"

And that's when it hit me. Tears flowed again, this time without restraint. "I don't know. I thought I understood Chinese culture."

"It's okay, Susan. There's a way out when you're ready. Where do you live?"

I tried to pull myself together enough to answer "San Francisco."

"And where is your family? Are they local?"

"No, Chicago."

"All right. Can you move back to Chicago?"

Between sobs I mumbled yes. My parents would take Jake and me in. When my mom suggested leaving Cai back in December, I knew she had implied that Jake and I could move in with them until I got back on my feet.

"You're going to need an attorney who specializes in interstate custody law. That's going to be our main priority now. If you'd like, I can give you the names of a few in San Francisco."

I agreed and took down the names, numbers, and addresses of three lawyers. She suggested trying one first.

"Joanne will be able to give you a lot of personal attention."

"Thank you," I whispered.

"Good luck, Susan. You've gotten into a mess here, but Joanne will be able to help."

I hung up and took a piece of tissue to blow my nose. The tears had stopped, and I suddenly felt like I needed to act quickly before I changed my mind or convinced myself that Cai would finally revert back to the person I knew in our Hong Kong dormitory. I couldn't wait another day.

Staring at the numbers I had just written down, I picked up the receiver and dialed the one for Joanne. A receptionist answered and put me through a moment later. I explained my situation, just as I had to the law professor.

"Wow," she said after I had finished my story. "We have to make sure this stays an interstate case, not an international one. Does your son have a passport?"

"No, not yet."

"Can you get his photos taken and apply for his passport this week? You should have it mailed to your parents in Chicago so your husband doesn't get his hands on it."

"That's no problem. I can take him for photos this Saturday when Cai's working all day and then apply for the passport on Monday during my lunch break." I hadn't thought about any of this until Joanne mentioned it, but as I spoke with her, these plans smoothly fell into place. My boss would be in Europe, so I could take all the time I needed on Monday to walk to the post office and apply for Jake's passport.

"Good. He can probably still apply for a Chinese passport for your son, but let's hope he hasn't thought of that. Can you come to my office during lunch another day so we can speak? But before then, I'll need a five-thousand-dollar retainer. Whatever you don't use, I'll return."

"That's fine. I can get you the money by the end of the week."

"What about coming in next Tuesday at lunchtime? Are you free then?"

"Yes. Is noon okay?"

"Sounds good. Do you have my address and full name to send the check?"

"Yes, the professor gave it to me. Thank you for everything."

"Hang in there, Susan. No matter what you decide to do, you need to know your rights so you can protect yourself and your son."

When I hung up, I opened my door and sent a quick email to my parents, detailing my conversations with the professor and Joanne. I asked if I could borrow money for the retainer. Ten minutes later, I received a reply from my mom. She agreed to overnight a check that afternoon and asked me to keep her posted.

Paranoid that Cai would learn I was consulting with a lawyer, I only told a few friends at work, like Anna and Doug, who had never met him. They already knew about our problems, so at lunch that day I filled them in on my phone call with Joanne.

That night I was determined not to let Cai's negativity get me down. When he returned after his radio show, I went about getting ready for bed, not bothering to ask about his evening. My mind focused on one thing: I had a way out.

On Saturday when Cai was teaching piano at the world music center, I drove with Jake to the Inner Sunset district, near my office, to a camera shop that handled passport photos. Jake sat still and smiled widely for the photo. I took him out to lunch, something I rarely did with our tight budget, to celebrate that accomplishment. On Monday I skipped lunch with Doug so I could apply for Jake's passport at the neighborhood post office. When I reached the window, the postal officer took my application, photos, and check.

"The next time you apply for his passport, you'll need both parents' signatures. A new law is going into effect in a few months."

"Thanks. I'll remember that." I took the receipt, my hands shaking, thankful I'd narrowly escaped this new law.

The following day, I boarded the N-Judah streetcar for Joanne's office near City Hall. When I entered her office suite, dark and bereft of furniture besides the receptionist's bent metal desk and Naugahyde chair, I wondered if I was at the right place.

The receptionist sat in the middle of the lobby, surrounded by half a dozen frosted doors. "Who are you here to see?"

"Joanne—"

She asked my name and picked up the phone, briefly speaking to someone on the other end. "It's the third door on the left."

I knocked and a middle-aged woman with frosted Janis Joplin hair opened it.

"Susan!" She hugged me as if we were old friends and closed the door. Walking back to her desk, Joanne motioned for me to take the chair before her. "I'm glad you're here."

"Thank you so much. Did you get the check?"

"I did. Thank you. As for your case, if you decide to return to Chicago, you will need to live there for six months to establish Illinois residency. However, if your husband takes any legal action against you in California before those six months are over, your case will be in California's jurisdiction and you will be required by law to return here. Assuming he doesn't take legal action and you remain in Illinois for six months, you can file for divorce in Chicago."

I nodded while scribbling notes on a legal pad she'd given me. "What happens if we divorce in California?"

"The courts will require you to stay in the state of California until your son is eighteen years of age. You won't be able to leave with your son unless your husband agrees."

I choked back tears.

"And if you're worried about him taking your son to China, I would advise you do whatever you can to stall your husband for six months to establish Illinois residency."

I wiped tears from my face with a few fingers. "I don't know how I'm going tell him we're leaving."

She handed me a box of tissues. "You don't have to. This isn't about him anymore. We'll work on a letter you'll leave for him."

I nodded, grateful for a clean exit.

Joanne looked me in the eyes. "Have you gone to couples counseling?"

"No. I asked him once and he said Chinese people don't do that. According to him, I'm the one with problems, not him."

She jotted something on her pad. "When you write the letter, it must indicate you've tried to get him into counseling. But you can't tell him you want a divorce. We need to make sure you come across as exhausted, scared, and frustrated because you did everything you could to work on your marriage, to no avail. The courts need to see that."

When the law professor mentioned the possibility of divorce, the word sounded threatening and grotesque. In the days since that conversation, I knew I had no other choice. Now when Joanne uttered the word "divorce," it felt like I'd been given a diagnosis I didn't want to hear but could learn to live with. As with many diagnoses, there's often a worse predicament. Seated across from her, I knew if I didn't go through with this now, I wouldn't have the strength to do it later. I nodded as she continued.

"You aren't taking your son from him. Your husband is free to visit Jake in Chicago whenever he wishes. Your letter has to be clear about that."

My eyes popped out at that last statement.

"Susan, if you keep your son from him, you are kidnapping him. Kidnapping is a felony. You are just visiting your family and don't know how long you'll stay. When you have a chance, draft a letter. Do you have access to a fax machine?"

"Yes, at work." I was lucky that my tiny office housed the only fax machine in the research center. It would be easy for me to fax my letter to Joanne without anyone seeing it.

"Good. Can you draft the letter during lunch or a break, when you're not around your husband? When you're finished, please fax it to me so I can make sure we cover all grounds."

"I'll have it to you by tomorrow after lunch."

"There's no hurry. You can take longer if you—"

"I'm leaving this weekend."

Joanne looked at me aghast, and it felt like I, too, was hearing this plan for the first time. It was if someone had taken over my body, someone who was determined and could think clearly. Starting with the call to the law professor, the momentum of this trajectory extended to phoning Joanne, applying for Jake's passport, and now stating without hesitation that I would leave this weekend. Cai was working all day Saturday, the only day I could guarantee he'd be away from home for a long stretch of time. I had to do it Saturday.

"You mean in four days?"

"Yes. If I don't do it now, I won't have the guts to do it later. He wants us to go to China in April. That's only a month away. I'm running out of time."

Leaning back in her chair, Joanne's eyes honed in on me. "You really want to do this? This weekend?"

"Yes. Is it possible?"

"Sure, but you need to fax me the letter by tomorrow. I'll be in court on Thursday and back in the office Friday. Your son is two?"

"Twenty months. Two in June."

"You're prepared to leave most of your things behind, right?"

"Yes, of course. I just want Jake."

"I don't advise you to do this alone. Can your mother fly out and help you? You seem very calm now, but you'll need help the day you leave."

Mom taught on Tuesdays and Thursdays, so I hoped she'd be free on Friday. "I'll call her when I get back to work. I think she'll be able to do it."

"One more thing: once you return to Chicago, I'm going to need a written statement documenting everything that went wrong in your marriage. If we go to trial, I'll need to know the details of your marriage so I can build your case. There's no great rush, but if you could send it to me a week or two after you arrive in Chicago, that'd be great."

As I stood to leave, she hugged me tightly. "You're very brave, Susan. But I hope I never see you again."

On the streetcar back to my office, I thought back to my first few months in graduate school. I could clearly visualize how Cai had spent his free evenings with me, talking to me as an equal, asking me to marry him, and kissing me in our dorm room. But when we traveled to China that first summer, he had showed that other side. What drove him to change? And how had I put up with his nightly visits to his professors' room or Yoshimoto's tight grip?

Since that summer, I had constantly struggled with the insoluble question of whether Cai's unkindness, his punitive temper, and his exclusion of me from his social life were a product of his Chinese upbringing or his increasing depression. Was it a cultural difference or a personality one? The longer we were married, the more I tailored my every move to avoid his outbursts and evade his criticisms. Constantly I wondered why he behaved this way and how I could help him. Now on the streetcar, thankful the end was near, the answer was finally clear to me: it didn't matter.

What mattered was me. I couldn't spend my life orbiting around him like a satellite. I would soon be free and would stop myself in the future from trying to be something I wasn't. Something I'd attempted to construct from notions about culture and marriage that I thought existed, but had made up myself all along.

Back in my office, I closed my door, locking it from the inside.

"Susan?" My mom sounded surprised to hear from me at work.

"I just came back from Joanne's office."

"What happened? What did she say?"

As much as I tried to remain calm, I started to sob. "Mom…I'm coming home."

"It's okay. Take a breath. Does Cai know?"

Sniffling, I reached for a tissue and wiped my eyes. "No. And he's not going to until Jake and I have left. Joanne will help me draft a letter so I'm absolved from kidnapping charges."

"Oh my God. I guess I was so worried about Cai taking Jake to China that I forgot about that possibility."

"It's okay. My letter won't say I want a divorce, just a break. And that Cai can visit Jake in Chicago anytime he wants."

"That sounds like wise advice."

"There's one more thing. Joanne doesn't think I can do this on my own."

"I see." My mom paused. "Do you want me to fly out to help you?"

"Could you? That's what she suggested. She thinks I'll be too frazzled to do it alone. I have to pack all of Jake's things, his strollers, the car seat, our suitcase." I blew my nose a couple of times. "Sorry."

"When do you want me to come out there?"

"Friday."

"You mean in three days?"

I sniffled again. "If I don't do it now, I won't have the strength later on. Can you stay in a hotel near the airport? We'll leave Saturday morning when Cai is out teaching."

"That's fine. Will you be okay in the meantime?"

"I think so, but Cai can't know any of this until he finds my letter on Saturday. So please don't call me at home about this. I think emailing my work address would be best."

"Sure. I'll make my travel arrangements and will email you with the details."

"Mom, can I ask you something?"

"Sure. What is it?"

"Are you disappointed it's ending this way?" My parents had been supportive about my relationship with Cai from the beginning. But no one in our immediate family had divorced.

Would they be ashamed to tell family and friends about my failed marriage?

"Of course I'm not disappointed. You tried your best and that's all you can do. Now it's time to focus on yourself and Jake."

"Thank you. I don't know what I'd do without you."

"Don't mention it. And don't worry. Everything will be fine."

"I hope so." But as we hung up, all I could wonder was how Cai would react to finding my letter that Saturday, realizing I had left with his son. Would he throw dishes or scream into the silence of our emptied house?

Chapter 44
PLANNING TO LEAVE

After I arrived home from meeting Joanne, I started to wonder if I actually had the resolve to leave Cai in a few days. That night—alone with Jake while Cai hosted his radio program—I was convinced I was a horrible wife for abandoning him in a strange country. Mama and Baba would be so disappointed in me. I was supposed to find Cai a job. I was supposed to be the dutiful daughter-in-law. And now I was giving up before Cai was able to settle into his new Californian life.

But by the next morning, all I could think about was how Cai had spent more time with his friends than he had with Jake and me. I'd patiently waited for him to find a job, to acclimate to San Francisco. If he couldn't help himself, how could I help him? How many more threats would I listen to before they would come true? I was right to leave.

Then the following day, on Thursday, I felt horrible for denying Jake his dad and Cai his son. No matter what he had done, Cai was still Jake's father. Would Jake suffer emotionally if I divorced Cai? I now understood just how difficult it was for women to leave abusive relationships when kids were involved.

When my mom phoned me at work on Friday afternoon from a hotel outside the San Francisco airport, my escape came one step closer to being realized.

"I've just checked into my hotel and have the car," my mom said. "I've also rented a cell phone, so let me give you the number."

I wrote it on a Post-it. The phone number stared at me naked, without a name or label. Tucking it away in my purse, I reviewed the plans with my mom for the next day. I prayed they would all go off without a hitch.

"Thanks so much, Mom. What are you going to do the rest of the day?"

"I was thinking of driving into the city since this will be my last time here for a while. Maybe to do some shopping—"

"No. Please don't. Cai could be anywhere today. It would be just my luck for him to see you downtown. Can you just stay at the hotel?"

"Sure, that's fine. I don't think he'd see me, but you're right. It's not good to take chances. I can read at the pool if the sun stays out."

That evening, I tried my best to act as if I wasn't about to leave my husband. As long as I didn't think about it, I didn't feel too jittery. But it was impossible to completely push it out of my mind. Later that evening we had a welcome distraction when Mr. Huang, Cai's friend from Wuhan, unexpectedly stopped by to drop off some concert tickets for a performance he was producing. He'd also come over the night of Jake's bris.

Cai joked around with Huang, mimicking the accent of a mutual friend. They spoke of the good old days in Wuhan, just following the Cultural Revolution, when they returned to study after many years outside the classroom. I couldn't remember the last time I had seen Cai laugh and joke around so much.

"I'm going to Russia in a few months," Huang announced, "with a group from San Francisco State."

Cai turned to me with kindness spilling from his eyes that I hadn't seen in ages. "Maybe we can visit Russia some day."

I felt my pulse deep in my chest. What could I say? No, I'll be long gone? Maybe I was wrong to leave when there was still a chance we could get along. Would Cai and I be able to enjoy a peaceful life together after all, traveling around the world on cultural exchanges?

I nodded but knew I was deluding myself in thinking he could still change. It was too late. I had to focus on what was best for Jake and myself. At that moment, I felt grateful that my mom was just a town over and would help me stay on track. Joanne was right about asking her to fly out. I cringed to think about leaving on my own and how easy it would have been to cancel my flight at the last minute.

Nervous about the next morning, I felt an urgent need to remove myself from Cai and Huang. "It's almost eight," I said to them. "Jake should go upstairs now. Nice to see you, Mr. Huang."

"You, too," Huang replied. "I'll see you at the concert next week?"

I pressed my lips together to stifle the tremors I could feel in my throat. Smiling, I peered at the tiled entryway floor. "Yes, of course."

Clutching Jake, I started up the stairs, unable to look back at Cai and Huang. It wouldn't be long before Huang would learn the truth about that night. I couldn't look, because if I did, I'd always remember the last moment Cai and I were a family in front of someone else.

We might meet together in the future with Jake, but never again would people come to our home to visit our family. I also worried I would start to lose focus if I lingered any longer with Cai and Huang. Or give myself away. Part of me knew I could go through with leaving the next day, while the other part felt vulnerable, impressionable, and unsure I would be able to pull this off.

Arise, and dress yourself with care.
Dress neatly, not showily.

—Ban Zhao
Instruction to Chinese Women and Girls

Chapter 45
THE MORNING OF DEPARTURE

I tossed and turned all night, nervous Cai would wake up feeling sick and cancel his class, or the school would call to say too many kids were out with colds so he shouldn't bother to come in. Even if Cai went to work as planned, my mom's rental car could suddenly have a flat tire that would make us miss our flight.

I wished I had thought about all the things that could go wrong when I decided to leave. Was there something I could have done to ensure a smoother escape? These worries weighed on my mind so much that I wasn't able to fall sleep until sometime before daybreak.

The next thing I knew, I woke with a start, the morning sun peeking through our bedroom curtains. Cai wasn't in bed next to me, but I could hear the water running in the bathroom. Without my glasses I squinted at my watch. 7:00 a.m. I had to get through these last two hours until Cai left to teach piano. But even then, I wouldn't be in the clear. There would only be a few hours between when my mom would arrive to gather Jake's and my things and when our flight to Chicago would depart at one that afternoon.

When Cai came out of the bathroom and got dressed in our room, I faked sleep. Then he left to go downstairs. He didn't suspect anything.

Jake woke about ten minutes later. I took my time changing his diaper and dressing him in an outfit warm enough to withstand the unforgiving Chicago winter. I then stuffed Jake's pajamas in my suitcase's side pocket. The green canvas case rested in a corner of our closet behind my clothes. I would deal with my toiletries after Cai drove off.

The smell of coffee flooded the kitchen, a familiar aroma since we'd moved into the house a little over two years earlier. Cai had acclimated to little American things like coffee in the morning and bacon, eggs, and toast for breakfast. I couldn't think about that now.

Staying out of Cai's way, I placed Jake in his high chair and cooked a pot of oatmeal. I'd lost my appetite since the day I saw Joanne and had been forcing myself to eat in front of Cai so my behavior wouldn't seem uncharacteristic. When he moved to the living room to watch the news from China, I exhaled for what seemed like the first time all morning.

The next hour dragged. Jake finger-fed himself small pieces of banana while I loaded the dishwasher and checked the clock. 8:15 a.m. I took Jake out of his high chair to give him more time with Cai before our nuclear family dissolved.

"Can you hold Jake while I clean up a bit?" I hadn't asked Cai for help with Jake since the night he first threatened to send him to China, but I had nothing to be afraid of now. Cai happily took Jake and held him on his lap. I returned to the kitchen, which was already spotless. Leaning against a counter and taking a deep breath, I scanned the back of the house. *I'll put the letter there*, I decided, looking at the naked cutting board.

Buying myself five minutes, which seemed like fifty, I returned to the living room. Cai's eyes were glued to the TV as Jake cruised the windowsills, lined with trinkets I'd bought on my travels through Eastern Europe in college. They would have to stay.

8:30 a.m. Walking upstairs with Jake was something I'd normally do, so I carried him up to the master bath to survey my toiletries. I didn't dare pack them with Cai still home, but I made mental notes, for the hundredth time since Tuesday, of what I would take.

When Jake and I returned to the living room, Cai was still in front of the TV. Then he stood up.

"I'm going now." He barely made eye contact with me before

heading downstairs to the garage. I looked at my watch. It was 8:45 a.m.

I stood by the window, my eyes fixed on the street below, waiting for him to pull his car out of the garage and turn down Newhall Street. I'd told my mom to park around the corner to the left because Cai usually turned right out of our garage. But as plans always changed, especially during crises, I crossed my fingers he wouldn't see her if he drove in the other direction.

It seemed like ten minutes had passed since Cai had headed downstairs to the garage.

And then his car appeared.

He turned right. Phew. I kept watch at the front window to make sure he didn't return. I pulled the Post-it with my mom's rented cell phone number out of my purse, picked up the phone, and dialed.

"He just left, but can you wait another ten minutes in case he comes back? I'll open the garage door then, and you can pull right in. I don't want the neighbors to see you. They would tell Cai you were here."

"Sure. I can see your garage. I'll wait until you open it before I start the car."

I continued to peek through the drapes, as Jake toddled around the living room. Each time a car turned onto Newhall from the intersection to the right, my heart skipped a beat. Worried about only having three hours to pack my things, return the rental car and phone, and check our bags, I thought about gathering some of Jake's things while I waited to make sure Cai was really on his way to the music center. But I couldn't risk leaving my post at the window. It would be a disaster if he were to return and surprise me while I was packing.

After ten minutes had passed and I felt fairly sure he hadn't forgotten something at home, I made my way downstairs with Jake and opened the garage door. My mom pulled in and I closed the door behind her.

"Jake!" My mom took Jake from me, latching on to him as if

she hadn't seen him in years. Her eyes revealed the same panic and nervousness as mine.

"Let's start packing the car," I said as I hugged her.

While my mom tried to collapse Jake's high chair, I scurried to retrieve my suitcase. Taking a plastic bag from under the bathroom vanity, I threw in my spare pair of glasses, my toothbrush, hairbrush, and Jake's baby scissors. I shoved the bag in the suitcase, then sprinted around the closet, taking more clothes and shoes, baby photo albums we kept stacked in piles on the closet floor, and my jewelry. Running into the guest room where Yoshimoto had stayed, I pulled Jake's clothes out of the dresser we'd bought for the room and piled them high in my arms. It was to be Jake's room once he moved into his own bed. After a few trips back and forth, I couldn't fit much else into the suitcase, so I zipped it and lugged it downstairs.

Jake walked around the kitchen as if my mom's presence were normal.

"I think I broke the high chair." My mom examined it, puzzled. "Something snapped that shouldn't have."

"It's okay. Just leave it. I'm going to bring my suitcase down to the car. Can you gather some of Jake's toys in the living room? I'll come back with a bag for them."

We spent the next half hour packing as much as we could in the trunk of the rental car. Jake's two strollers, diaper bag, and a bag of his toys joined my suitcase and my mom's carry-on.

I scanned the garage. A blue tricycle my parents had bought for Jake stood parked in the corner. We'd have to leave it behind. "I think we have as much as we can fit. After I put Jake in his car seat, I'll go upstairs to leave the letter in the kitchen."

With my final task completed, I closed the door to the upstairs, locking it with my key for the last time. My mom pulled out of the garage so the car just cleared the door frame. I stepped outside and reached back into the garage to press the opener on an inside wall. I then slid into the backseat next to Jake while the garage door slowly closed.

Apart from the broken high chair, this part of the escape couldn't have been executed better. My mom seemed calm and Jake looked content in his car seat, oblivious to this harrowing event. I even felt confident the rest of it would go just as well.

But when I looked back onto Newhall Street, my eyes clouded as I saw for the last time the house I thought would bring us so much joy.

Chapter 46
DELAYED IN SAN FRANCISCO

At San Francisco International Airport, my mom pushed Jake in one stroller while I pushed another stroller carrying his car seat. Dressed in our winter coats in anticipation of the cold Chicago weather, we checked our bags, received our boarding passes, and cleared security. In the departures area, my mom waited with Jake while I brought his two strollers to our gate to receive gate check tags. Because I'd bought Jake a seat on the plane, I wanted to keep both strollers to transport Jake and the heavy car seat through the airport.

Just as it was my turn at the desk, the gate agent shook her head. "I'm sorry, ma'am, but this flight has just been canceled."

"What?" This couldn't be happening, not today. I could feel my knees start to buckle.

"I'm sorry. After I make the announcement, you can come back here to book another flight."

I quickly looked at my mom, who was holding Jake in her lap, guarding the car seat and carry-ons. Then I turned toward the gate agent and lowered my voice, speaking in almost a whisper. "I have to get to Chicago today. When's the next flight?"

"Just the red-eye. But please take a seat now."

The red-eye? When did that leave? Midnight? It wasn't even noon yet. If we stayed at the airport for twelve hours, Cai would find us. He knew my family only flew ATA. When he found my letter, he could make one phone call and learn that the midday flight had been canceled and the next one would take off at midnight. He would have nothing to lose and everything to gain if he camped out at the airport to observe the passengers before they boarded the red-eye flight. (This was a year before 9/11 and anyone could pass through security to meet or bid farewell to people at the gate. Or intercept a wife who was about to abscond with his child.)

I fought back tears as I tried to think of a solution. There had to be a way to leave San Francisco sooner than midnight. "Can you book me on another airline before this evening?"

"Ma'am, please have a seat. I have to make the announcement and then I can reschedule you on an ATA flight. Please."

I walked in defeat back to Jake and my mom, collapsing in the chair next to them.

"Our flight," I choked. "It's been canceled."

"*What?*"

"They're going to—"

And then we heard the overhead announcement. "—and if you can't get on another flight today, you'll receive a hotel voucher. Please come to the gate to reschedule—"

"I'll be right back." My mom placed Jake in my lap and grabbed the boarding passes from my hand. She dashed over to the long line that was forming in front of the desk. What if Cai's afternoon classes were canceled and he found my letter earlier than I expected? We might have less time than I thought. So I quickly scanned our end of the terminal, terrified that I would find him storming our gate in fury to snatch Jake away from me. What if he showed up with the police?

"Susan." My mom touched my shoulder, startling me. "There's only a red-eye at eleven or a flight tomorrow morning at six. I'll do whatever you want."

"We can't wait until tomorrow," I snapped. "Can you get us on the red-eye? And a hotel voucher? We can't stay here. He'll find us."

My mom waited in line again as I kept watch. When it was her turn to speak to the gate agent, I could see them discussing something but couldn't hear or read their lips. It seemed like an hour passed, all in slow motion.

"We're on the red-eye and have a room at the Marriott. Let's find the shuttle."

Pushing Jake in one stroller while my mom maneuvered the other stroller holding the car seat, we raced through the terminal to the outside transportation area. As the time got later, I grew certain that Cai would find us one way or another.

While we stood outside for the Marriott shuttle, I started to shiver even though I was still wearing my heavy winter jacket. The wait seemed to take all day, but in reality the bus arrived within five minutes. It wasn't until we'd safely reached our hotel room, closed the door, and locked it that I could relax until we had to return to the airport later that night.

By then, Cai would surely know I had left with Jake. It would also give him time to learn about the canceled flight and the next scheduled one to Chicago, the red-eye for which we now had reservations. Over the years, I had called airlines to check if friends or family were on certain flights. The airlines claimed they wouldn't divulge that information, but after much pleading they always gave the information I sought. So Cai, with his charming voice and pleasant manners, wouldn't have a problem either.

At that time, most cell phone packages made it prohibitively expensive to call long distance. That was the reason my mom had rented a cell phone at the airport the day before. We had returned it hours earlier with the rental car, so to call my dad, my mom took out her calling card to use on the phone in our hotel room. I listened closely as she explained the whole ordeal to him. "If Cai calls, tell him that Budgie went to meet us at the airport. Stall him as long as you can, but call us as soon as you hang up with him."

I tried to rest but could barely close my eyes. Expecting Cai to phone any moment after 3:00 p.m., when he usually returned home, I fidgeted and paced the small room. My mom ordered a few sandwiches through room service. I fed some to Jake, but I had no appetite, not even for a sip of tea.

"Why isn't Cai calling? Maybe Dad forgot to call us." Or perhaps

Cai wouldn't call my parents. If he found out about our canceled flight, there would be no need to call my parents. He would care more about intercepting us at the airport, even if it meant waiting for hours in the departures terminal.

My mom reached for the room phone. "I'll call Dad again."

They spoke for a few minutes. "Nothing yet." It was almost 4:00 p.m. Maybe Cai had stopped to rent porn, I thought wryly.

By 6:00 p.m. I finally felt hungry, so my mom ordered room service again. Just after she placed the call, the phone rang. My mom and I looked at each other as it rang again. Without speaking, we knew it was my dad. And that he was calling with an update.

"Do you want me to get it?" my mom asked.

The phone rang for the third time. Without answering her, I grabbed the receiver. "Hello?"

"Cai just called," my dad said. "He was very upset and could barely speak."

My heart raced. "Was he angry? Did he sound violent?"

"No, no. He was crying. He sounded heartbroken."

I slumped into a chair next to the bed. This wasn't how I had expected him to react. Given his violent outbursts and love of the silent treatment, wasn't he supposed to lash out at dinner plates or water glasses after reading my letter? Or maybe he would feel relieved, happy I'd left and given him the chance to return to China carte blanche.

My dad continued. "I told him you weren't going to arrive for a couple of hours. I tried to stall and say you'd call him in the morning, but he insisted on phoning back tonight. What should I tell him?"

I gazed at my mom, who sat with Jake on the bed and stared at me. "Dad, can you say I'm exhausted and I'll call him in the morning?"

Room service arrived and I forced myself to eat something. I wondered why Cai's reaction seemed harder to digest than hearing he had been angry or violent about it. Then I realized it was guilt. I was abandoning him in a country he didn't like, taking away his son, and leaving him with a house, two cars, and no way to pay the mortgage or the other bills.

My mom suggested we rest up before heading back to the airport for our red-eye departure. She phoned down to the reception desk for a 9:00 p.m. wake-up call that evening. Jake had already fallen asleep in the middle of the bed, so my mom and I lay on either side of him and tried to close our eyes. Images passed through my mind of Cai slumped over the kitchen counter, the tear-soaked letter in his hands.

By the time we entered the departures terminal hours later, I no longer felt guilty. The terror that I had experienced earlier that day returned in full force. Eerily quiet on a Saturday night, the airport exuded tranquility in contrast to the throngs loitering around the gates earlier that day. I feared Cai would be lurking around the corner after we passed through security.

The one consolation was that it would be easier to spot Cai at this late hour, but that turned out not to be true. Each tall man with dark hair who came into vision looked just like him from afar. I could no longer differentiate between paranoia and rational concerns.

Even when we reached the gate without incident, I positioned myself at all times so I could view passersby. After my mom checked the strollers at the gate, she insisted that Cai was probably too upset to think about calling the airport, but I wouldn't take any chances. When the gate agent called for families traveling with young children to board first, I sprinted to the gate with Jake held tightly in my arms. My mom followed us, loaded down with the car seat and our carry-on bags. It wasn't until the plane's doors closed and the flight attendants announced takeoff that I felt the tension from that day—and the last few years—begin to leave my body.

As the plane ascended, the flight attendants turned off the lights in the cabin. My mom sat in the aisle seat, finally able to sleep. Seated next to her, I turned to peer over Jake's car seat in the window row and down at the lights peeking through the midnight fog.

I was going home.

Chapter 47

SWEET HOME CHICAGO

A knock on my parents' guest room door stirred me from the short nap I had taken after arriving in Chicago at five o'clock that morning. Jake slept soundly next to me.

My dad opened my door an inch. "It's Cai. What do you want to do?"

"Can you tell him I'm resting and will call in a couple of hours?"

Deprived of a night's sleep and years of energy, what *could* I say to him? I didn't know what kind of mood he'd be in. Remembering the mixed emotions during my last week in San Francisco, I wouldn't have been surprised if Cai had moved on to anger and lashed out at me over the phone. I needed more rest before I could think clearly. But as Jake dozed soundly next to me, I found that I couldn't fall back to sleep.

Even though I had originally left Chicago in search of the excitement I thought I could only find in Hong Kong, it felt good to be back. I reflected back on my years in Hong Kong and my marriage to Cai, and everything I thought I wanted back then. Now what I craved was stability. Cai couldn't give that to me, and this was the reason I had returned to Chicago. My childhood in the Midwest suddenly didn't seem so bad anymore. It was the kind of upbringing I now wanted for Jake, rather than the turbulent way in which Cai was raised.

Many of my friends and colleagues didn't know Jake and I had left San Francisco. So as I lay in bed next to Jake, I made a mental list of everyone I would call in the next few days. I hadn't talked to Janice in months, so she went to the top of the list. If anyone would be sympathetic, it would be her. She had moved back to New York a month after I left Hong Kong, and it would be easy to phone her.

And then there was the narrative Joanne had asked me to write, describing how and when my marriage first started to fail and what led up to this point. Other than those two things, I planned to spend the week doing nothing but relaxing with my family, unraveling from years of tiptoeing around Cai.

When Jake woke two hours later, I knew I had to call Cai. I had put him first all these years and found it difficult not to think about his needs now. He must be terribly upset, whether sad or angry, and deserved an explanation from me. Or maybe Cai should wait. He rarely put me first during our marriage.

My dad was reading the newspaper when I walked into the kitchen holding Jake. He looked up. "Are you going to call Cai?"

"I think so. Yes. I'll do it now. Is Mom still sleeping?"

My dad nodded and happily took Jake from my hands. Reaching for the phone, I could feel my pulse in my throat.

Cai answered on the first ring, as if he was standing by the phone waiting for my call.

"*Susan.*" The sound of his cries came through clearly. "I'm so sorry if I did something wrong. I never thought you'd leave."

"Cai, it's okay." Wait, it was not okay. I had to stop being a peace-keeper at my own expense. "I mean, I can't go on like this."

He could barely get the words out. "D–d–do you want a divorce?"

"No… I don't know. I just need a rest. I need to think about what I want."

"Please come back." He pleaded with a gentle voice I hadn't heard in years. "I'll do anything. *I love you.*"

"I'm really tired. I didn't get much sleep last night. Can we talk tomorrow?"

"Sure, yes, call anytime you want. If I'm not home, call my cell phone."

"I'll call tomorrow morning at ten your time." Argh! I mentally hit myself on the forehead. Again, I put him first in making those plans. I didn't want to call too early, lest I cut short his sleep.

The narrative I wrote for Joanne spanned sixty-seven handwritten sheets of lined paper, taking me a week to complete. Things I'd buried for years emerged like wriggling earthworms from the dirt after a stormy night: the STD, the red bathing basin in Wuhan, the Shanghai Railway Station, and the subsequent silent train ride to Suzhou, talking to prostitutes, putting porn watching before spending time with his family, and running off with Japanese Father. Those shameful events seemed like a lifetime ago. When I read about them on paper, I wept not because they'd happened, but because I'd allowed them to happen. By leaving San Francisco, I wasn't just bringing Jake to a safe and supportive environment; I was also saving myself from a marriage that had become defined by fear.

My daily phone conversations with Cai left me exhausted and wishing for a reprieve from his heartbroken pleas. Every time I spoke with him, he claimed he finally realized what had gone wrong. First it was his poor English and inability to find a good job. The next day he said our marriage was strained because of the late nights he kept while producing the Chinese concert. On the third day, he suggested I ask my mom to come live with us so I'd have a close family member nearby.

He never spoke about the silent treatment, the threats to hit me or to send Jake to China, the arguments over Jake's sleeping habits, or the times he had locked Jake in the dark guest room or had held him over the second-floor staircase. When I brought these things up—and asked him about the STD and hinted at his relationships with Yoshimoto and Xiaohong—he changed the subject and cried about how he was losing weight and was alone in the house. I felt overwhelmed by these conversations and sensed that no matter how much I asked, he'd never come forth with the truth. That first week I checked in with Joanne multiple times.

"I just can't talk to him every day like this. I'm worried I'll lose my cool and drive him to hire a lawyer."

"It's all right to set some boundaries. Why don't you cut your conversations down to once a week and limit them to ten minutes? You'll sleep better. More importantly, do you think he's already gone to a lawyer?"

"No, divorce seems to be the farthest thing from his mind. Of course that could change or maybe he's trying to trick me. I don't know what to believe."

"Has he said anything about visiting you and Jake in Chicago?"

"Nothing."

Cai never did ask to visit us, even though my letter made it clear that he was welcome. Each time I spoke with him, I asked if he would like to talk to Jake. But Cai usually said it was too upsetting for him to do that. Maybe next time. When I asked him the following week, he said the same thing. I still felt guilty that I had taken Jake away from his father, and I was frustrated that Cai wasn't doing everything he could to keep up contact with his son. Jake could only put a couple words together, but he missed talking to his father. As the months passed, Jake rarely heard Cai's voice.

Stalling Cai from afar wasn't easy, even after I limited our phone conversations to once a week. After three months, he started demanding I make a decision—either to come back or to file for divorce—and saying that he couldn't stay in limbo anymore.

"I want to stay here for the summer," I finally told him in early June. "I'll have an answer after Labor Day." That would bring me to just beyond the six-month mark.

He agreed to wait for my decision in early September. In the meantime, I found a lawyer in Chicago who took over from Joanne as September approached. Once I reached my sixth month in Illinois, my case would no longer be in California's jurisdiction, thus the need to find a lawyer who was licensed to practice in Illinois.

At the beginning of the summer, Jake started preschool near the University of Chicago and I began to temp at advertising agencies, copyediting and proofreading. We were still living with my parents, but I had put a down payment on a condo that would break ground later that year. I hoped to pay for it with the equity from the future sale of our house on Newhall Street.

On the Fourth of July, I informed Cai I would no longer pay the mortgage from our savings. A couple weeks later, he told me he'd found a full-time job at a Chinese publishing house just south of San Francisco. He'd be working in their music department, acquiring new titles, overseeing the production process, and collaborating with the publicity department to market the books.

When he revealed he now earned more than I made in my first job in San Francisco, I put my head in my hands. Why hadn't he found this job earlier? Would he have looked harder if I'd been strict, or did it take a crisis for him to become serious about working? In any case, it was too late. I knew I could never go back to him, and I was pretty sure he would treat me even worse if I returned to San Francisco. So it was pointless to ask why he hadn't tried harder before I left.

Just before Labor Day, Cai grew exasperated for the first time since I'd left. "Please tell me what you want. I don't care if you come back or stay there. I just have to know. I can't go on like this, not knowing what you want."

"The summer's not quite over yet. I'll decide soon."

The following week, a process server handed divorce papers to Cai at his office. It was my thirtieth birthday. Cai could hire a lawyer, but our case was now in Illinois' jurisdiction. Any legal proceedings would take place in Chicago, not San Francisco. I could finally get on with my life.

My Halloween divorce court date came and went without more than a quick squeal from Cai back in San Francisco. I arrived at the courthouse with my lawyer and my mom and left an hour later with sole custody of Jake and half of my marital assets. The following month Cai finally flew out to Chicago to visit Jake. My mom, Jake, and I picked him up at Midway Airport and drove him to my aunt and uncle's home where Cai would sleep for the two days he stayed in Chicago.

Cai gushed over Jake as the two sat in the minivan's middle row. Although Jake hadn't seen his father in six months, he still remembered him and took to him right away. But once we arrived at my aunt and uncle's house, Cai perched himself in a corner of the living room, squatting on the floor and weeping softly. Jake wasn't two and a half yet, but he caught on to his dad's distress and brought some toys over to Cai in an attempt to cheer him up. And yet Cai continued to cry.

Whether or not Jake understood that his parents were separated, it was clear that Jake loved his father. In one way I hoped Cai would stop crying so he and Jake could play in peace, but on the other hand it seemed like a valid reason to cut our visit short that day. It was also emotionally taxing for me to see Cai after six months. A couple hours later, I told him that Jake needed to return to my parents' for his early bedtime. He didn't protest.

The next morning when I returned with Jake to my aunt and uncle's house, Cai smiled as Jake and I entered the front door. But ten minutes later he was back in the corner, crying like he had on our first day in San Francisco when he was overwhelmed by the newness of our lives there. Now I imagined he wished we were back in San Francisco. Or perhaps he regretted flying out to Chicago. He'd spent years apart from Ting-Ting, so maybe that was an easier way for him to cope with separation from his child.

We stayed inside for the rest of that day, Cai breaking away from the corner when my aunt announced lunch. The third morning, my mom, Jake, and I drove with Cai to the airport. Although Cai's tears ran down his cheeks as he kissed Jake good-bye outside the departures terminal, I had a feeling Cai wouldn't be rushing back to see his son any time soon.

And as it turned out, Cai's visits to Jake would continue to be quick, annual forty-eight hour visits in the years to come, until he started only visiting every two years. Two years after we divorced, Cai passed his naturalization exam to become a U.S. citizen. That month he boarded a plane to move back to Hong Kong where he would be working as the music director at the Taoist temple up by the China border.

My lawyer purposely left the terms of Cai's visitation vague. He could see Jake whenever he wished as long as I agreed. And each time Cai asked to come to Chicago, I said yes and arranged for him to visit Jake's school, Sunday school, soccer matches, and Little League games. I would always be amenable to Cai's visits to Chicago, as I hoped for the best for Jake and his relationship with his father. I was past rancor and bitterness. After all, Cai had given me the great gift of my son.

EPILOGUE

It was a hot summer day the first time Cai met my fiancé, Tom. A dozen kids scrambled around my parents' back porch for Jake's seventh birthday party while Cai quietly videotaped our son playing with his friends, the Sears Tower looming in the background. That evening Jake, Tom, Cai, and I drove to Chinatown for dinner at a Malaysian restaurant. It was the first time the four of us had been alone together. The din of the restaurant camouflaged our wavering conversation. After dinner, Jake and Cai walked ahead while Tom draped his arm around my shoulder.

"It looks like Jake is leading his dad," Tom said as father and son crossed the street ahead. Patient and calm, Tom had known about Jake before he asked me out at work—a hospital where I was temping at the time—a couple years earlier. Months before Cai arrived in Chicago for this visit, Jake had casually mentioned in an email to his father that Tom and I were engaged.

And then it was Cai's turn. He revealed over the phone in early 2006, a month after my wedding, that his girlfriend Mimi thought it was time that they marry. I'd never expected to feel sad to hear Cai was going to remarry. I didn't even know he had a girlfriend. So I phoned Janice, who still lived in New York and was engaged to a German businessman. "I shouldn't care about Cai's new marriage, but I can't help feeling somewhat dejected."

"It's not just you. I've heard it's always upsetting when an ex finds someone else. I'm sure Cai felt the same when he learned about you and Tom. Just give it some time. Soon you won't think anything of it."

As usual, Janice was correct. Cai had been back in Hong Kong for four years and had met Mimi at a Western opera, in which she had been a performer. She'd lived in New York for almost a decade and had recently returned to China to teach at the Shanghai Conservatory of Music, yet still traveled around the world to sing opera. Theirs would be a long-distance marriage, Cai told me, but eventually he'd move back to China, to a Shanghai that resembled very little of what we had experienced eleven years earlier.

It was during this time that Cai also mentioned he'd resumed contact with Ting-Ting. Now a teenager, Ting-Ting had moved back to Wuhan to attend boarding school. After she'd lived in the dorms for a few semesters, Ting-Ting asked Cai to pay her rent for a three-bedroom apartment off campus.

"She's only sixteen and doesn't need such a big apartment," Cai said to me on a forty-eight-hour visit to Jake in Chicago.

"What did you tell her?" I asked, not wanting to sound too curious. I'd tried to maintain a professional rapport with Cai since our divorce, devoid of emotion or attachment. But I did want to know what had become of Ting-Ting. Cai hadn't mentioned her before then.

"Of course I agreed. I'm her father."

"Do you see her often?"

"No. I'm in Hong Kong. She's in Wuhan. But I wanted to help her, so I'm paying her rent."

Poor Ting-Ting. After all these years, her father still wasn't a constant presence in her life. Paying her rent could never make up for their lost time together. And as infrequently as Cai visited Jake, he did schedule consistent visits every year or two, even if they only lasted two days.

While we were on the subject of Ting-Ting, I suggested to Cai that she and Jake could start corresponding. Jake was old enough to write letters, and Ting-Ting must surely be able to read simple English or know someone who could translate a letter from an eight-year-old.

"I'll ask her," Cai said.

Months later, when Cai phoned to speak to Jake, I asked again about Jake writing to Ting-Ting. "Can you give me Ting-Ting's address?" Cai must know it since he paid her rent.

"Sorry," he said, pausing a moment. "Ting-Ting doesn't feel comfortable writing to Jake. She thinks she's too fat."

Huh? Too fat to write letters? How had Cai responded to his daughter's heartrending assertion? I felt bad for Jake because he was losing a relationship with his sister, yet Cai wasn't eager to foster that bond.

Several years later, Cai would mention on another quick visit to Chicago that Wei Ling had married a banker and was living in New York. And Ting-Ting had joined them, enrolling in college somewhere in the New York area. As luck would have it, Cai was headed to New York the following day to see his wife, Mimi, sing an opera there.

"So you'll see Ting-Ting?" I said more as a statement than a question.

"No. I don't know how to find her."

"You could surely find Wei Ling's phone number from old classmates. It's always worked in the past."

He shook his head. "I don't know where they live." Then he changed the subject and asked about the Mandarin class Jake attended after school once a week.

Just as I was about to bring the conversation back to Ting-Ting, I suddenly felt like I was slipping back a decade to when I was married to Cai and encouraging him to reach out to his daughter. But that wasn't my place anymore. I couldn't be the one to push for this relationship. My idea of the right thing to do differed from his, and I knew I'd have to leave it at that. Tuning back to his questions about Jake, I waited for him to finish, then went on to tell him about Jake's Mandarin teacher and the types of sentences he'd been learning.

In the winter of 2008, Cai announced that he would be making another one of his quick visits to Chicago. This time he'd bring his wife, Mimi, along.

I braced myself for an uncomfortable meeting and lost my appetite a few days before they flew to Chicago. Tom stayed home with our baby daughter, Rachel, while I drove Jake from our new home in a Chicago suburb to meet Cai and Mimi in Chinatown.

Jake and I entered a dim sum stadium, my hand gripping his. We paused before a stream of middle-aged women pushing metal carts piled high with bamboo steamers filled with dim sum: dumplings, sticky rice, and juicy beef balls. One of the dim sum ladies ruffled Jake's hair, remarking that we'd returned. "*Huí lái le*," she said, remembering I spoke Mandarin. It was Jake's favorite restaurant and we'd been regulars over the last eight years.

I smiled, too nervous to chat. Holding Jake close, I peered through the crowded tables to locate Cai, who had come in from Shanghai where he and Mimi lived together with a miniature pinscher. From behind a cluster of young couples, Cai ran up to Jake, lifting his eighty-pound bulk and embracing him like an oversized teddy bear.

"You're so big!" Cai set ten-year-old Jake back down, his eyes sizing Jake up and down. It had been two years since father and son had met.

Cai peered at me, nodding congenially. My shoulders taut, I watched him with caution. I immediately noticed he was wearing a platinum wedding ring, something he refused to do when we were married. It felt like a little punch to the stomach. I wondered if this meant he had never really taken our marriage seriously. Or perhaps it wasn't him at all, but his new wife. I imagined Mimi was probably more assertive than I was when she got married to Cai.

Just then a tall woman with short hair and lipstick to match her red cashmere sweater hurried past Cai and greeted me with a firm handshake, her diamond rings sparkling in a stream of sunlight flowing through the windows behind me.

"It's so good to meet you. I've heard so much about you." Her

English was perfect and her smile genuine. "I'm Mimi." I wasn't expecting her to be nice. Was this how Wei Ling felt when she met me?

Mimi led me to their table as Jake and Cai followed. I studied Jake's face. He walked stiffly beside Cai, and his eyes stayed focused on me. What did he think of his dad, someone he knew mostly from phone conversations every few months?

"Please sit." Mimi took the chair next to me. "Jake looks so much older than in his photos. You're doing such a good job with him."

As the carts of dim sum passed, Jake and I took turns pointing to choice dishes: eggplant stuffed with white fish, shrimp dumplings, beef rice rolls, and chicken congee. During lunch Mimi sashayed between cultures, conversing comfortably with Cai about Chicago's version of dim sum compared to those in China, Hong Kong, and elsewhere, and about American movies with Jake and me.

Then Mimi turned to me. "I'm surprised your husband and daughter aren't here. Why didn't they come?"

"Rachel still naps a couple times a day, so Tom stayed home with her. Believe me, it wouldn't have been pleasant if she'd missed her naps." I tried to sound lighthearted, never revealing how difficult it had been for me to show up that morning, let alone subject Tom and Rachel to something I'd been dreading since Cai announced this trip a month earlier.

Tom had told me he'd do whatever I wanted—accompany Jake and me or stay home with Rachel. I felt it would be best for them to stay home, in case Mimi was unfriendly. But just as with Wei Ling, I grossly miscalculated Mimi's lovely personality. Still, it was nice for Jake to have this time alone with Cai, without having to share the spotlight with his baby sister.

While we ate, Cai told us about Mama and Baba's new apartment and how he and Mimi visited them in Hidden River whenever they got the chance. Although grateful I no longer had to make those trips to Hidden River, I did feel bad for Mama and Baba. They hadn't seen Jake since they left San Francisco nine years earlier. I also felt a bit guilty because it was my fault that Jake couldn't see his grandparents—I refused to go back to China with him. They'd only spoken on the phone a couple times, and only when Cai stayed with them and asked us to call his parents' number. One consolation was that Cai always took plenty of photos and video of Jake on his visits to Chicago so he could show his parents how much Jake had grown.

After lunch, we headed to a children's museum along the Chicago lakefront. To give Cai time alone with Jake, I sat with Mimi on a bench along the sidelines, learning about her early years in Shandong, how she discovered Western opera, and her path to New York and reviews in the *New York Times*. Every once in a while, I glanced over at Cai and Jake engaged in a giant game of chess or standing in line for a ropes course.

Jake smiled often and seemed more at ease with his father now. With the help of Mimi's calming presence, I relaxed and chatted with her. Later I drove Cai and Mimi to their shabby hotel in Chinatown, aghast that Cai would allow Mimi to stay at such a location. It didn't even have a private bath, she told me with a chuckle, as if amused by the simplicity of the place.

Before Jake and I headed back home, Mimi hugged me tightly. I looked forward to seeing her the following day, again for dim sum, before their flight to New York, where she was going to perform in an opera. Up until I'd met Mimi, it was easy to wish the worst for her and Cai. I had felt resentful that Cai had treated me as an enemy during our marriage. Now here was another woman who was probably gaining from what Cai had learned from his mistakes with me.

But once I got to know Mimi, I couldn't help but hope that her marriage would work. I finally knew what it was like to have a caring spouse and a happy life. If Mimi and Cai were happy, it could only benefit Jake's relationship with Cai, no matter how little they saw one another.

On the way home, Jake rehashed the events of the day. "Baba's wife is much better than I thought."

"I thought the same thing," I said, pulling onto the highway ramp at Chinatown.

It was then that I started to appreciate what I had gained from my marriage to Cai. Throughout those five years, I had tried to be a good Chinese wife but had ended up almost losing myself. There was more than enough of the bad for me to dwell on, but there also were glimmering rays of good that shone through.

Because of everything I had been through, my life seemed so calm and easy now with Tom. Though in another untraditional marriage, I could be myself and know that Tom would love me for it. I had matured and become stronger, but I could also put into perspective little things that might have bothered me before. If Tom needed to stay at work late, I wouldn't get upset—I knew he wouldn't be out with other women or driving God-knows-where to find an adult video store.

Most times, he would jump in to help with the kids or start cooking dinner. But if he wanted to sit back with a beer in front of the TV, I was fine with that, too. I relished this peace and stability that had been absent in my first marriage. And if Tom's mother wanted to see the kids—I had another son named Martin a couple years after Rachel was born—I knew she wouldn't threaten to keep them for a few years.

The calmness I felt in my marriage allowed me to be a better mother to my children. I could see the difference between how I behaved when Jake was a baby and when Rachel and Martin were the same age. While Cai's moods dominated my first two years as a mother, not allowing me to truly focus on my son, I felt no such stress during Rachel's and Martin's early childhoods.

Tom was a first-time father when Rachel was born, and was happy to let me make big decisions for her: which foods she would eat, what time she would go to sleep, and how to dress her for each season. These things were all sources of distress in my marriage to Cai, but with Tom they were never up for argument.

With a peaceful family life, I could spend time with my kids doing things I thought they would enjoy. I took them to Chinatown to try out new dim sum restaurants and shop for moon cakes at the

Mid-Autumn Festival. We read books about Chinese culture and decorated our house with red posters of fish and smiling children at Chinese New Year. I knew I could never do these things with the kids if I had still been married to someone who continued to drain my energy until I was solely operating in survival mode.

And in the ironic way in which history tends to repeat itself, I learned something else from Cai. Twelve years earlier, he had phoned me at work one winter day, enthusiastic about booking a trip to China before Jake turned two. Cai had stressed the urgency in purchasing these tickets so we wouldn't have to pay for Jake's airfare. Cai's call had come out of the blue, leaving me frightened and panicked to act quickly. That phone call ultimately sparked the events that led to our divorce.

Just as Cai had surprised me with that call, one winter day in January 2012 when Martin was also two years old, I paged Tom at the hospital where he worked as a cardiologist. No matter what he was doing—rounding on patients, reading stress-test results, or performing postoperative procedures—he never failed to phone me back at his earliest convenience. I could always tell from the way he started the conversation whether he had time to talk for a bit or if we had to keep it short. My heart thumped when the phone rang a couple minutes after my page.

"Hey, what's up?" he asked leisurely. Although he didn't seem in a hurry, I suddenly felt rushed to get it all out.

"I have a crazy idea. The deadline is tonight, and my mom said she could stay with the kids for a week. Although we'd have to buy the tickets now, we wouldn't have to fly until sometime before May first. The airfare is just too good to—"

"Wait a second," Tom said, not impatiently. "What are you talking about?"

"Hong Kong."

"Hell yeah! I'd love to go there."

Although Tom knew all about my time in Hong Kong—and after—I had never suggested traveling there in the decade since we'd met. Looking back, I could see that I wouldn't be able to return until I felt comfortable with myself and grounded in my new family. Having Rachel and Martin helped with that. And seeing Jake grow into a confident young man did, too.

Yes, now that I felt secure in my new life, I could return to the home of my twentysomething self and experience it afresh. I expected to see changes in Hong Kong since I'd left. After all, it had been fourteen years. But then again, I had changed, too.

ACKNOWLEDGMENTS

Years ago, I attended a writing conference in Chicago and met a woman who warned that others might steal a book idea if it's revealed too early. I followed this advice for years, but it was only when I started talking about it that this book started to become a reality. And I learned that writing is anything but a solitary endeavor.

A million thanks to my brother, Jonathan Blumberg, for inspiring me to write the book in the first place. To Xu Xi, Kathy Carter, Paula Bernstein, Bruce Tracy, Kathleen Herbach, Jennifer Barron, Sara Rubin Agahi, Chandrika Marla, Czes Tubilewicz, and Sharon Woodhouse for early feedback. To Jean Oram, Glenn Stewart, and everyone at AgentQuery Connect.

To my friends on Authors of Asian Novels, Facebook, and Twitter. To the many writers who have provided invaluable support and a warm shoulder: Ilan Greenberg, Ceil Miller Bouchet, Linda Furiya, Dana Sachs, Rachel DeWoskin, Kim Fay, Janet Brown, Chris Thrall, Tom Carter, Pete Spurrier, Stuart Beaton, Caitlin Shetterly, Jean Kwok, Susan Conley, Shannon Young, Tracy Slater, Anju Gattani, and of course Jocelyn Eikenburg.

To Erica Lyons, thank you for your support, friendship, and the Hong Kong charm. I wear it with honor.

Jean Hao-Hirt, thank you for being a champion of my story and my best friend all these years. Annie Galpin, *do jeh, do jeh*. And a huge thank-you to all my friends from CUHK, both in Hong Kong and Chicago. Friends and saviors from my San Francisco days: Adrienne Robillard, Tim Booher, Adria Arteseros, and Bren Ahearn among many others.

A thousand kowtows to Wendy Nelson Tokunaga, who taught me how to write.

To Carrie Pestritto, dream agent extraordinaire and dear friend. Thank you for believing in this story at first glance and for finding it the perfect home. I can't imagine my life without you. Thanks also to Emily Sylvan Kim at Prospect Agency.

And to my amazing editor, Stephanie Bowen at Sourcebooks. Thank you for your unwavering support and vision for this book. It has been a joy and an honor to work with you and others at Sourcebooks: Jenna Skwarek for answering my many questions and keeping me on schedule; Liz Kelsch, Heather Moore, and Jennifer Sterkowitz in publicity and online marketing; Adrienne Krogh, Dawn Adams, and Kelly Lawler for creating such a fabulous cover; Heather Hall and the out-of-this-world copyediting team; and Todd Stocke and Dominique Raccah. I wouldn't want to be anywhere else.

I couldn't have written this book without the support of my family. My dear husband, Tom, thank you for your patience and for accepting me as I am. Jake, thank you for allowing me (not always by choice) to share our story. To Rachel and Martin, my little dim sum companions. To the Kasons for accepting a Jewish, divorced, single mother into your family and treating Jake and me as your own. Thank you, Budgie and Grandma. And to my mother: our family would look much different if it weren't for you.

ABOUT THE AUTHOR

Susan Blumberg-Kason is a freelance journalist in Chicago. As a child growing up in
suburban Chicago, she dreamed of the neon
street signs and double-decker buses of Hong
Kong. In her late teens, she left for a year
abroad in Hong Kong and ended up spending most of her twenties there. She studied
Mandarin and completed a master's degree
in political science at the Chinese University
of Hong Kong.

Photo credit: Tom Kason

Susan is now back in the Chicago area, where she lives with her
husband, three kids, and a surly cat. Her work has appeared in affiliate
papers of the *Chicago Sun-Times*, *Chicago Parent* magazine, and the
Journal of the American Dietetic Association. She has been interviewed
in *TimeOut Chicago* and on ABC News Chicago and WTTW
Chicago, the local public television channel. You can find her online
at www.susanbkason.com.